STRIKING AT THE ROOTS

A Practical Guide to Animal Activism

First published by O Books, 2008
O Books is an imprint of John Hunt Publishing
Ltd., The Bothy, Deershot Lodge, Park Lane,
Ropley, Hants, SO24 0BE, UK
office1@o-books.net
www.o-books.net

Distribution in:

UK and Europe
Orca Book Services
orders@orcabookservices.co.uk
Tel: 01202 665432 Fax: 01202 666219 Int. code
(44)

USA and Canada
NBN
custserv@nbnbooks.com
Tel: 1 800 462 6420 Fax: 1 800 338 4550

Australia and New Zealand
Brumby Books
sales@brumbybooks.com.au
Tel: 61 3 9761 5535 Fax: 61 3 9761 7095

Far East (offices in Singapore, Thailand, Hong
Kong, Taiwan)
Pansing Distribution Pte Ltd
kemal@pansing.com
Tel: 65 6319 9939 Fax: 65 6462 5761

South Africa
Alternative Books
altbook@peterhyde.co.za
Tel: 021 447 5300 Fax: 021 447 1430

Text copyright Mark Hawthorne 2008

Design: Stuart Davies

ISBN: 978 1 84694 091 0

A CIP catalogue record for this book is available
from the British Library.

Printed in the US by Maple Vail

O Books operates a distinctive and ethical publishing philosophy in
all areas of its business, from its global network of authors to
production and worldwide distribution.
No trees were cut down to print this particular book. The paper is
100% recycled, with 50% of that being post-consumer. It's processed
chlorine-free, and has no fibre from ancient or endangered forests.
This production method on this print run saved approximately
thirteen trees, 4,000 gallons of water, 600 pounds of solid waste,
990 pounds of greenhouse gases and 8 million BTU of energy. On its
publication a tree was planted in a new forest that O Books is
sponsoring at The Village www.thefourgates.com

STRIKING AT THE ROOTS

A Practical Guide
to Animal Activism

Mark Hawthorne

BOOKS

Winchester, UK
Washington, USA

CONTENTS

There are a thousand hacking at the branches of evil to one who is striking at the root.
– Henry David Thoreau, *Walden*

For a certain cow in India, who showed me a kinder way of living.

ACKNOWLEDGEMENTS

The animal-rights movement is comprised of some of the most supportive human beings imaginable, and I am indebted to many of them from around the world for their invaluable contributions. A typical example is Paul Shapiro who, when I called him at home one evening for his insights and apologized for interrupting his downtime, responded, "Hey, Mark, there are still hens in battery cages, aren't there?"

In addition to Paul, my humble thanks to Carol J. Adams, Pam Ahern, Chris Anderson, Josh Balk, Monica Ball, Jenny Barsby, Joel Bartlett, Gene Baur, Georgina Beach, David Benjamin, Beverly Lynn Bennett, Olga Betts, Earle Bingley, Tony Bishop-Weston, Shari Black Velvet, Sienna Blake, Sarahjane Blum, Jenny Brown, Andrew Butler, Jenna Calabrese, Suzanne Carey, John Carmody, Jon Camp, Erika Ceballos, Alka Chandna, Phil Clayton, George Clements, Nick Cooney, Lauren Corman, Aurelia d'Andrea, Jason Das, Karen Davis, Margo DeMello, Jennifer Dillard, Jason Doucette, Joyce D'Silva, Adam Durand, Monica Engebretson, Matthew Engelhart, Kathleen Farley, Kate Fowler-Reeves, Camilla Fox, Lisa Franzetta, Juliet Gellatley, Derek Goodwin, Kathy Guillermo, Dian Hardy, Megan Hartman, Michael Hayward, Alison Hermance, Josh Hooten, Michelle Johnson, pattrice jones, Justin Kerswell, Aaron Koolen, Nora Kramer, Sarah Kramer, Tammy Lee, Lana Lehr, Julie Lewin, Karl H. Losken, Haviva Lush, Mia MacDonald, Erik Marcus, Patty Mark, Mary Martin, Tim I. Martin, Caroline McAleese, Erica Meier, Peter Milne, Dawn Moncrief, Christine Morrissey, Liberty Mulkani, Jack Norris, Glenys Oogjes, lauren Ornelas, Jake Oster, Heidi Jury Parker, Wendy Parsons, Colleen Patrick-Goudreau, Bryan Pease, Fiona Pereira, Clare Persey, Michele Pickover, Karen Pilling, Annie Potts, Eric Prescott, Debra Probert, Rochelle Rees, Mark Reinfeld, Isabel Reinhards, Karin Ridgers, Dallas Rising, Angela Roberts, John F. Robins, Helen Rosser, Nathan Runkle, Marcy Schaaf, Dan Shannon, Jill Simpson, Deirdre Sims, Kelly Slade, Charles Stahler, Jo Stepaniak, Angie Stephenson, Kim Sturla, Jennifer Surrette, Anthony Terry, Bob Torres, Jenna Torres, Eric Tucker, Kate Turlington, Don Walker, Yvette Watt, Zoe Weil, Sue Werrett,

Anna West, Freeman Wicklund and Erin Williams for patiently enduring my endless questions and transforming them into the practical advice that is the heart of this book.

Many thanks to Bruce Friedrich, a fearless activist, for immediately embracing the vision of this book, for wading through early drafts of the manuscript and suggesting changes and for contributing the foreword.

My research also led me to experts not necessarily associated with animal rights, and I appreciate the insights of reporter Henry Lee of the *San Francisco Chronicle* and reporter Wendy Suares of WTOK-TV. Thanks to Chip Heath, co-author of *Made to Stick: Why Some Ideas Survive and Others Die*, for reviewing my thoughts on "sticky" communication.

I am exceedingly grateful to Kymberlie Adams Matthews, Cat Clyne, Beth Gould, Sangu Iyer and everyone else at *Satya* magazine for allowing me to express my thoughts about animals and activism in writing over the years and for kindly granting permission to reprint the standalone quotes found in each chapter. Sadly, *Satya* ceased publication as this book was being completed. This voice for animals, the environment and social justice will be missed.

A special thank you to activist and fellow bunny hugger Julianna Baker for her input and unwavering encouragement. It is fitting that we met at an animal-rights conference, and I am proud to call you my friend.

It is my great privilege to be a volunteer at Animal Place, an education center and sanctuary for farmed animals in northern California. Although co-founder Kim Sturla and the other staff think I am helping *them*, in reality, it is I who benefit from my time there (please do *not* tell them I said that!). It was a tour of Animal Place that inspired me to make the transition from vegetarianism to veganism, and every hour I spend with animals rescued from agribusiness, 4-H projects, vet schools and other abuse adds to my knowledge and resolve. Thank you, Kim, for allowing me to help.

My friends outside the movement (yes, I do have a few) have offered their kind support, and I thank in particular Wes Andrues, Deb Kling, Kavita Salvado-DaRocha and Steve Tarani for their help.

I owe much gratitude to John Hunt of O Books for taking this book on and understanding its importance.

Finally, a great big gold-embossed, gift-wrapped thank you to Tim Ward for believing in this project from the very beginning and for mentoring me through the entire process of bringing it to fruition.

Mark Hawthorne

PREFACE

WHAT ARE WE FIGHTING FOR?

When activists speak out against animal suffering, they are generally referring to the exploitation of animals in the production of food, clothing, entertainment, consumer products, pharmaceuticals and pets, such as:

- Chickens in factory farms who are bred to grow so quickly that their brief lives are filled with misery: fragile bones, lung congestion, limb deformities and heart failure are common.
- Egg-laying "battery" hens who spend about two years packed into wire cages with other hens without room to spread a single wing. If she doesn't die from untreated illness or uterine prolapse pushing out an egg, the exhausted hen is slaughtered as soon as her egg production declines.
- Male chicks hatched in the egg industry who are immediately gassed, ground up while fully conscious or flung into garbage bags to eventually suffocate.
- Pigs who spend their lives in crates so small they are unable to even turn around.
- Cows who are strapped into what the dairy industry calls a "rape rack" and artificially inseminated each year so they will give milk. Their newborn calves are taken away, the females going back into the dairy system while many of the males are crammed into small crates and later sold as veal. Mother cows are slaughtered when their milk production declines.
- Ocean-dwelling animals who are scooped from the sea by the billions each year to slowly suffocate or be boiled alive.
- Baby seals who are savagely clubbed for their fur and frequently skinned alive.
- Bulls, horses and baby calves who suffer the intense pain of spurs,

electric prods and cinch straps used to make them appear "wild" so rodeo cowboys will seem like heroes.

• Mother elephants who are killed so their babies can be exported and used in animal acts like circuses or to languish in zoos around the world. Other wild animals suffer the same fate.

• Companion animals who are bred into a hopelessly crowded pet population in which millions of them are abandoned, abused, neglected and euthanized every year.

• Rabbits, non-human primates, mice, dogs, rats and other animals who are annually tortured and killed by the millions in the course of needlessly testing drugs, chemicals and household products.

• Cows who have their throats slit and their skin ripped off while they are fully conscious in developing countries like India and China, source of most of the world's leather.

• Australian sheep who undergo "mulesing," a gruesome mutilation in which large chunks of skin and flesh are cut from their backsides without any painkillers. Sheep no longer producing enough wool are packed onto export ships and sent to the Middle East for slaughter.

• Birds and mammals hunted for "sport" who may suffer prolonged, painful deaths when they are injured but not killed by hunters. Animals in "canned" hunts, meanwhile, are killed in an enclosed area by hunters who pay to shoot these "trophies."

• Fur-bearing animals who are caught in traps or raised in fur farms and then gassed, suffocated or electrocuted (done anally or through the mouth so the blood doesn't ruin the fur).

• Chimpanzees, bears, lions and other wild animals who are physically and psychologically abused so they will perform tricks for human amusement.

• Horses and dogs used for racing who are treated as "running machines," not sentient beings with needs of their own. These animals are routinely killed when they are no longer deemed profitable.

FOREWORD

IS ACTIVISM THE MEANING OF LIFE?

Right now, raccoons are chewing off their paws to escape from
steel-jaw traps.
Right now, baby chicks' beaks are being burned off by the egg industry.
Right now, animals are being beaten and whipped in circus
training schools.
Right now, millions of dogs, cats, sheep, pigs, chimpanzees, rabbits, mice,
fish, and other animals are being abused in myriad ways by "scientists."
Write now.

This reminder about the horrors suffered by other animals every moment – and for the most frivolous of human whims – graces PETA's guide to letter-writing. The reminder serves two purposes: First, it keeps any problems in our own lives in perspective. Second, it reminds us of how easy it is to take action one behalf of other animals. Writing a letter is just one powerful way among many that we can expose abuse and make positive changes for animals. Letters can literally mean the difference between life and death, as Mark Hawthorne discusses in this important book.

Anyone who shares his or her life with a dog or cat understands that the human species is not the only one whose members are worth knowing as individuals. My wife and I share our lives with the world's most perfect cat, Gracie, and she motivates us as activists. Every day, when we return from work, she greets us at the door, often rolling over so that we can scratch her belly. We know that she feels a full range of emotions – from joy and sadness to fear and self-confidence. She helps us remember that other animals are individuals who have needs, desires, and the capacity to experience rich emotional lives.

Although we are less likely to know them personally, other animals – whether they are mammals, birds, or fish – are just as intelligent and interesting as any dog or cat. As philosopher Henry Beston writes in *The Outermost House*, "In a world older and more complete than ours, [other animals] move finished and complete, gifted with extensions of the senses we have lost or never attained, living by voices we shall never hear. They are not brethren, they are not underlings; they are other nations, caught with ourselves in the net of life and time..."

Three more keen observers of other species are Dr. Jeffrey Masson, author (with Susan McCarthy) of *When Elephants Weep: The Emotional Lives of Animals*; Dr. Jonathan Balcombe, author of *Pleasurable Kingdom: Animals and the Nature of Feeling Good*; and Dr. Temple Grandin, author of *Animals in Translation: Using the Mysteries of Autism to Decode Animal Behavior*. All three books are highly recommended for their ability to help us tear down the barriers that we have constructed between ourselves and other species.

Recognizing that other animals have the same basic capacities as human beings is not anthropomorphism; it is simply common sense if we take the time to observe other species. It is also what science is increasingly beginning to acknowledge. Grandin shows, for example, that other animals "have the same core feelings people do" and that "all domestic animals need companionship. It's as much a core requirement as food and water." All three authors discuss the fact that other animals love to play and that adult animals will, like human animals, often allow children to "win" when they're playing. Grandin discusses her belief – which is based on ample scientific rationale – that the psychological trauma of fear in animals is even worse than physical pain because it is thoroughly debilitating in a way that physiological pain is not. This should give us all pause when we consider the lives of animals in factory farms, fur farms, vivisection labs, circus training camps and so on. Try to imagine their abject fear.

All three authors – and many more – show that every time we think that there is something unique about the human species, further research proves that – as Darwin taught us – humans are not unique in our various capacities; whatever differences exist between humans and other animals are differences of degree, not kind. Because some scientists continue to deny Darwin's observations and to focus on trying to find differences between humans and other species, Grandin argues that perhaps *they* are the ones who have real trouble learning. Time and time again, contrary to the assumptions of certain scientists, we learn that animals can anticipate the future, delay gratification, dream, play, use language and tools and do everything else that we thought they couldn't do. When scientists fail to identify animals' capacities, *scientists* have failed – not animals.

In April 2007, *The New York Times* reported that chimpanzees have better short-term memories than do human beings; chimpanzees have consistently far outperformed humans on short-term memory tests. But it's not just chimpanzees who have impressive capacities that defy the common misconception of animals as beings who lack self-awareness. Consider these recent quotes from mainstream media stories:

- "Chickens do not just live in the present, but can anticipate the future and demonstrate self-control, something previously attributed only to humans and other primates, according to a recent study."
  – *Discovery*
- "Elephants can recognize themselves in a mirror and use their reflections to explore hidden parts of themselves, a measure of subjective self-awareness that until now has been shown definitively only in humans and apes, researchers reported yesterday."
  – *The Washington Post*
- "Rats appear capable of a complex form of thinking before known to exist only in humans and other primates – the capacity to reflect on what they do or do not know."
  – *University of Georgia news release*
- "[Pigs] have proved they are at least as clever as chimpanzees with their first forays into video games."
  – *The Daily Telegraph*
- "...scientists have now confirmed what pet lovers have always known: that each animal has its own distinct personality. More than 60 different species, from primates and rodents to fish and even insects, have been scientifically documented to exhibit individual differences in characteristics such as aggression or shyness."
  – *The Independent*

Anyone looking for more of these kinds of stories will find a steady stream of them. We now know that chickens, pigs, fish, rats, mice, and all other vertebrate animals are interesting individuals in their own right. Of course, they also feel pain in the same way – and to the same degree – as human beings. Civil rights icon Dick Gregory explained, "Dr. King taught us that the fight against oppression is never an easy one. It is even harder when you have no voice.... Because I am a civil-rights activist, I am also an animal-rights activist. Animals and humans suffer and die alike. Violence causes the same pain, the same spilling of blood, the same stench of death, the same arrogant, cruel and vicious taking of life. We shouldn't be a part of it."

Walker Percy suggests in *The Last Gentleman* that insanity is the most rational response to reality. What do we do about the fact that more than 1.3 billion human beings are living on less than a dollar a day? What do we do about the war in Iraq or the genocide in Darfur? What do we do about vivisection laboratories, factory farms and slaughterhouses? It seems reasonable to assume that it is the insane among us who are fully grasping – and accepting responsibility for – both the degree of suffering in the world and the inability of any of us to put an end to it. The rest of us are suffering a psychological malady that is summed up nicely in one word: "denial."

But is the final word really that we're all in denial? I think that it's true that denial and insanity are the two options for human existence only if you neglect another possibility: changing reality and making things better – or at least less horrible. That is the subject of Mark Hawthorne's vital book: how to improve the lot of animals, who are the most exploited and least considered beings on the planet. Animals exist with us in the world and are more like us than unlike us, yet we devour their corpses by the billions for a momentary palate sensation, we steal their fur and skin from them for vanity and we drive them insane and injure them in laboratories to "test" another toothpaste – or simply to find out what will happen when we hurt them.

In this book, you will find ample corroboration for Alice Walker's thesis in *Possessing the Secret of Joy*: The secret of joy is resistance to evil. The point of human existence, Walker contends in perhaps her most powerful novel, is to move beyond ourselves and fight to make the world a kinder place. Refusing to support cruelty and suffering is crucial, but the next step

– resisting injustice – is even more important. Mark gives us the tools that we need to put this thesis into practice.

It is not enough to withdraw our support of cruelty. If it were, the most ethical lifestyle would be that of the hermit in the mountains – or whoever consumes the least resources. But there is another important factor that must be considered: our impact in the world. For example, if you adopt a vegetarian (or better yet, vegan) diet, you will save approximately 100 animals every year. That's wonderful, but consider this: If you convince one *more* person to adopt a vegetarian diet, you (in that moment) double the positive impact of your entire life as a vegetarian. I'll repeat that, just in case you were skimming: Handing *one* leaflet to *one* person who changes his or her mind on the basis of that leaflet will *double the positive impact of your entire life of choosing exclusively vegetarian options*. And we can do a lot more than distribute just one leaflet.

The story in this book that I find the most inspiring is the one about Nathan Runkle picking up a brochure at a table, studying it, conducting further research, and then launching Mercy For Animals, an extremely effective animal-rights group that has saved millions of animals from abuse. As I write this, Nathan has just broken the news of an undercover investigation into a turkey slaughterhouse that will awaken millions of people around the world to the dark underbelly of their Thanksgiving dinners. One brochure, taken from one table, did it. One hour of someone's time literally changed the world for millions – if not billions – of animals.

This book is packed with tips and advice that will help all of us become better advocates for animals. It will help us take our own compassionate lives and multiply them exponentially by reaching out more effectively and influencing other people. Mark's words will give us ideas and tools that will allow us not just to double our positive impact but to multiply our positive impact by thousands. The sky, as they say, is the limit.

Make no mistake: Activism is changing the world right now. In addition to the growing body of evidence that other animals are interesting individuals – just like the dogs, cats and human beings we know a little bit better – big changes on the health and environmental fronts are also taking place.

As just one example, in December 2006, the UN hammered home the point that eating meat is bad for the environment by releasing a 408-page analysis of the environmental impact of raising animals for food. The report concludes, "The livestock sector emerges as one of the top two or three most significant contributors to the most serious environmental problems, at every scale from local to global." Raising animals for food is the number-one source of greenhouse-gas emissions, releasing more gases into the atmosphere than all the world's planes, trains, trucks, and automobiles combined. Other studies have made the same point.

On the health front, we have pro-vegetarian books from respected researchers and physicians, including Drs. Dean Ornish, Caldwell Esselstyn, Neal Barnard, T. Colin Campbell, Andrew Weil and many more. The American Dietetic Association, the American Medical Association (AMA), and even the US Department of Agriculture now conclude, based on scientific evidence, that vegetarian diets are healthier than diets that include meat. *Not one* respected physician or nutritional or medical association (not one) says that eating any meat or animal products, ever, is essential for good health. The dietary regime of the sole well-known pro-meat doctor, Robert Atkins, was denounced by the AMA as "dangerous." As if in tacit endorsement of the AMA's statement, Atkins keeled over dead at 260 pounds (118 kilograms). Some "diet."

As we work to make the world a kinder place, it helps to keep constantly in mind that we in the animal-rights movement have science and rationality on our side. We have justice on our side, and we also have public opinion on our side. Our goal is simply to help people understand the ways in which their own actions may not be congruent with their ethics. Everyone opposes cruelty, but the general public has no idea how animals used for food, clothing, experimentation and human entertainment suffer. Our task, then, is not to change people's ethics; it's simply to educate them about the reality of other animals' suffering as vigorously as we are able, using the tools provided by this book.

We can do it, and we can do it in our lifetimes. Not long ago – a mere historical blink of an eye – society believed things about government and human behavior that are diametrically opposed to what we believe with equal certainty today. Just 200 years ago, no one would have believed that we would abolish slavery in the developed world, give women the right to work and vote, abolish child labor and establish largely democratic systems of governance. "But the Bible dictates the treatment of slaves, women, and children," they would have protested. "It is natural to treat other people this way; it's how we've always done it," they would have said – much as many people argue today about humans' relationship to other animals.

The animal-rights movement is young, and we have new savvy and new tools. We also have a growing following among the world's youth. I have no doubt that in 100 years – if we are all as active as we can be and work as hard as we possibly can – human beings will look back on past generations' mistreatment of other animals with the same horror that we now reserve for historical injustices like slavery and other deeply immoral transgressions against human beings.

Our ethics concerning animals are changing, and this book will play an important role in accelerating that change. It is deeply empowering to know that by wearing T-shirts, putting bumper stickers on our cars, adding an auto-signature to our emails or doing some other very small things, we can save lives. The more deeply that we're willing to devote ourselves, the more good we can do. This book gives us the tools and the motivation, and nothing is more important.

Dr. Martin Luther King taught us that "The arc of history is long, but it bends toward justice."

Thank you for being a part of the movement toward a more just world.

Bruce Friedrich
Vice President, International Grassroots Campaigns
People for the Ethical Treatment of Animals

INTRODUCTION

The power to act for animals – to work for change on behalf of the voiceless – is within all of us. It does not require a vast amount of knowledge, although understanding the abuses animals suffer will make you more effective. Activism does not demand a lot of time, either: you can make a difference even if you limit your involvement to an hour a month. You needn't be an extrovert or polished speaker – although such traits may come in handy and indeed may develop as you become more accustomed to addressing friends and the public about animal issues.

Animal activism only requires a desire to help and that you follow that desire with action.

Striking at the Roots: A Practical Guide to Animal Activism is intended for the person who agrees with the premise that animals are mistreated in our society, believes that the public has a moral obligation to speak out against this cruelty and who wants to be directly involved in opposing animal exploitation in its many forms. This is a guide to the most pragmatic opportunities available for speaking and acting on behalf of animals. We will examine tried-and-true models of activism and explore some modern tactics that are gaining traction among advocates with a talent for using technology.

You may wonder if animal activism itself is even worth it. Does it have an impact at all? Since 1950, worldwide meat consumption has increased more than fivefold. A rise in the Earth's population can account for some of that expansion, but such a spike occurring concurrently with an increase in animal-rights activism and vegan outreach is troubling at the very least. Worldwide, an estimated fifty-five *billion* animals are now raised and killed for their flesh each year. How are we to account for this? Part of the answer lies in how animals have come to be mass produced, commodified and marketed in the last half century. Today's industrialized farming practices mean that most of the pigs, cows, chickens, sheep, turkeys, goats and other animals raised and slaughtered for food are regarded as little more than units in a massive corporate enterprise designed to make meat, eggs and dairy as cheap and accessible to consumers as possible. Make no mistake: This is a multi-billion-dollar industry, giving the companies that exploit animals the deep pockets and political influence necessary to keep the killing machine moving forward at an ever-growing pace.

The same is true for businesses that use animals for their skin and fur, as well as for product testing, medical research and entertainment. Even the pet industry, which contributes to the constant cycle of breeding and selling, is responsible for making animals suffer.

Yet, animal activists *do* make a difference, and those who blatantly disregard animals are nervous. A recent editorial in *Feedstuffs*, the weekly agribusiness newspaper, reads: "Why are [animal activists] winning? It's simple. They have their game together, while animal agriculture and its allies have a fragmented, hopelessly under-funded, ineffective, reactive approach. The activists are engaged and taking their campaign to chefs, foodservice managers, dairy and meat case managers and policymakers from city councils to the US Congress."[1]

Animal activism is a struggle for change, and the reality is the human species is hard-wired to fear change. But we have two powerful weapons in this battle: the public's innate sensitivity and a tremendous amount of animal abuse as evidence. Most people believe animal abuse is wrong; in fact, a Gallup poll found that ninety-six percent of people living in the US oppose cruelty to animals – I doubt you could find that level of unanimity on many other issues.[2] Similar results have been published in New Zealand, where a survey by the New Zealand Centre for Human-Animal Studies found that *one hundred percent* of participants (meat-eaters and vegetarians alike) are against factory farming, regarding the practice as cruel and indefensible.[3] A poll of Canadians, meanwhile, revealed that seventy-three percent of those surveyed regard the humane treatment of farmed animals as very important.[4] Australia's *Sunday Mail* published results of a national survey that asked people what they wanted to see in 2004: eighty-three percent wanted improved conditions for battery hens.[5] And polls conducted by the British research firm Ipsos MORI reveal that the majority of citizens in the United Kingdom favor the hunting ban (by a three-to-one ratio), are against fur farms (seventy-six percent) and the trapping of animals for their fur (eighty-eight percent) and believe the use of wild animals in circuses should be banned (eighty percent).[6]

People are revolted by animal exploitation – once they learn about it. So, if we can educate people enough so that they can see that their daily choices are supporting practices that they actually oppose, then we can change them, one by one. And as more people change, eventually society will change.

When we consider how long humans have been using animals, the history of animal-rights activism is surprisingly brief. Of course, the world has always had those who abstained from eating animals, though they weren't always known as vegetarians or vegans. And there have long been people who have spoken out in favor of animal welfare; that is, a concern for the well-being of animals, who were still regarded as useful to society. But an organized movement – or, more accurately, a movement consisting of many organizations established to advance the interests of animals – is really only about two centuries old.

True, the Massachusetts Bay Colony enacted what is likely the first law to protect animals in Western civilization in 1641, but the Puritans were motivated less by a belief in the intrinsic rights of animals than in safeguarding their property and the ideal of Christian charity.

It was not until the nineteenth century that philosophical principles and an increasingly industrialized society would inspire the first Society for the Prevention of Cruelty to Animals (later renamed the Royal Society for the Prevention of Cruelty to Animals) in England in 1824, a concept that would span the Atlantic in 1866 with the founding of the first chapter of the American Society for the Prevention of Cruelty to Animals (ASPCA) in New York. Other milestones soon followed, including additional SPCA chapters across the US and the founding of the American Anti-Vivisection Society. Reformer Henry Salt published *Animals' Rights: Considered in Relation to Social Progress* in 1892 (and still in print), setting forth his argument against the exploitation of animals and influencing the beliefs of vegetarians like George Bernard Shaw and Gandhi, who credited Salt with guiding his thoughts on civil disobedience.

Although Salt decried the public's mentality of entitlement that continued to subjugate animals and espoused his belief that animals have innate rights, most of the groups and voices of his day were advocating animal *welfare*. Organizations such as the ASPCA and its many chapters established animal shelters and worked to improve the conditions for urban workhorses, for example, rather than struggling to liberate animals altogether from being used for food, medical research, clothing and blood sports. Of course, one need not accord animals the status of having rights to treat them with compassion, but the idea of animal rights argued that animals have an intrinsic right to exist on their own terms, free from any human exploitation.

What we think of as the modern animal-rights movement took shape late in the twentieth century, with new groups like People for the Ethical Treatment of Animals (PETA) and Friends of Animals, as well as charismatic individuals such as Henry Spira, speaking out and asserting that animals should not be treated as property. Spira was active in the American civil-rights movement in the 1950s and '60s before becoming one of the most vocal and influential advocates of animal rights in the 1970s. His campaigns for the abolition of animals were radical for their time, and many activists today refer to him as the father of the animal-rights movement.

In the UK, committed pacifist Donald Watson started the Vegan Society in 1944. Watson took to heart a Welsh maxim: "When everyone else runs, stand still." It is in that spirit that he spent most of his life advocating a plant-based diet and a way of life that embraces compassion for all species. In the first issue of the Society's newsletter, *The Vegan News* ("Quarterly magazine of the non-dairy vegetarians," reads the masthead), Watson ponders what they should be called. "As this first issue of our periodical had to be named, I have used the title 'The Vegan News,'" he writes. "Should we adopt this, our diet will soon become known as a VEGAN diet, and we should aspire to the rank of VEGANS." A vegan for sixty-one years, Donald Watson died in 2005 at the age of ninety-five.

Another figure often credited with jumpstarting the animal-rights movement by writing his seminal work on behalf of animals is the Australian ethicist Peter Singer. Published in 1975, Singer's book *Animal Liberation* described the institutionalized abuse of animals on farms, in vivisection laboratories and more, and it became for many activists the movement's manifesto. In fact, it was Singer's book that inspired Ingrid Newkirk and

Alex Pacheco to found PETA in 1980.

Thus, by the early 1980s, animal activism was becoming entrenched in Western society. *Animal Liberation* shocked a generation of readers with an inside view of factory farming practices, veganism offered an ethical alternative to an omnivorous diet and organized groups like PETA galvanized animal advocates, helping to convince the average conscientious consumer that their eating and buying habits *do* make a difference in the lives of animals. The term "animal rights" entered the international lexicon, and soon people were debating the fundamental rights of animals to exist for themselves, rather than as tools for scientific research, sporting events, product testing, clothing, amusement and the human palate. This is not to suggest that those supporting animal welfare or reform simply faded away – in fact, the welfare-versus-liberation argument has never been more vociferous – but in the last thirty years there has been a dramatic shift toward embracing the notion that animals do not belong in cages, laboratories, crates, circuses, rodeos or dairy farms, and that the best way, indeed the only way, to effect change is through activism.

Being an advocate for animals is not always a popular activity, but that should not dissuade you from doing what is right. Every social movement that had any impact – whether it's the abolition of slavery, the suffrage movement, civil rights, the child-protection movement or reforms for farm workers – was initially backed by a person or a group thought to represent the minority opinion, and those opposed to them tried to provoke the fear that overturning the status quo would lead to chaos: the end of slavery would result in economic ruin, granting women the right to vote or banning child labor would weaken national strength, passing laws against child abuse would dissolve families and so on. Animal-rights activists are now hearing the same sort of nonsense from those who profit by abusing animals. According to them, the only way to feed the world, cure diseases or advance scientific knowledge is by using animals. To them, animals are not sentient individuals with their own interests, but commodities to be exploited for human profit, amusement, convenience or taste.

The following pages will guide you through the fundamentals of grassroots activism. We will begin with what I and many other animal advocates believe to be the most effective model of activism, and then we'll progress, chapter by chapter, through the more involved tactics and meet some of the activists who find them successful. Each chapter will end with a list of resources for the model or models discussed. Four appendices will cover milestones activists have won for animals, animal-rights groups worldwide, recommended books, civil rights, a cruelty-free shopping guide, suggested actions you can take today to help animals and other relevant material. The time is ripe for change. More defenseless beings than ever before are suffering and in need of a voice. All we need are the passionate humans to turn these opportunities into dramatic improvements for billions of animals. Remember: Reform simply does not occur when people stand idly by. Let's get started.

Notes

[1] *Feedstuffs*, page 9, April 2, 2007.

[2] Gallup Poll, May 21, 2003. *Public Lukewarm on Animal Rights*, David W. Moore, Gallup News Service.

[3] Annie Potts & Mandala White, *Cruelty-Free Consumption in New Zealand*, May 2007, New Zealand Centre for Human-Animal Studies, University of Canterbury.

[4] www.humanefood.ca/docs/Poll2005.pdf

[5] *Sunday Mail*, pgs 12-13, December 28, 2003.

[6] www.ipsos-mori.com

CHAPTER 1

ANIMAL TRACTS: LEAFLETING

Dissent is the essential aspect of patriotism.

Thomas Jefferson

It is two o'clock on a sunny Texas afternoon, and Jon Camp is pulling another stack of vegan leaflets from his bag. As students here at Sam Houston State University hustle to their next class, Jon greets each one within speaking distance. "Brochure to help animals?" he asks, proffering a pamphlet to a young woman hurrying past. She shifts the large book bag on her shoulder and quietly takes the literature, walking as she looks at it. Then, a few paces beyond, she stops, turns on her heel and heads back. "This is horrible," she says, clearly upset by the information she's taken in about factory farming. "Yes, it is," responds Jon. "Most people have no clue how bad today's farmed animals have it." She asks for a few additional leaflets and thanks Jon for being on campus that day.

You're not likely to meet a more dedicated leafleter than Jon Camp, nor a more successful one. As an employee for Vegan Outreach, Jon travels the US, handing out the organization's literature at college campuses. He estimates he distributes about one hundred thousand vegan leaflets a year, giving him a unique perspective on this model of activism.

"I went vegetarian in early 1995 after taking an ethics course at my local community college, The College of Lake County in Grayslake, Illinois," he says. "I had always felt a sense of empathy for animals and was also concerned with being a kind and ethical person. As a kid, I'd ask my parents about what kind of conditions farmed animals lived under, and my father, who grew up on a small farm in Iowa during the '30s and '40s, told me that farmed animals lead good lives – lives worth living."

Jon's ethics class taught him that farming conditions had changed dramatically since his dad was a boy. Indeed, it was in 1955 that two economics professors from Harvard University, Ray Goldberg and John Davis, developed a food-production model that used profits as its guide, moving away from the family farm and vertically integrating all the production, distribution and sales of food products. This industrialized approach allowed animals to be exploited in an economically efficient manner, intensively confining farmed animals and regarding them, like never before, as commodities and units of production. Goldberg and Davis called this new enterprise "agribusiness." Most activists refer to it as "factory farming."

Jon Camp distributes about 100,000 leaflets a year on college campuses.

Soon after Jon went vegetarian, he learned about the abuses animals suffer in the egg and dairy industries, and he realized making the full commitment to veganism was the most ethical choice.

"I learned about Vegan Outreach by reading a book by [PETA president and co-founder] Ingrid Newkirk about easy ways to help animals," Jon says. "I ordered some booklets from Vegan Outreach and started to receive their newsletters and literature. What I liked about Vegan Outreach was their cost-benefit analysis of everything, including focusing on farmed animals and approaching the general public in a level-headed, kind manner – a manner that builds bridges. Their approach was in accordance with my way of viewing the world: rationally and calmly. I started ordering more and more of their booklets, putting them out in bookstores, record stores, and such, and finally, around 2001, I built up the nerve to leaflet."

Jon quickly saw the value of leafleting and was soon among Vegan Outreach's most active volunteers. "In the spring of 2004," he says, "Jack Norris, Vegan Outreach's president, asked if I would like to leaflet colleges for the organization as a means of employment. I said that I gladly would, and I've been doing this work on a full-time basis."

A History of Success

By a happy coincidence, leafleting is both one of the easiest models of activism and one of the most effective. It is also one of the oldest. Thomas Jefferson and Thomas Paine were among the "pamphleteers" who helped create a new nation, the United States of America, in part through their effective use of the leaflets, or pamphlets, they wrote and distributed in the eighteenth century. Pamphlets such as Paine's *Common Sense* took a decidedly radical stand on the political issues of colonial America, stirring colonists to defend their liberty and fomenting a revolution for their independence from Britain.

This proud tradition continues today as activists use leaflets to decry the tyranny of morally bankrupt animal oppressors and to advocate the liberation of millions of non-human animals. Leafleting has been a tremendous boon to the animal-rights movement, which does not have the budget to wage an advertising war with those industries that exploit animals; McDonald's spent more than two billion dollars on ads last year, many times the combined budget of every animal-protection group – and that's just one example.

Getting our message out there often means face-to-face meetings with the public. The good news is this personal interaction is tremendously successful at affecting the hearts and minds of people, and this can be much more effective than advertising or legislation; after all, an ad can be ignored and a law repealed, but once someone is enlightened about the harrowing abuses that occur every day within factory farms, biomedical labs, circuses, puppy mills and more, it is unlikely that a compassionate human being could forget what they've learned. You might not convince someone overnight to give up eating meat or wearing leather, but on the other hand, you just might. At the very least, you are planting seeds of change.

Leafleting is often described as a numbers game, working to influence as many people as possible. An average leafleter at a busy spot, such as a concert or packed festival, can pass out one hundred and fifty to two hundred leaflets in an hour. In that same amount of time, a superb leafleter can pass out as many as five hundred leaflets – about one leaflet every eight seconds. If you commit with a friend to hand out leaflets for an hour each week, you will reach about thirty thousand people a year with the message of compassion for animals. All of these people's lives will have changed, and some of them will change their behavior.

While an activist can leaflet in support of any animal cause, from spreading the word about animal shelters to asking local residents not to visit the circus that's coming to town, leafleting in support of vegetarianism is probably the most popular tactic. That makes sense, because every person you convince to adopt a vegetarian (or vegan) diet saves about one hundred animals a year and doubles your impact as a vegetarian. Think about that: Each person you sway to embrace vegetarianism is just as important to animals as your lifetime commitment to vegetarianism.

"I consider the cost of the outreach effort in measuring its effectiveness," says activist Tammy Lee of Bay Area Vegetarians, a grassroots organization located near San Francisco. "Leafleting is a very inexpensive form of advocacy – all that is involved is the cost of literature, whereas other forms of activism do have fees associated, like tabling space, or running commercials or having a program on TV. What's great is that leafleting can be a very spontaneous activity, and effective even with small increments of time."

> Rather than daydreaming about perfect and absolute solutions, activists need to push for the most rapid progress. Above all, we need to continually assess what differences we are making. Are we accomplishing all that we can to reduce the total universe of animal pain and suffering? Clearly, we have the tools. Do we have the will?
>
> **Henry Spira**
> *Satya* magazine, June 1996

One of the key points to remember when handing out vegetarian literature is to not complicate the issue by engaging in too much rhetoric about animal rights, if you can help it. Paul Shapiro, who founded Compassion Over Killing and currently manages the Factory Farming Campaign for the Humane Society of the United States (HSUS), observes that most people already oppose animal abuse, so when leafleting, it is a more efficient use of your time to focus on how animal factories and slaughterhouses abuse animals, rather than constructing an abstract argument about how animals' rights are being violated.

Vegan Outreach

One of the most active groups engaged in vegetarian and vegan leafleting is Vegan Outreach (veganoutreach.org). Activists Jack Norris and Matt Ball founded what would become Vegan Outreach in 1993 after discovering that handing out literature promoting veganism was a better use of their time than protesting or staging media events.

From its office in Pittsburgh, Pennsylvania, Vegan Outreach makes a variety of leaflets available to activists, including a vegan starter kit, a guide to cruelty-free living and its popular *Even If You Like Meat* pamphlet, which distills the argument for a plant-based diet into sixteen pages and depicts some heartbreaking images of animal exploitation and abuse.

Many people just starting out with leafleting feel nervous. Before I handed out my first pamphlet, I worried about how I would respond if someone became angry at my leafleting efforts. This is a very common concern, but I discovered that very few people are antagonistic toward me while I'm engaging in this model of activism. Those few who do get angry are often upset by having their lifestyle choices challenged. (I believe that at some level most meat-eaters feel guilty about consuming animals, and it is sometimes easier for them to strike back, rather than thoughtfully examine their contribution to animal suffering.) I asked Jack Norris how he responds when confronted by someone's anger.

"I generally try to diffuse people's anger by affirming their feelings," he says. "If they're angry about something, I'll recognize their anger. Often, they have misinterpreted something that I believe and when I set the record straight, they feel less attacked and thus feel less like attacking. I try to find common ground — and usually the common ground is that people agree that unnecessary suffering is bad."

Among Vegan Outreach's programs is Adopt A College, which encourages volunteers to focus their leafleting efforts on a nearby college campus. This is the campaign Jon Camp works on, covering a lot of miles every year in support of animals. Clearly, not every person we leaflet is going to become vegan. So it makes sense to leaflet to those who will be the most receptive to the message of compassion that veganism offers. Young people, particularly college-age women, are more open to new ideas like veganism and thus are more inclined to embrace the vegan lifestyle. Countless people spend their entire lives in ignorance about what goes on behind the closed doors of factory farms and slaughterhouses. The learning atmosphere of a college, with students challenging old beliefs and embarking on new experiences, is ripe for positive, life-affirming

> Animal advocacy is, in a certain sense, standing up to tell true life stories that are not being heard; true life stories that most people are ignoring. The first step in animal advocacy is to help people see things differently. Animals are somebody, not something.
>
> **Tom Regan**
> *Satya* magazine, August 2004

changes. That's not to say you shouldn't hand out vegan literature elsewhere – train stations, concerts, busy street corners, festivals, street fairs and other public places with high foot traffic are all great – but you're unlikely to find a more effective location than a college campus.

"At the moment, I don't think the animal protection movement is even reaching ten percent of college students," says Erik Marcus, who uses his weekly podcast on Vegan.com to promote activism. "Given that leafleting requires no special background and is something that anyone can do, I can't think of a better starting point for new activists who want to make a difference."

Voices of Experience

Crisscrossing the country as a full-time vegan leafleter, Jon says his two main goals are creating new vegans and encouraging more people to leaflet. "All of our most prolific leafleters have seen firsthand the tangible impacts of leafleting," he says. "Those of us who do this on a regular basis continue to come across individuals who have been vegetarian or vegan as a result of our work, who have gotten active for the animals, who have said that this work has changed their outlook on life, etc. Our work is not sophisticated or glamorous, but it does create significant change."

Following is Jon Camp's advice ...
On starting out:

- Without question, the first booklet is the most difficult to give out. Some find it best to make their leafleting debut with another person – either an experienced leafleter or someone starting out for their first time as well. However, some don't have that option, as they might not know of any others interested in doing this. My suggestion for them is to just take the plunge and give out that first booklet.

On a new leafleter's concerns:

- There are a few main concerns with individuals considering leafleting. One is that they will be asked a bunch of questions and they will not know how to adequately respond to them. The good news for these people is that the vast majority of individuals will either take a booklet or say, "no thanks." And for those who do wish to ask questions, we don't need to be encyclopedias. Our answers to most questions can be as simple as, "Animals suffer unnecessarily on factory farms and slaughter-houses. We can reduce this suffering by opting for more vegetarian fare." Or if someone has health questions, we can always just give the person a starter guide such as Vegan Outreach's *Guide to Cruelty-Free Eating.*

On negative responses and rude people:

- Some new leafleters worry that individuals are going to be rude, yet only a very tiny number of people are, and we can always just respond to those few by telling them that we're sorry that they don't agree with us but to have a nice day.
- The most common negative response is, "I like meat," and this usually isn't stated in some vitriolic manner. Many of our leafleters have found that simply saying, "You can still read the booklet," "This booklet is for those who like meat," or, if they don't seem at all interested, "Well, have

a nice day." We created our *Even If You Like Meat* booklet with this in mind.

• Some might make a nasty or belittling comment, but those who do are a very small minority. Leafleting is a statistics game – if you give out X amount of booklets, you're most likely going to reach many receptive individuals and help animals significantly. I've found it best to not let nasty comments get to me, just smile it off, and focus on the good we can do. One thing that animal advocates have on our side is a sense of compassion and kindness. Responding to nasty comments with kindness presents us with a great opportunity to make people think; frequently individuals who make a rude comment at first will come up later, apologize and ask for a booklet.

• And some may worry about irritating those they leaflet. But if done in a polite, friendly manner, this shouldn't be an issue. Many people are excited to get a booklet on this issue, and even if we do create a slight inconvenience, it is only for a second. The flip side is that this work can help spare animals an enormous amount of suffering. A minor inconvenience to one might mean warding off a major inconvenience to many animals.

Leafleting Tips from Paul Shapiro, HSUS:

• Always look professional and clean-cut. Activists have found that the general public is much more receptive if we look as mainstream as our message of compassion should be.

• While leafleting, try to be outgoing and friendly. A simple smile can have a dramatic effect on how people perceive you and serve as an encouraging invitation to take a brochure. If someone is wearing a team shirt, commenting positively about their team is a quick ice breaker that makes it hard for them to refuse your leaflet, and leaves them with the impression, for example, "That animal rights person is an Orioles fan, too."

• Try to place the leaflet directly in front of the passing person's stomach so it's less effort for them to take the brochure from you if they so choose.

• If you have a conversation with someone, make sure to stay focused. Never lose sight of why you're there: to expose the misery endured by farmed animals and to promote veganism as a solution.

• Be overly polite and make it easy for them to take the literature. When we refer to people as "ma'am" or "sir" and say "thank you" or "have a great day" to those who take literature, we are seen as polite, well-meaning individuals concerned about the issue, rather than "radical militants" who the public is all too eager to dismiss.

Other Leafleting

Veganism isn't the only topic your leafleting efforts can focus on. Fur, circuses, vivisection, rodeos and companion-animal issues are just a few additional animal-rights concerns about which activists can educate the public by handing out literature. PETA, an excellent resource for getting active in leafleting campaigns, organizes at least one leafleting campaign every month, targeting a specific issue, such as "Kentucky Fried Cruelty" or its efforts to free the dogs and cats languishing in animal-food test labs at Iams Company. Each one of these monthly campaigns results in the face-to-face distribution of about thirty thousand leaflets, and as a whole, PETA's

activist network hands out millions of pieces of animal-rights literature every year. Joining this network is a great way to get started. Check it out at animalactivist.com.

Leafleting may also be an adjunct to other forms of activism. For example, a few other activists and I recently demonstrated against the Canadian seal slaughter. We each stood at separate corners of a busy intersection holding a protest sign; when drivers paused to ask questions like "Didn't they outlaw

Alex Bury finds plenty of people to educate about fur outside the San Francisco Opera.

that already?" we'd offer them a pamphlet provided by the Humane Society of the United States explaining the latest facts about the annual massacre and what they can do to help end it.

In addition to handing out leaflets, you can also post them on bulletin boards in public areas such as apartment buildings, companion-animal supply stores, laundry facilities, libraries, student unions, super-markets and veterinary offices. Your leaflet will stand a better chance of staying in place if you can get permission before posting it in a public area. Often, vegan and vegetarian restaurants and health food stores will allow you to leave a small stack of pamphlets near the register or in a designated literature rack. Leaving stacks of leaflets out is a great idea because everyone who picks one up is actually interested in the topic – you're reaching the lowest-hanging fruit, and with almost no time

Leafleting in Cyberspace

Activist Nora Kramer suggests posting an ad for a "Free Vegetarian Starter Guide" on Craigslist.org:

1. Go to Craigslist.org.

2. Click on your (or any) city on the right-hand side.

3. Click on the section titled "free" in the "for sale" section.

4. Click on the link titled "post" (in the upper right-hand corner).

5. Type out and submit your message explaining where they can get a Free Vegetarian Starter Guide, using as a link http://www.veganoutreach.org/st arterpack/free-vsp.html or a similar veggie guide link from PETA, Mercy For Animals, etc.

6. Click "post" and follow the final directions, then repeat once a week, as the posts get removed.

expenditure on your part. If you leave some there, be sure to check back frequently and restock the supply – the leaflets go fast!

Some activists like to set up a table in a public area with lots of foot traffic, such as outside a grocery store, and offer a variety of pamphlets on animal issues (permission is usually required for setting up a table, and a permit may be needed). This model of activism takes a little more time and effort, and we'll address it in Chapter 3.

Getting Started

Like any model of activism, leafleting takes a certain level of commitment. "It's important to take things slowly at first," says Jenna Calabrese of Vegan Outreach. "Some great activism has been done in just thirty minutes on a campus. We want leafleters to be able to continue to do this for years to come, rather than burning out within the first few months because they tried to put in eight-hour days right off the bat."

Although it is a very easy tactic, walking around handing out booklets to passersby can sometimes feel routine, and you may encounter a few rude people. As Jon Camp points out, it's important to remember how much good leafleting does for animals.

"In just a matter of an hour," he says, "we can oftentimes reach hundreds of individuals with this information. Even if just one individual goes vegetarian out of this, we're looking at approximately thirty-five birds and mammals spared a life of suffering per year. This is not including the number of people who will be more empathetic to farmed animal issues and such. In short, this is a highly effective and efficient use of time. So while it might be easy to dwell on the worst-case scenario, the likeliest of scenarios is always that leafleting will be relatively painless and that as a result, many more individuals will consider the animals' plight."

To emphasize his point, Jon likes to share his favorite example of how powerful vegan leafleting can be. About fifteen years ago, Matt Ball – now executive director for Vegan Outreach, but then a student at the University of Illinois – was distributing vegan literature at his campus when he was approached by two men: a dairy farmer and a fellow student named Joe Espinosa. Rather than berating the dairy farmer for exploiting animals, Matt used a very respectful tone and discussed the positive aspects of veganism. Joe was so impressed by Matt's civil approach that he got some information himself, went vegan and has gone on to hand out more than one hundred thousand booklets on behalf of Vegan Outreach and farmed animals. "So," says Jon, "Matt's decision to get out that day and speak up for the animals has yielded some enormous benefits!"

Resources:

Compassion Over Killing
www.cok.net

PETA (activism site)
www.animalactivist.com or peta.org

Vegan Outreach
www.veganoutreach.org

CHAPTER 2

ANIMAL WRITES: LETTERS, OPINION PIECES & ARTICLES

Our lives begin to end the day we become silent about things that matter.
Martin Luther King, Jr.

It took only a few weeks and the power of the computer to help Fortnum & Mason, one of London's oldest department stores, change its business practices. When word reached activists that Fortnum's was selling clothing trimmed with rabbit, fox and mink fur, the UK office of the Coalition to Abolish the Fur Trade quickly organized a campaign that began with emails to the company's director and further plans to protest outside the store in Piccadilly Circus. Citing "the unspeakable cruelty involved in the fur trade," Isabel Reinhards was just one of many activists who wrote to express their disgust and remind the store's director that fur farms are so horrific the parliament voted in 2000 to ban them in the UK. Bombarded with correspondence, and not very keen on the idea of a protest outside its doors, Fortnum's agreed that what is good for animals is good for the company's bottom line. "After considering the subject they decided to comply with our requests for ethical reasons," says Isabel, who notes that politely educating companies about animal cruelty can go a long way. (We'll discuss this point in Chapter 6.)

Indeed, courtesy is a key element of activism, and letters afford us the opportunity to choose our words carefully. "Although anger gives backbone to compassion, legitimate emotional responses to animal suffering and abuse must be transformed into a mature and compelling statement of the problem, why it matters and what you want the recipient to do about it," says Karen Davis, who probably spends more time writing than any animal activist I know.

Many people consider writing an art – and a lost one at that. Long gone are the days when we regularly drafted letters to friends and family to stay in touch. We rely so much on technologies like spell check and text messaging that, left to our own devices, composing a complete sentence can be a daunting experience for some. But don't let this wonderful way to campaign for animals slip past you. Writing letters to editors, policymakers and companies is not difficult, and this tactic can be very effective.

"Letter-writing appeals to activists who may not feel comfortable standing on the sidewalk holding a poster or confronting a fur-coat wearer standing in the grocery store line," says Anna West, director of written communications for PETA. She adds that letters can have far-reaching effects. "When you send a letter to the editor of a newspaper or magazine, you are not only sending a message to those editors that animal rights is an important issue that readers want to see more of, but if your letter is printed, you can potentially educate millions of people."

Letters to the Editor
Since the Letters page is one of the most highly read sections of newspapers and magazines, a letter to the editor is one of the best tools animal activists have for making our message heard. Letters to editors are easy to write, and every community has at least one newspaper. Sending letters to the editor is effective because they:

- reach a very large audience
- can be used to rebut information not accurately addressed in a news article or editorial
- create an impression of widespread support or opposition to an issue
- are widely read by community leaders and lawmakers to gauge public sentiment about current issues.

There are essentially two kinds of letters to the editor: "soapbox" letters in which the writer expresses an opinion but is not responding to something in the paper, and letters that are in direct response to an article, editorial or another letter that recently appeared in the publication.

As president of United Poultry Concerns, a non-profit haven for domestic fowl, Karen Davis has devoted her life to working toward a better future for chickens, turkeys and ducks. The Virginia-based sanctuary is the focus of most of her waking hours, and yet this former English instructor understands the importance of effective communication, so she also writes brochures, white papers, articles, opinion pieces, letters to editors and books such as *More Than a Meal: The Turkey in History, Myth, Ritual, and Reality* and *The Holocaust & The Henmaid's Tale*. Karen estimates she spends about ninety-eight percent of her activist time and energy formulating ideas, strategies and calls for action in the medium of words.

"A lot of time is spent researching the information needed to craft an effective piece of writing," she says. "For me, even a letter to the editor is a painstaking process in which every word, phrase and sentence is carefully weighed for content, clarity, concision, rhythm, sound and style. Form and content are inseparable parts of the process."

While not every activist spends as much time as Karen crafting a letter, it is important to think carefully about the message you want to convey and do so in as few words as possible, especially for a letter to the editor. Being knowledgeable about the subject helps, which is why Karen advises that activists learn all they can about the issues and arguments surrounding animal rights. "When you take time to learn about the issue, you can add relevant details to your writing that enrich it beyond mere venting and generalities. This makes your letter more interesting and increases your credibility."

She observes that our culture pays particular attention to "what science says." When writing letters or opinion pieces (an "op-ed"), Karen often quotes poultry scientists, and she cites these examples:

- "Bruce Webster of the University of Georgia says factory-farmed chickens are 'treated like bowling balls.'"
- "Bird specialist Lesley Rogers writes: 'I am convinced chickens are not animals that should be kept in mentally and socially deprived conditions. They are as complex as the cats and dogs we share our homes with.'"

Writers Groups

Joining a writers group, such as those offered by PETA, Mercy For Animals and Compassion Over Killing, is a great way to get started with letters to editors. Heidi Jury Parker, a writer for PETA, suggests activists start off by writing letters to the editors regarding animal issues in response to the group's action alerts. "Frequent letter-writers can join the Volunteer Writers E-Mail Network to be alerted to opportunities to write additional, time-sensitive letters," she says. "PETA's Writers Group seeks volunteers who are familiar with animal-rights issues, have writing experience or enjoy writing, have regular access to and working knowledge of the Internet and email and who are able to respond to email alerts within two days." PETA notifies writers when a newspaper publishes an animal-related story in their geographical area, tells them where to send the letters and offers fact sheets for the given issue.

Adds Anna: "We have seen an increase in the amount of animal-related letters to the editor that are printed in newspapers and magazines, and we have every reason to believe that is because more people are taking the time – maybe on their lunch break or after dinner – to jot down a letter and email it to their local paper or to a national publication, like *Time* or *Newsweek*."

> **Google Alerts**
>
> An easy way to find out if your letters have been printed is by setting up a Google Alert at www.google.com/alerts. Just enter your name in the "Search terms" field, choose how often you'd like to receive the results and then enter your email address. Links to letters signed by you and published in newspapers that are searchable on Google's news page will be emailed to you automatically.

Tips for Getting Your Letter to the Editor Published

• Be concise. Start with a strong introductory sentence and follow it up with short, clear facts. Focus on the most important issue rather than trying to cover everything. Most newspapers publish letters that are no more than three hundred words.

• Always include your first and last name, mailing address and daytime and evening phone numbers in case the newspaper or magazine wants to

> Thankfully, the enthusiasm and passion of new activists push, prompt and inspire us to constantly be mindful of why we do what we do and consider innovative ways to bring about lasting change. By adding their earnest voices to the collective cry demanding an end to animal suffering, they are the future of the movement.
>
> **Miyun Park**
> *Satya* magazine, October 2002

verify that you submitted the letter (though generally only the larger publications will contact you). Only your name and hometown will appear in print.

• Stay professional. Polite, proofread letters are far more effective than personal attacks.

• Mention anything that makes you especially qualified to write on a topic. For example: "As a cancer survivor, I understand the importance of a diet that avoids animal flesh."

• Readers care about how an issue will affect them personally. Including information on the local economic or other impacts of an issue will draw readers' interest.

• It is just as important to respond to positive stories, like pro-vegetarian articles, as it is to respond to the negative ones, such as a pro-vivisection article. Generally, people writing letters to newspapers are more likely to voice complaints rather than give compliments, so complimentary letters may be valuable and more likely to be printed.

• Letters to editors sent via email arrive promptly and don't need to be re-typed. Type your text into a word processing program (i.e., Microsoft Word) and then paste the letter into the body of the email – do not send attachments.

• Remember who your audience is. Direct letters to readers, rather than the newspaper or author of the piece you are responding to. Write your letter so that it makes sense to someone who did not see the piece. Avoid long sentences and big words that the average reader may not understand (unless you're writing to a scientific or technical publication).

Tips for Effective Animal-Rights Letters to Editors

• Tell readers something they might not know – such as that most hens are confined in battery cages or how dairy cows are treated to produce milk – and suggest ways readers can make a difference (stop buying eggs and dairy products).

- Include information about the issue(s); do not assume that readers already know. For example, rather than writing "Foie gras production is bad," be specific: "In order to create 'fatty livers,' foie gras producers subject ducks and geese to an invasive feeding technique that forces into their stomachs up to thirty percent of their body weight every day. That's like a two-hundred-pound (91-kilogram) man being forced to swallow sixty pounds (27.3 kilograms) of food a day."
- Watch your language. Instead of referring to an animal with an inanimate pronoun ("that" or "it"), use "who," "she" or "he." Also, use "animal advocates" rather than "animal-rights groups," "farmed animals" rather than the friendly "farm animals" and "painkiller" rather than "anesthesia."
- Use positive suggestions to help readers make a difference. For example, rather than simply writing "Boycott the circus," you can suggest events that don't use animals, such as Cirque du Soleil, or direct them to Web sites like circuses.com.
- Do not use overly dramatic language, which may turn some readers off. Let the facts speak for themselves.
- Use an affirmative voice. For example, rather than writing "Vegans are not wimps," write "Vegans have a much healthier body-mass index than most meat-eaters, and they live years longer."
- Promote the friendly side of veganism/vegetarianism ("veg*nism") and animal advocacy, and refrain from insults, which will hurt your credibility and perpetuate a negative opinion of animal activists.
- Like humans, animals have a wide range of emotions. Try to depict this in your letters and help people understand how similar animals are to us. For example, "Like all animals, pigs feel pain and fear ..."

Don't be discouraged if your letter is not printed. Every letter you submit educates the editorial board of newspapers and magazines worldwide and paves the way for future letters to be printed. Monica Ball, a volunteer with

PETA's Writers Group, estimates she writes about eight letters a week to editors. "Of course, only a small percentage are published," she says. "Nonetheless, I feel it's important to write the letters because it keeps topics alive in editor's minds and lets them know there is interest in animal rights and animal welfare issues. Also, even when my letters aren't published, they may play a role in getting someone else's letter on the same topic published. And any letter published represents potential for change and is a small victory for animals."

Letters to Legislators

Like newspaper editors, public officials get lots of letters. But unlike letters to editors, letters to a senator, assemblyperson, Member of Parliament, etc., could have an immediate and long-lasting impact on a piece of legislation to protect animals. Think of a letter (or email, fax or phone call) to a politician as a vote: the more they receive in support of or opposition to one issue, the more interest the legislator is likely to pay to that issue. Public officials appreciate hearing about the concerns of their constituency, and they have the power to make changes. For example, Compassion in World Farming (CIWF) and the Royal Society for the Prevention of Cruelty to Animals organized a massive letter-writing campaign to Members of Parliament in 1991, which led to a ban on sow stalls (gestation crates) in the UK.

Most activists agree that when writing to an elected official, it's best to take the time to draft something either by hand or using the computer (or typewriter). Don't rely on a pre-printed piece created as part of a specific campaign. "Members of Parliament prefer a personally written letter over postcards that people just sign and post," says Joyce D'Silva of CIWF. "They take the issue more seriously. And a letter usually requires an answer – or they might not get the vote next time round!"

If you want to go the extra mile, especially if you know officials will be voting on an animal issue soon, send a follow-up email or call the legislator's office after sending your letter. Karen Davis offers this example: "Recently I urged council members in San Diego to vote to ban foie gras. A council meeting was scheduled for the next day. So I wrote and emailed a letter, which I then printed out on [United Poultry Concerns] letterhead and faxed to each council member. Then I called each council member to introduce myself and to alert them that I had emailed and faxed a letter about the upcoming meeting on foie gras. That way, I covered my bases and felt reassured that I'd done what I could under a time constraint, and I like making direct contact with people I'm trying to influence."

> When we were debating gestation crates in the Westminster Parliament in 1991 at the time of the first Gulf War, several Parliament Members stood up and said "I've had more letters from the people in my constituency on pigs than I have on the war!" This is because we wrote to everyone saying that if you only write one letter this year, write this one. And they did! It's the case of democracy actually working for once.
>
> **Joyce D'Silva**
> *Satya* magazine, June/July 2005

Karen will even send a letter by express mail or some other method requiring a signature, and she believes a letter on an organization's letterhead can carry a weight in the corporate or legislative domain that an email does not. "As in all things," she says, "the situation should dictate by what means you send your letter."

Of course, the average activist probably doesn't even have imprinted stationery, let alone work with an organization, and that's fine – grassroots activism does not require a big budget. A sincere letter to your elected official, addressing one piece of legislation or a single issue that concerns you, is a powerful method for speaking up for animals.

Here's a suggested format for a simple letter to a public official:

Paragraph 1 – introduce yourself in two or three sentences ("I am a college student and avid hiker who recently learned of a plan to shoot non-native deer in our state as way to reduce their population....").

Paragraph 2 – develop your point and position on this issue ("You may not know that there are non-lethal ways to control wildlife population, including...").

Paragraph 3 – conclude your position on this issue and ask the legislator to support it ("Furthermore, the National Park Service has not demonstrated that the eradication of these beautiful animals is even necessary.... I hope you will agree that there is no reason to kill the deer and will do what you can to ensure that a more humane solution is found").

Sign-off – ask for a reply ("Thank you for your time, and I look forward to your response").

Tips for Effective Letters to Legislators

- Include your name and address on both your letter and envelope.
- Deal with only one issue or one piece of legislation at a time.
- If you live within the boundaries served by your elected official, let them know you are a constituent.
- Remember that your legislator's job is to represent you. Be respectful, but don't be afraid to take a firm position.
- Avoid detailed personal stories.
- Handwritten letters seem to hold more sway with legislators. The action of writing a letter by hand tells the official you feel passionate about the issue.
- A typed letter, or one written on a computer, and signed in ink invokes a similar feeling of deep personal concern.
- Politicians know it is easy to create mail-merge documents, and form

letters tell the recipient "I am not vested enough in this issue to write an original letter to you."

- Proofread your letter for grammar, spelling and punctuation errors.
- Ask for a reply. Ending the letter with "I look forward to your response" will let him/her know that you want a reply. (But don't be surprised if the reply you receive looks like a form letter.

Phone It In!

When the matter is urgent – such as an issue legislators will be deciding on in a day or two – it is advisable to call your elected official right away. Also, many letters to lawmakers now go through a security screening, which can delay their arrival to the recipient.

The legislator may have received numerous letters on the same issue you contacted him/her about and may have a prepared response.)

Activist Tim I. Martin believes that letters to editors and legislators work in concert to achieve advances for animals. "Policymakers often have a vested interest in what readers write to editors," he says. "A series of letters to legislators, multiplied using the power of the press, can have more leverage in getting those leaders to open up their ears, if not their hearts and minds. Letters to the editor are a good example of leverage, in addition to getting a lot of exposure for a small effort."

"Needless to say," adds Karen, "not all policymakers are receptive and not all letter-writing campaigns succeed. Getting Congress to move on an animal protection bill, especially a farmed-animal protection bill, is very hard, even with many letters over a period of years. The thing about writing letters and making phone calls is that you improve your communication skills. You become more confident, and confidence is crucial to effective activism."

Honorifics
Show respect for policymakers by using the proper form of address in your letters.

Members of Congress:
The Honorable John/Jane Doe

Member, Senate:
Dear Senator Doe
Member, House of Representatives:
Dear Congressman/woman Doe

Prime Ministers:
Dear Prime Minister Doe

Other Officials and elected representatives:
Dear (Title) Doe

Opinion Pieces

Opinion pieces, known as "op-eds" because they generally run opposite a newspaper's editorial page, are another popular venue for advancing the interests of animals. Op-eds are written by a reader on a topic that is relevant to the newspaper's audience. Because op-eds run longer than letters and the paper prints only one or two in an issue (sometimes more on Sunday), getting one accepted and published is a little trickier. Since they are longer than letters to the editor, they offer an opportunity for a better-developed argument. Op-eds (sometimes called "guest columns") are formatted like an essay, with the writer taking a position and elaborating on that position in about seven hundred words – longer if the writer is well known or represents a well-known organization.

"To improve your chance of publication, it's important to know something about the publication you're submitting your piece to," says Karen. "I think it can also help to call the editorial page editor in advance and present your idea to him or her and make use of whatever advice they give, before submitting your piece. My writing has benefited enormously from editorial advice and editing."

Kathy Guillermo, a writer for PETA and author of countless op-eds, recommends emailing the editor a day or two after submitting a piece. "If you get no response to that," she says, "then call the editor and ask if the piece was received and if the editor had time to read it. Always be very polite and professional. Sometimes a phone call can make all the difference because it can prompt an editor to take a look at a piece that he or she hadn't noticed before." Kathy cautions writers not to get upset if their submission isn't printed. "Understand that editors have many issues to deal with and though we know that our issue is literally a matter of life and death, not everyone else sees it as urgent. And if your op-ed isn't chosen this time, your next piece may be, so it's not a good idea to burn any bridges by, say, accusing an editor of being biased or unreasonable."

For Karen, a rejected op-ed simply means she rewrites it a bit. "Over the years, I've published many guest columns about the plight – and delight – of chickens and turkeys. I've also written letters and op-eds that were turned down. Usually in such cases, I rework the piece and eventually submit it elsewhere with success. Also, it's good to establish a relationship with an editorial page editor. Not to ramble on and take up their valuable time, but a brief friendly phone call about your submission can increase your chance of being published, and you may be pleased to learn on occasion that the editorial page editor cares about animals and values your concerns."

Tips for Getting Your Op-Ed Published

- Let readers know your view by getting to the point. The first sentence should reveal what you intend to write about.
- Make your argument accessible to a general audience, not just an academic one.
- Bring a local connection to a national issue if possible.
- Know something about the paper you are sending your piece to and the type of pieces they print and adjust accordingly.
- Check the newspaper's guidelines online for their rules regarding op-eds.
- Include a call to action – something that the readers can do, such as visiting a vegetarian Web site for more information or calling their legislator to voice concern.
- As always, use correct grammar, spelling, sentence construction and

other essentials of composition. Lack of attention to these details discredits the author.

- Editors receive fewer op-ed submissions right before major holidays and toward the end of summer, so these may be opportune times to get yours published.
- Unless you're submitting to a news service, your op-ed should be an exclusive to the publication – no simultaneous submissions. (Though by all means send it to another paper if the first editor declines it.)

Articles

There's something extremely rewarding about writing for a publication: having an idea for an article, pitching your idea to a magazine editor, writing the piece and then seeing it in print, knowing that thousands of people will be reading your words. It's especially gratifying to me when the piece I've contributed helps educate people about animal abuse or focuses on a solution to it, like veganism.

A good place to start is with the publications you already enjoy. Which of these publish articles, media reviews, interviews and profiles with a perspective on animal rights? Such magazines are always looking for contributors who can bring a fresh viewpoint to activism, animal issues, veganism, etc. "I look for honesty and, if it fits the tone of the story, humor," says Sienna Blake, editor of *Vegan Voice*. "There are a few different types of articles, and I try to get a good selection into each issue. I try to keep the bulk of the magazine positive these days. My advice to contributors would be to write from your heart and write what you know."

Herbivore editor Josh Hooten encourages writers to have fun. "We love lively, humorous, passionate writing," he says. "We aren't all that concerned with formal training or refined journalism, though we appreciate it. We're more interested in a great story being told with guts and energy. So many publications have no strong voice. We want some fire and some passion." Josh notes that one thing that sets his magazine apart from others is that *Herbivore* runs stories few publications will touch. "There are so many things going on out there that are related in some way to veganism, vegetarianism and animal rights that would just never make it on to other publishers' radars, but that we find fascinating. We've run features on topics ranging from a vegan trapeze artist to a vegan bicycle maker to the SHAC 7, who are in prison for their activism. While most magazines wouldn't see the connection in those things, any project or outlet that is coming from the viewpoint of a veg person is connected to what we're all about." Though he looks for pieces that address activism, art, humor, music, travel and personalities within the animal-rights movement, Josh says the field is wide open to contributors. "We really like pieces that empower our readers to take more control of their consumption and lifestyle, and we hope to do more of these in the future."

Over at *VegNews*, managing editor Aurelia d'Andrea emphasizes that writers should know a magazine well before pitching an idea to them. "For instance," she says, "a five-thousand-word manuscript on the wonders of beeswax wouldn't be a good fit for *VegNews* because (a) it's not vegan, and (b) we don't run five-thousand-word articles. It's clear that many writers who pitch us don't really have a good handle on length or appropriate subject matter, which shows they haven't done their homework." Aurelia's plea is a familiar refrain in the publishing business: she's looking for fresh ideas. "Many pitches we receive aren't novel ones," she says. "We get a lot of 'It's easy being vegan – here's how' and 'Kale (or another vegetable): How this miracle plant saved my life/cured my cancer.' What we, and other publications, look for are smart ideas that haven't been done a thousand times before, but that still fit the general voice and format of our publications. A great piece of advice I would give to aspiring writers wishing to be published in *VegNews* is to keep abreast of veg issues. Read the big papers, the indie press, gorge on magazines and public radio, and look for ideas and inspiration that could be shaped into an article that fits our unique voice and style."

But animal activism requires that we reach beyond our comfort zones, so also consider publications outside the movement for story submissions. Because animal exploitation is literally everywhere, you will likely find an animal-rights angle for any magazine, and the more mainstream it is the better. A publication on health may be interested in a submission having to do with animal testing or the benefits of soy, while a travel magazine may publish your article on veggie vacations or a profile of a local animal sanctuary that's open to the public. Just remember that writing articles for such consumer publications requires a lighter touch than writing for animal-rights magazines. Unless it's an opinion piece, when writing about any animal abuse, just let the facts speak for themselves.

There's also a middle way: approach a magazine that is not specifically an animal-rights publication, but is open to promoting the movement within its pages. Vegan Shari Black Velvet, for example, started her eponymous magazine in 1994 to cover the UK's music scene. "*Black Velvet* is first and foremost a rock music magazine," she says. "However, as I believe in animal rights, I have included a couple of animal rights-based interviews over the years and a lot of the time try to mention if a musician is vegetarian, vegan or a supporter of animal rights."

Volunteer Your Skills

Finally, if you're truly inspired by the writing muse, consider using your skills to help a local animal organization with their written material. This could be a newsletter, email alert, press release, bylined op-ed (you "ghost write" the piece for someone else), brochure, fundraiser letter, Web site text* – just about anything. A funny thing about non-profits, though: they are not always prompt about responding to people who volunteer their time and services. If this happens to you, try not to take it personally. Non-profit organizations are notoriously understaffed, and animal groups are no exception. It's best to call and speak to someone rather than email them with your offer to help.

Good writing is indeed an art, and it has incredible power. Whether you can compose brief letters to editors or longer pieces for newspapers, magazines or an animal-rights group, your ability to translate your passion for compassion into words will raise awareness and help advance the interests of countless animals.

* For some beautifully written prose about farmed animals, read the posts by Joanna Lucas on the Peaceful Prairie Sanctuary's blog at http://peaceful-prairie.blogspot.com.

Resources:

Black Velvet

www.blackvelvetmagazine.com

Coalition to Abolish the Fur Trade

www.caft.org.uk

Compassion in World Farming

www.ciwf.org

Compassion Over Killing Writers Group

www.cok.net/camp/writers

Herbivore

http://herbivoremagazine.com

Mercy For Animals Writers Group

www.mercyforanimals.org/writers_group.asp

PETA's Action Center

www.peta.org/actioncenter/letter-writing-guide.asp

THOMAS

In the spirit of Thomas Jefferson, THOMAS provides federal legislative information from the US Library of Congress.

http://thomas.loc.gov

United Poultry Concerns

www.upc-online.org

Vegan Voice

http://veganic.net

VegNews

www.vegnews.com

Also:

Online listings of print and other media throughout Australia:

www.abyznewslinks.com/austr.htm

Online listings of print and other media throughout Canada:

www.altstuff.com/newspapr.htm

Online listings of print and other media throughout New Zealand:

www.abyznewslinks.com/newze.htm

Online listings of print and other media throughout South Africa:

www.abyznewslinks.com/safri.htm

Online listings of print and other media throughout the UK:

www.wrx.zen.co.uk/alltnews.htm

www.thepaperboy.com/uk/

Online listings of print and other media throughout the US:

http://newslink.org/topstate.html

www.usnpl.com/

Online listing of print and other media throughout the world:

www.onlinenewspapers.com/

www.world-newspapers.com/

CHAPTER 3

ANIMAL TALK: TABLING

In a time of universal deceit, telling the truth becomes a revolutionary act.
George Orwell

The first time Nathan Runkle visited an animal-rights information table, set up inside a local shopping mall, he went away with more than a handful of pamphlets – he went away with a new lifestyle. "The information was presented by an animal-rights group here in Ohio called People/Animals Network," he recalls, "and I took a bunch of literature. I remember reading it and feeling sick to my stomach. I had never heard of factory farming or vivisection or veal crates or battery cages. It was so clear to me then that this was the problem." Nathan promptly researched and presented a report on animal rights to his class and went vegetarian. He was eleven years old. Four years later he founded Mercy For Animals, one of the most highly regarded animal-rights organizations in the world. Mercy For Animals is among a handful of groups actively investigating the exploitation of animals in factory farms, and Nathan has become a vocal thorn in the side of agribusiness. And to think it all began because some activists were tabling at the mall.

As Nathan will attest, tabling (also called "holding a stall" in some countries) is one of the most effective outreach activities you can do for animals; it will put your knowledge of animal exploitation and its remedies to good use.

To table or hold a stall is simply to arrange a selection of leaflets, fact sheets, stickers and other printed information on a folding table, or something similar, for the public to take with them. Your table can also display a banner and even show a video – anything to attract people and help them understand the extent of animal abuse in our culture. You remain at the table, answering questions and selling related merchandise, if you have any.

Animal Aid's popular street stall.

Most of the larger non-profit animal-rights groups will supply you with all the literature you need. Although it takes a little more time than handing out leaflets, tabling gives you the chance to share a lot more information, collect names for your database and give people a glimpse of what animal activism is all about – not the skewed image they may have gleaned from negative press stories or a Web site devoted to animal exploitation.

Opportunities for tabling are as varied as the tables themselves: concerts, school events, health food stores, parks, festivals and shopping centers are among the many places you can set up a table. The first time I ever tabled was during an animal-rights conference in Berkeley, California. I was representing Animal Place, and I thought it was just about the easiest gig in the world. Countless people stopped by to learn about the sanctuary, pick up literature and add their names to our sign-up sheet. "This is great," I thought. "Everyone loves Animal Place."

Then I tabled at the county fair amid the pony rides and livestock auctions. At first I was surprised that the table wasn't attracting as many people. I wondered what was wrong: Did our banner fall down? Were the chicken photos not clearly visible? Was I having an especially bad hair day? Then I got a whiff of the barbecued pig flesh from a nearby stall. It was a different audience and a completely different experience. But how many more hearts do you think might be won over at the fair versus a venue filled with animal-rights activists? Most of the people who did stop at the table were surprised to learn there was such a thing as a sanctuary for farmed animals, which made the fair an ideal place for addressing the many problems with factory farming. And I sold more of Animal Place's vegan cookbooks that day than I've ever sold at progressive events.

"Having a stand or table is always so beneficial whatever way you look at it," says John Carmody of Animal Rights Action Network Ireland. "We tend to organize national tabling events from time to time, and in this we have a fantastic display of literature which is always displayed in a really cool, eye-catching way. We love to use a banner to highlight the group's name, but what gets people going is a fantastic DVD that shows many exciting demos and events we have held, and the background music is Elvis singing 'A little less conversation, a little more action, please.' My number-one tip for having such a successful display is to be hugely warm, friendly, knowledgeable and always understanding with the other person in order to ensure they don't feel alienated."

There are a number of ways that individual activists and their friends can get in on the tabling fun:

- You can volunteer with an organization that regularly tables at local venues. If you've never tabled before, this is a great way to get your feet wet. Search the Web for vegetarian groups in your area and ask them about upcoming events.
- Many animal advocacy groups such as Farm Sanctuary, PETA and Viva! have everything you'll need to table in your neighborhood, including literature, displays and signage.
- Set up your own table. Ask a like-minded, outgoing friend to join you and the experience will be more enjoyable. One person can stand behind the table while the other mingles with the flow of foot traffic, handing out leaflets and directing people to your display.

"Tabling for animal rights does not require any activism experience," says Dan Shannon, PETA's manager of youth outreach and campaigns, though he does recommend that activists plan well. "It is always helpful to prepare for outreach events by researching your topic; setting goals; dressing appropriately; mentally preparing to present the best possible image for animal rights, veganism and any organization with whom you're affiliated – like peta2 – and staying focused on the goals and sticking to your script."

"We really enjoy tabling at peace fairs or any kind of community event like a street party or art festivals," says Adam Durand of Compassionate Consumers. "We try to table at events that don't charge a fee, and it's really important to find the right kind of event and craft your message to that event. You know, if you're going to an environmental event, you can bring some more information on how animal consumption impacts the environment."

Knowing your venue ahead of time can save time and money, warns Erica Meier, executive director of Compassion Over Killing. "One of the biggest concerns for us when we consider tabling is the number of attendees at the event," she says. "We've been to some community events that were very, very small and that time probably would have been better spent leafleting on a busy street corner and reached many more people." Adam agrees, noting that some venues charge a tabling fee that may be beyond the budget of individuals or even some animal-rights groups. "Sometimes we find it's actually easier to leaflet an event," he says. "Bringing backpacks full of leaflets and talking to people at these events sometimes works just as well as actually setting up a table."

> Animal activists should also build stronger bridges with the environmental movement, as we share many common goals, specifically with regard to fighting factory farms.
>
> **Erica Meier**
> *Satya* magazine, June/July 2005

Bruce Friedrich, who is in charge of international grassroots campaigns for PETA, says some of the best locations in the US for setting up activist tables are government-owned property like metro stations, public streets and even some convention centers. "They may try to tell you that you can't table there," he says, "but they have no right to." Even government-owned zoos have to let you pass out anti-zoo literature, right at the entrance, if you like. "They'll try to shunt you to the sidewalk," Bruce says, "but legally, they can't do that. PETA is ready to consult with anyone, anytime, if they're told they can't table or leaflet in a certain place."

Getting Permission

Pick a good location for your table – one with plenty of foot traffic – and then investigate whether or not you'll need permission to table there. For example, if you'll be holding your stall at a concert or other performance, contact the show manager. To table on campus – either at your school or another one – check with the student activities office. If you want to table at a shopping center or outside a theater, you'll need permission from the manager, as this is private property. (UK-based Animal Aid says that in practice, many people do stalls in the street without getting permission, and as long as the police do not deem you to be causing an obstruction and they do not get any complaints from businesses near the stall, you may be okay.)

You may not need permission to table in a park or other public space, but it's best to first check with a city official, such as the local council or mayor's office, before setting up your stall. Be sure to ask:

- If you need a permit to table in your chosen location.
- If there are rules regarding the sale of merchandise at your table. (If there are restrictions, you can simply ask for a donation instead.)
- If there are any restrictions to what you can display or make available to the public.

When asking for permission, let the person know you will bring all your own material and will take care to clean up afterward.

Setting Up

Having an attractive table means more than just being organized or making sure your banner is straight. Though having quality leafleting and datasheets is always a good idea, Nathan Runkle stresses the importance of not having too many pieces of literature to choose from. "We like to keep the table relatively simple," he says. "When I first started doing activism and tabling, I thought, 'The more literature the better. We'll have a thousand brochures on everything!' Not only was it difficult to transport all those different brochures, but we found that usually when somebody comes up to the table they would only pick up one or two pieces of literature. So we consolidated our materials into our thirty-two-page vegetarian starter kit, our newsletter and our vegetarian guide to Ohio. We'll leaflet with the *Why Vegetarian?* pamphlet, and we'll have DVDs of [PETA's video] *Chew On This*. Basically, everything we want to get across in just a few important pieces of literature.

> **Holiday Tables**
>
> For extra impact, time your tabling effort to coincide with a holiday and then draw a connection between them. For example, you might table against veal on Mother's Day to protest the dairy industry's practice of taking male calves from their mothers immediately after birth, while Easter season is a perfect time to address the horrors of egg production or to educate the public about the many ways rabbits are exploited – and urge parents to do their homework before giving their children bunnies as Easter gifts!

We focus on what is going to be compelling – what we want people to walk away with."

Nathan suggests a vegetarian starter kit, available from many of the larger animal-rights groups, is a tabling must. "This gives people the tools and resources they need to get started right away. And these things work," he adds. "I was recently at a check-cashing place wearing an MFA shirt, and one of the girls who worked there said she'd stopped by a table at an animal-rights event last year, picked up one of the DVDs and watched it and hasn't eaten meat since then. So tabling really does have an impact."

Anthony Terry of Save Animals From Exploitation (SAFE) highly recommends offering free items at your table as a way to promote the movement. "People love free stuff," he says, "and the more animal-rights stuff out in circulation the better. For example, you can work hard and sell ten bumper stickers for twenty bucks or easily give away a hundred and get your message out there. Chances are your generosity will be rewarded by donations or new members, earning you more than from simply selling. Besides, you will look great for offering free stuff!" Anthony also recommends making your message clear, simple and to the point. "People are busy and can't be expected to digest and understand Animal Rights 101 in thirty seconds of passing your stall!"

Tabling Items

In addition to a table, you'll want to have:

- Driver's license or school ID
- Literature: vegan leaflets, stickers, data sheets and other pamphlets
- Name and phone number of your contact person at the venue
- Banner, if you have one, to go along the front of your table
- Sign-up sheets and clipboard
- Tablecloth – large enough to cover anything stored beneath the table
- Shirt and buttons with an animal-rights message
- Pens
- Clear tape
- Rubber bands
- Paper weights
- Donation can
- TV with VCR or DVD combo (or a laptop) for showing videos like PETA's *Meet Your Meat* or *Testing... One, Two, Three*
- Lamp (if the venue is at night or indoors)
- Extension cord and power strip or a power generator to run a TV
- Petition (if you'll be collecting signatures for an issue)
- Bottled water
- Wheeled cart (trolley) large enough to haul your literature and other material – but small enough to fit under the table (the collapsible kind works great for this).

Table Manners

Chances are people walking by your table are going to be sizing you up as well as your display, so look approachable. This means you're standing straight, you're not eating or smoking and you're giving the impression that you're happy to be there: a smile goes a long way and will make people more relaxed. Also, if you're tabling outside, avoid wearing sunglasses, if possible – making eye contact is important! If you must shade your eyes, wear a billed cap with an animal-rights message on it (see Resources at the end of this chapter).

Greet people who approach your table, and be attentive to those who express an interest in whatever issue your table is addressing. Ask visitors to add their name and email address to your sign-up sheet. If you're tabling for

> The last thing animal advocates should do is give people another reason to ignore animals. If we present ourselves as self-righteous and pure, and view everybody else in the world as impure, we are just going to turn people off. I can't even count the number of people who have been turned off to animal rights when we behave this way.
>
> **Tom Regan**
> *Satya* magazine, August 2004

an organization, tell people who add their name that the group will be emailing them with news and alerts.

Don't feel dismayed if someone asks a question for which you don't know the answer. Be honest: tell them you don't know, but you will find out. Get the person's email address, or make a notation next to this information on the sign-up sheet if they've added their name. Later you can research the question and respond – even with links to online details!

Be patient and treat everyone with respect. Remember that you too were once unaware of the egregious abuses animals suffer. Learning how you made the connection between animal exploitation and your consumer behavior may help someone else see the relationship and make changes in their lifestyle as well.

Although you'll want to keep an eye on your table at all times – tabling with a friend makes it easy to take bathroom breaks or see the rest of the event – you don't necessarily have to stand behind it. If he notices that people seem too intimidated to approach his table while he's there, Jack Norris of Vegan Outreach will stand somewhere else. "I just stand far enough away so that I can keep my eye on the table, but without it being obvious that I'm staffing it," he says. "Maybe ten yards [about 9 meters] or so. And I return when someone starts to look around like they want to talk to someone."

Do not linger speaking with those who obviously stopped by your table to argue; it only wastes your time and makes other visitors to the table uncomfortable. Of course, people may not be inclined to give up habits like meat-eating right away – don't mistake such reluctance for belligerence. Someone who is genuinely interested may still disagree, and perhaps you'll say something to them, or they'll walk away with a pamphlet, that will engender more contemplation on the issue. But if someone is clearly being confrontational, you won't be helping the animals any by arguing your point. Remain calm, stay focused and simply say you're sorry he/she feels that way. Sending them off with a smile and "Have a nice day" may feel less satisfying to you at that moment, but you're doing more good in the long run.

After Tabling

If you've been tabling at an event, concert or other organized venue, thank everyone when it's time to go home: the venue owner, manager, staff members and anyone else you dealt with, such as the band's tour manager. If your tabling was on behalf of an organization, they will have given you specific instructions, which will probably include returning the donation can, sign-up sheets, any petitions and the table sign. They will also tell you how to send in any donations you have collected or funds from merchandise you may have sold on their behalf.

Sticky Tables

In his essay "Effective Advocacy: Stealing from the Corporate Playbook," Bruce Friedrich gives some advice so simple and obvious that one may be tempted to ignore it. Don't. Bruce is one of the most effective vegan advocates you'll ever

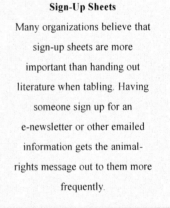

Sign-Up Sheets
Many organizations believe that sign-up sheets are more important than handing out literature when tabling. Having someone sign up for an e-newsletter or other emailed information gets the animal-rights message out to them more frequently.

meet or hear speak, so when he suggests that every activist should read *The Seven Habits of Highly Effective People* by Steven Covey and *How to Win Friends and Influence People* by Dale Carnegie, you have to assume the guy knows what he's talking about. "If these two books can be used to make money and sell products, then they can be used to help animals," Bruce writes. "I highly recommend that every animal-rights activist take the time to read them both. We must take our animal advocacy as seriously as corporate America takes making money." (I urge you to read his essay at www.goveg.com/effectiveadvocacy.asp.)

In this discussion of effective advocacy for animals, I'd like to add another title to the mix: *Made to Stick: Why Some Ideas Survive and Others Die* by Chip Heath and Dan Heath. This 2007 book is being touted as a must-read marketing text, but the principles behind it are as applicable to animal advocacy, and indeed can be applied to teaching, the work of spiritual leaders, environmental advocacy or persuading volunteers to donate time to a non-profit. Moreover, I believe *Made to Stick* can be used to emphasize the critical role of the individual animal activist.

The Heath brothers were inspired by Malcolm Gladwell's *The Tipping Point* (another book Bruce credits in his essay), which refers to the idea that certain behaviors and ideas are "sticky" and catch on with society. But Chip and Dan take the idea a step further, and they give many examples of ideas that have become viral and part of our culture's collective consciousness. A professor at Stanford University, Chip had spent a decade asking why bad ideas sometimes win out in the social marketplace of ideas – and what idea could be worse than any of the inhumane ways we treat another species and damage our planet? He wondered why a false idea could displace a true one, and what made some ideas more viral than others. As an entry point into these topics, he dove into the realm of "naturally sticky" ideas such as urban legends and conspiracy theories.

What sticky ideas have in common, according to the Heaths, is a Simple, Unexpected, Concrete, Credible, Emotional Story. So, how can we apply this "SUCCES" strategy to animal activism and not only make our message resonate with the public, but make it *stick*? What can we say to someone while tabling that will have a lasting impact? Anyone who has tabled has encountered a broad mix of society. Some people go slack jawed in utter shock at the sight of an undercover video, while others politely (or maybe not so politely) walk away, preferring ignorance. How can we employ the Heaths' principles to increase our tabling (or other outreach) effectiveness, transforming it from the realm of mere rhetoric into an easily comprehensible message that will inspire the public to take action? The key to success is in the delivery: making the core message understandable and memorable in a way that retains essential elements.

The good news is that most tabling displays are doing a lot of these things right. Take a table exposing factory farming as an example. It has, for most people, an unexpected message: the suffering of animals in factory farms. It has simplicity: go vegan to not support animal abuse. It uses concrete images that vividly illustrate exploitation and cruelty. The person tabling appears credible, provided he or she has done their homework and maintains a respectful attitude. And what could be more emotional than the misery of innocents? I believe that whatever the animal-rights issue, such displays are fairly typical, though I realize I am generalizing here – every activist or group presents their table or stall a little differently.

What I suspect could use more development among most animal outreach efforts, especially tabling, is the principle of stories, and it's in this area that the activist can truly shine. Effective stories can act as a catalyst for change, elevating an idea into something tangible. We certainly have no shortage of compelling stories. Among the most famous stories concern pigs, sheep, goats and cows who have managed to flee an abattoir, transport truck or auction yard, eluding their pursuers in a frantic bid for freedom. Animals like the two Tamworth pigs, who became international celebrities after escaping a UK slaughterhouse and spending a week evading recapture, attract media attention and teach the world that (surprise!) farmed animals do have feelings and don't want to die. These clever pigs, incidentally, named Butch and Sundance, were given a home for life at sanctuary in Kent and even became the subject of a BBC movie, *The Tamworth Two*.

The key to using stories is keeping them simple and making sure they reflect our core message. Of the types of stories the Heath brothers discuss, I believe "springboard" stories – so called because they provide the listener with a leap in understanding and stimulate action – offer animal activists the most promising opportunity to change the public's perception and behavior toward animals. Springboard stories communicate ideas and accelerate change. As the Heaths put it, "In addition to creating buy-in, springboard stories mobilize people to act." True stories with happy endings work best, since people want to feel they can make difference. A story about failure – though perhaps effective in other circumstances – is not going to empower somebody.

Kim Sturla of Animal Place shares a story about how a pig named Bruce

A committed activist who won't burn out needs three important things: facts, confidence and passion. When we know our subject and can articulate our issues, our confidence grows along with our credibility, and we become stronger and more effective every time we speak. But facts by themselves may not be persuasive. If we lack or fail to convey passion for our subject, we will have a hard time getting people's attention.

Karen Davis
Satya magazine, July/August 2001

came to live at the sanctuary. A woman living up the hill from the property on which Bruce lived drove by one winter day and saw this emaciated adult pig lying motionless in the mud. It wasn't the first time she'd seen Bruce: a year earlier she'd called Animal Control to report this obvious case of neglect and nothing had been done. Now she was mad. So she called Kim, who drove out to the property to see what could be done for Bruce. "He was like a skeleton," Kim says. "He was skin and bones, and he never moved. I started driving home, and I just couldn't leave." After speaking with the owner, she made a number of calls to Animal Control, telling them she wanted custody of Bruce. When the return call finally came, Kim was shocked: "Okay, you can have custody of the pig," the officer told her. Bruce's owner (I cannot bring myself call him his guardian) suggested the Animal Place crew would have to pull him into the stock trailer with a rope around his neck, but Kim knew better. "We had a bucket of apples, bananas, pastry buns and all sorts of goodies for him," she says. "It took us three minutes to coax him into the trailer." Today this gentle animal is lavished with love and produce, and Kim credits the compassionate person who finally took action on his behalf. "This *one woman* had evidently been the only person who ever complained to Animal Control – and she pursued it. All it takes is one person saying 'This is wrong' and doing something about it. She just made some phone calls. I feel so lucky to have that pig here."

I am not suggesting that telling compelling stories is the definitive strategy for approaching activism. But it may help the public embrace the concepts of the animal-rights movement and think, genuinely and deeply, about the suffering of animals – and then make changes in their lifestyle. There is a tenet in the advertising business regarding the power of emotionally connecting with a message: People remember only one-third of what they read and one-half of what they hear, but they retain *one hundred percent* of what they feel. All I am proposing is that we implement a new tabling tactic – a fresh way of framing our argument that inspires a more emotional connection – and see if we increase our success. I observe progress in the movement every day, but making our position, and our tables, sticky would advance the interests of animals even more quickly.

Mobile Tabling

Akin to the tabling model is FaunaVision, a van that has been transformed into a rolling media center for advocacy by showing video footage of animal atrocities. Created by New York activist Eddie Lama, the FaunaVision van is equipped with color monitors, speakers, a computerized message board and a public-address system.

Eddie also builds portable kiosks called Faunettes that are designed to hold audio and video components for use in playing video footage to a street audience. Faunettes are high quality, but they're not cheap, so some resourceful, financially challenged activists like Adam Durand have fashioned their own.

"We find the Faunette is great for sidewalk outreach," says Adam, "especially at night when you don't have to worry about sunlight reflecting off the screen. We've found that if we're going to be out on a well-traveled sidewalk, bringing the mobile TV unit with us is the way to go. I cannot recommend the Faunette enough. People will stand there for ten or twenty minutes, just watching the looping footage we have, sometimes crying, wanting to know what they can do to help stop the cruelty they're seeing – how they can change their own lives and habits. Being on hand to answer questions is great too. I can say that if you're going to be on a public sidewalk, try to stay away from bars or any place where people are going to come out any maybe be argumentative, because you don't want to spend all your time arguing with somebody when you could be distributing literature or talking to people who are willing to listen. For the Faunette, we find the best locations are outside coffee shops, especially near a college campus."

Nora Kramer uses an even more modest approach to achieve the same results. On any given Friday night, you'll find her and a friend outside the Metreon-Loews, a popular cinema in downtown San Francisco. On the sidewalk they set up a small folding table with some literature and a combination TV/VCR that plays *Meet Your Meat*. "We plug the TV right into a portable generator," Nora explains. "One person stays at the table with the video and the other hands out leaflets as people walk by. Some people look at the video for just a moment, wince and walk away. But I still feel that's a positive step. That's probably way more than they've ever seen how animals raised for food are treated, even in those two seconds. It sounds cliché, but it's like we're planting seeds that may some day sprout."

Nora, who founded VegSF to promote the cruelty-free lifestyle in the Bay Area, understands that many new activists worry about not being able to answer all the questions they might be asked while tabling. Her advice is simple: "Educate yourself. In order to be effective, you need to be a good spokesperson. Go online and check out the information offered by groups like PETA, Vegan Outreach, Mercy For Animals, Farm Sanctuary, the Humane Society of the United States and Compassion Over Killing." She recommends an hour on the Internet will get your confidence up, and it's doubtful the typical passerby is going to stump you. "It is *highly* unlikely that someone is going to ask a detailed question that you won't know the answer to," she says. "Just remember why you're out there and what's important to you. For most people doing this kind of activism, it's going to be that they don't want to support cruelty to animals."

Activist coach Dallas Rising agrees. She keeps her answers simple when doing outreach, and she counsels others to do the same. "I don't get into the details about gestation crates or the science behind vivisection or anything like that," she says. "I always encourage people to speak from their heart about what their convictions are – your real motivations. It all comes down to ethics and compassion and our sense of right and wrong in how animals should be treated." She acknowledges that some people may want to argue specifics, but an activist does not have to play along. "It's very easy to say,

'You know, I don't feel we need to mistreat animals in order to be healthy – or whatever it is – and keep it very simple. If people want more information, offer them a resource like a Web site or leaflet. Just speaking simply from your heart about why you made this choice is the most powerful way to talk about it, and it's also a way people can't really argue with, because it's your values."

Emphasizing a point you've read earlier in this book, Nora adds: "What's just as important as the message is the messenger – how you present yourself. Be kind. Smile and be friendly. If someone gives you a hard time, you do not give them a hard time back. It does no one, especially the animals, any good for us to be judgmental or hard on people."

Tips for Effective Tabling

Effective activism, whether it's tabling or any other model of animal outreach, educates the public about the atrocities animals suffer. Consistent exposure to the truth reinforces our message and helps consumers understand not only how serious the issue of animal exploitation is, but their role in it. Such knowledge can be shocking to a compassionate person, who may never have considered how, for example, their "harmless cheese habit"

Mercy For Animals frequently tables at events. Note the sign-up sheet and the volunteer mingling with foot traffic.

directly impacts the lives of dairy cows, all of whom end up slaughtered when they are no longer deemed to be profitable commodities. Outreach is often a slow and multifaceted process, and tabling is just one of the many essential models for informing the public.

Let's sum up this chapter with Dan Shannon's advice for successful tabling:

1. Set Goals

   Effective outreach can only be judged by the goals activists set. That goal could be to engage a certain number of people in conversation about the routine cruelty on factory farms and in slaughterhouses, or to register as many voters as possible for a pro-animal ballot initiative. Peta2 focuses on petition and email address gathering, so whether it's a petition asking KFC to stop cutting the beaks off of baby birds or demanding that the US Department of Agriculture end experiments on primates in laboratories, peta2 can, at least, judge our success by how many petition pages we fill.

2. Be Accessible

   Positive body language is a must for effective communication. Smile, relax, keep your hands out of your pockets and your head up. Each person reached has the potential to save one hundred lives a year by going veg, so treat people accordingly. Doing the little things to create a good outreach environment can make even a slow day a successful one.

3. Offer Something for Free

   Always make sure there is something that people can bring home with them. The best items to give out are DVDs that include PETA's *Meet Your Meat* or other videos with footage of chickens, pigs, turkeys and cows on factory farms and slaughterhouses. Even literature as small as stickers can be enough to create foot traffic in front of an animal rights table.

4. Pick Your Battles

   There is no need to argue with anyone while tabling for the animals. Effective tabling depends on activists' ability to recognize when someone simply wants to argue, and responding accordingly. The response must be polite but firm, but at no time should we engage in heated debates. Confrontation with potential supporters creates a negative outreach environment, and no matter how right activists are, if we're arguing, the animals are losing. We want to create the impression that animal advocates are friendly, non-judgmental people who simply care about animals and want to prevent their unnecessary suffering.

5. Mohawks and Lingerie

People will always judge a book by its cover, and as sad as that is, animal activists must always dress appropriately. Clearly the animals don't care what you look like, but the people who eat them do, so match your clothes to your audience, and when in doubt, dress a little more conservatively than you think they will.

6. Know Your Facts

Effective outreach for animals depends on activists being knowledgeable about every aspect of the topic at hand. If the tabling is focused on how chickens are raised and killed for food, an effective advocate will know chickens' lives from the moment they are hatched to the moment they are packaged for sale. It is also very helpful to have some knowledge of chickens themselves, their social behaviors and some general facts about them. It's a great idea to ask people if they know that chickens are one of only a few species that can communicate to one another that a predator is coming on two legs or four.

7. Sitting Is for Breaks

Demonstrate your commitment to animal rights by standing up while doing outreach. Sitting behind the table makes advocates less visible, but more importantly, it limits the volume of people we can reach with our message.

8. A Beautiful Table Goes a Long Way

Organize the table itself in an attractive way. Make sure to have space for every piece of literature to maximize the effectiveness of each leaflet, sticker or booklet. An attractive table sends the message that animal-rights activists are organized and focused.

Tabling is a pretty low-key way to do animal-rights outreach, but you'll still see surprising results. Dan shares a story about a night he was tabling at a

Morrissey concert: "We were in New Jersey," he says, "and this huge guy walks up looking very skeptical. For a while he stood silently in front of my table watching *Meet Your Meat*, the video peta2 always shows when tabling. I fully expected this guy to say something nasty or insensitive about what was happening on the video, so I braced myself. Finally he turned to me with this awful look on his face and said, 'How did you get this video?' I told him about PETA's undercover investigators working on farms and in slaughter-houses all over the country – that the investigators wear spy cameras and send this footage to us regularly. He said to me, 'This is disgusting. You know, I have a cat, and if someone tried to hurt my cat, let alone do these things to him, I would fucking kill them. I think I'm going to have to go vegetarian.' And with that, he took a vegetarian starter kit and went into the show."

Resources

Animal Place
www.animalplace.org
AnimalRightstuff
www.animalrightstuff.com
See Appendix D for additional sources of hats and other apparel with animal-rights messages.
Compassion Over Killing
www.cok.net
Compassionate Consumers
www.compassionateconsumers.org
Dallas Rising
www.dallasrising.com
Farm Sanctuary
www.farmsanctuary.org
Faunette construction
www.cok.net/lit/faunette
The Humane Society of the United States
www.hsus.org
Made to Stick

www.madetostick.com

Mercy For Animals

www.mercyforanimals.org

PETA (activism sites)

www.animalactivist.com

www.goveg.com/getActive.asp

peta2

www.peta2.com

SAFE

www.safe.org.nz

Vegan Outreach

www.veganoutreach.org

VegSF

www.vegsf.com

Viva!

www.viva.org.uk/campaigner/stall.html

CHAPTER 4

ANIMAL ATTRACTIONS:
PROTESTS & DEMONSTRATIONS

We must always take sides. Neutrality helps the oppressor, never the victim.
Silence encourages the tormentor, never the tormented.
Elie Wiesel

At three hundred and seven feet (93.6 meters) high, Sather Tower, in the middle of Berkeley's University of California campus, is the tallest structure in the city and offers spectacular views across the bay to San Francisco. The easiest way to enjoy this sweeping vista is an elevator ride up the tower, nicknamed "the Campanile," to the observation deck. A more challenging – and attention-getting – way is to climb up a rope, which is what activist Mike Kennedy did to protest the university's plans to construct an animal-research facility. Of course, like any complex protest, Mike had some help.

"This action was a joint effort between In Defense of Animals and the Animal Rights Direct Action Coalition," explains lauren Ornelas, who was among five activists who went up the Campanile the easy way and barricaded themselves inside the observation deck, which has bars across the windows. "We brought up Mike's food and water and tossed the rope down to him." Once Mike reached the observation deck, he unfurled a narrow, sixty-foot-long (18.3 meters) banner proclaiming "End Vivisection – Animal Liberation" and set up a snug rock climber's hammock that would be his home for eight days. "The protest received a lot of media coverage," lauren says, adding that they were all arrested and charged with misdemeanor trespassing.

Protests like this one are a dramatic way to focus the public's attention on the plight of animals in our society, but one need not break the law to make a point. Indeed, a protest can be as simple as one person holding an anti-circus banner outside a circus venue – or as complicated as thousands of people marching and chanting slogans to voice their disapproval of a planned factory farm in their community.

Although some activists may regard protests and demonstrations as disparate efforts – and they may have subtle or distinct differences – for the purposes of this chapter let's assume that protesting and demonstrating on behalf of animals are similar enough activities to be interchangeable. They both involve planning and a clear message to the public and the target (i.e., a research facility or store selling fur).

Bird's Eye View of a Protest

As I write this chapter, a number of issues concerning the welfare of farmed animals are being addressed by legislators, activists and the general public in the US. Chief among these are the practices of confining egg-laying hens in battery cages, keeping veal calves in tiny crates and forcing breeding pigs to spend nearly their entire lives in metal cages barely larger than their bodies. All of these inhumane business models are being scrutinized and, in some cases, reformed; however, every animal activist I know agrees that animals do not belong in factory farms in the first place.

Also the subject of heated debate is the foie gras industry, which uses an invasive technique to force-feed ducks and geese until they have become so obese their livers are engorged with fat. The diseased livers of the slaughtered birds are considered a delicacy in many high-end restaurants, which have attracted protests from outraged activists who regard foie gras as a frivolous appetizer inseparable from the egregious abuse of animals. Among the activists campaigning against this gourmet cruelty is Nick Cooney, director of Hugs for Puppies, a small animal-rights group in

> Anger is one of the major pitfalls of being an animal activist and it does burn you up inside. But what starts out as anger has to get transformed into something that's more positive for you and for what you're trying to do.
>
> **Mary Lou Randour**
> *Satya* magazine, July/August 2001

Philadelphia. To give you a fuller view of the role protesting can play in a major campaign strategy, I asked Nick to describe his efforts to eliminate the sale of foie gras in his city.

Although a city council member introduced legislation in 2006 that would eventually ban the sale of foie gras in Philadelphia, Nick saw no reason why he shouldn't take action right away to ensure the bill's passing. He mobilized a campaign that includes:

- postcards to city council members from their constituents (signed at tabling venues)
- letters from local free-range duck farmers supporting the ban
- meetings with council members and pledges from restaurateurs not to sell foie gras
- petitions signed by business owners in favor of the ban
- a plan for submitting op-eds to newspapers just before the bill comes up for vote
- emails, faxes and letters to legislators
- endorsements from other animal groups in the city.

The highest-profile aspect of the campaign targets restaurants that continue to sell foie gras, and that means protesting. Nick and his fellow activists use the Internet to identify restaurants offering foie gras. "Many upscale restaurants have their menus online," he says, "and there are thousands of restaurant reviews online for every city. It's not hard to find restaurants that serve foie gras." He also uses resources offered by national groups like Farm Sanctuary, which keeps track of businesses selling foie gras, and looks at menus posted outside restaurants.

"We have tried contacting restaurants in advance through letters or phone calls," Nick says, "but typically this doesn't yield any results. Letters are usually ignored, and so far phone calls have not led anywhere. So we organize evenings of demonstrations – usually on a Friday or Saturday, as that is when the most customers are dining out. We'll have one individual go into the restaurant and ask to speak with the manager or owner about the issue. He or she will inform the owner that we would like to set up a meeting to discuss the issue with them, but that if they are not willing to meet with us we will be protesting the restaurant. Occasionally they have been willing to meet and at the meeting have decided not to serve foie gras, but typically they are not interested in meeting with us or discussing the issue. They see no practical need to, and the ethical issues are not usually important to them."

So, Nick and the others give

> **Everyday Protesting**
>
> You can protest each time you shop for food and clothing: just go vegan. By pulling support from industries that profit from sales of meat, eggs, dairy, fur, leather and other products made from animals, you are saving lives and protesting against the use of such products.

restaurant owners a powerful, practical reason to consider the issue. "We hold very loud protests in front of the restaurant," he says, "holding signs, distributing leaflets from In Defense of Animals and Farm Sanctuary and chanting at the top of our lungs. The more of a scene we create outside the restaurant, and the more of an annoyance we become for the restaurant and its customers, the more likely they are to agree to no longer serve foie gras." Nick reasons that the restaurants are not making much profit from foie gras, which is used to showcase a chef's talent and attract hard-core foodies. "On the other hand, our presence will deter both current and future customers. After all, people going out for a relaxing meal don't want to walk through a line of angry picketers or hear chants all through the course of their dinner."

The activists return to the same restaurant every weekend, often protesting two or three restaurants each night they go out. "By exercising your First Amendment rights in a very vocal and very consistent fashion, you create a situation where the best practical decision for the restaurant owner is to take foie gras off the menu. And nine times out of ten, that is what happens – sometimes right away, sometimes after weeks or months of protesting at a particular restaurant, and sometimes longer than that."

When owners do come out to speak with the protesters, Nick and his colleagues politely assert that they would like to discuss the issue, but they will not end the protest until some progress is made. "On numerous occasions this has led to very productive meetings and the end of the sale of foie gras," he says. "Presenting a professional image, being courteous and friendly, showing that you take your issue seriously and will persist as long as necessary, and making clear that you are intelligent, thoughtful, and respectful, are very key. Dress the part, speak the part, and you will be respected. Also, be sure to make it clear that you wish no harm to the restaurant itself, and hope that it does well, but you simply have one point of contention and that is the sale of foie gras. Having materials to present to owners and managers such as literature, lists of other restaurants that have dropped foie gras, news articles on the issue and DVDs is also very important."

Nick sees the foie gras industry as so pointless – tremendous animal suffering in exchange for a fleeting gustatory pleasure – that he is confident any dedicated activist or group will see the same results he has. "With some animal rights issues, you can try your hardest and still see little or no results," he says. "This is one issue where the results are waiting for you, where the animals are waiting for you. You merely need to make the commitment of several hours a week every week and victory is yours."

Keep Your Cool

No doubt one reason more activists do not engage in protesting is that this model of activism can be more confrontational than distributing leaflets or tabling, especially when you are directly challenging a business that exploits animals. Tempers can flare and angry words may be exchanged.

When protesting, it's inevitable you will encounter someone who's not as interested in learning about the animal-rights cause as in arguing with you. Maybe your protest makes them feel guilty about eating meat or wearing fur. Maybe they're just having a bad day. Whatever the case, it's important that you not engage in an argument. Animal Liberation Victoria's Patty Mark puts it this way: "Even if someone in the public becomes aggressive or abusive, do not return their verbal violence with more anger or violence. Our main message is non-violence and we must demonstrate this at all times, even though this does get hard to do! Animal activists are animal ambassadors, and during any actions, tabling or protests we must do the best job we can to represent them in the strongest way possible. Depending on your age group there are various ways to approach this. If you are younger, think how you would want your parents to defend you: how you would want them to act, what you would want them to say? If you're older, think how you would want a lawyer to defend you in court. Are you prepared? Have you got your facts straight? Always speak with authority, conviction and determination, but *always with respect* for whoever you are talking with. Try to develop a type of empathy even with those least willing to listen to your message."

Dian Hardy of Sonoma People for Animal Rights (SPAR) recalls a particular protest at a livestock auction yard in the Bay Area that got out of hand. She organized the protest to draw attention to the lack of any legislation that protected animals at auctions, and SPAR was joined by a large number of activists from another local animal-rights group. "We blocked the entrance to the auction yard so all the trucks coming in from the nearby ranches and farms with their calves and spent dairy cows could not enter," she says. "SPAR had determined that this would be a non-violent protest, but pretty soon these other activists were climbing all over the trucks, spitting on the windows and frightening people. I found myself detaching protesters from these trucks, telling them that we're trying to be non-violent. It was all very heated. These things can take on a life of their own. This is why communication among activists beforehand is so important." (This protest eventually led to some legal protection for animals at auction yards in California.)

Although physical danger at protest sites is extremely rare, it does occur. Perhaps the most infamous example of this occurred in England in 1995, when Jill Phipps, a thirty-one-year-old activist, was killed beneath the wheels of a truck delivering veal calves to Coventry Airport. Jill was among thirty-three activists who had gathered to protest the export of calves to Amsterdam. It was common practice at the time to ship these calves in small

> To be successful, we need a thousand small organizations addressing hundreds of thousands of issues. Strength is to be found in diversity of approaches and a diversity of ideas, tactics, actions and philosophies.
>
> **Paul Watson**
> *Satya* magazine, March 2004

crates to be distributed to farms across Europe. Jill and some of the other protesters had broken through a police barricade to sit in the road or chain themselves to the trucks. Soon after Jill's death, Coventry Airport vowed to never allow veal to be exported from its runways.

Media Attention

There is no question that news coverage has played a critical role in countless protests. While we'd love to think that important issues alone draw media attention, it's often the unusual and dramatic demonstrations that get

the headlines: undressing to protest fur ... someone costumed like a crippled chicken to draw attention to KFC ... a man pretending to suckle from a life-sized fiberglass cow with a "Milk Sucks" banner on her side ... a woman painted with markings that mimic a butcher's diagram of body parts to illustrate the similarities shared by humans and non-humans.

Lisa Franzetta gets primeval to protest fur.

Activist Lisa Franzetta engaged in more than her fair share of whimsical, attention-getting demonstrations for PETA. In fact, the first time Lisa ever attended an animal-rights demonstration, she was center stage, her nearly naked body painted with tiger stripes and confined in a cage to protest the treatment of animals in the Ringling Bros. and Barnum & Bailey Circus. "I probably did several dozen different 'naked' or body painted-type demonstrations," she says. "'Tiger lady' to protest the circus, 'leopard lady' to protest the fur industry, 'lettuce lady' in a lettuce bikini to promote vegetarianism, 'commando chick' in a showgirl chicken-type bikini ensemble to protest KFC. I was even painted pink, put on pig ears and posed in a faux gestation crate to protest some fast-food restaurant or other. This kind of activism was certainly effective in attracting the attention of passersby and also the media, and so in that regard, it was quite effective."

These protests are controversial, though, and many people – activists and non-activists alike – have criticized them as demeaning to women. Lisa, who is now the communications director for Animal Legal Defense Fund, laments that women's bodies have a different meaning in our culture than men's bodies, and she recognizes that we live in a society that does objectify women. "However," she says, "I think it is a backward logic that would, as a result of this, require women – or men – to keep covered up, rather than quite boldly expressing themselves, their bodies and even their sexuality any way they want to – particularly if that is going to be the end of raising attention for a social or political issue, like animal rights. Other organizations, like Code Pink, also use nudity to get attention in their demonstrations, and I don't generally see them getting the same kinds of criticism from feminists, and I'm not sure why. Perhaps it's because their upfront mission is more obviously aligned with feminism."

Lisa believes these events have a powerful potential for creating publicity, though she admits the media coverage they garner is generally superficial. "But the premise we operated under was that superficial coverage that might pique some interest was better than no coverage at all," she says. "I still agree with that premise." She notes that this kind of activism became less effective as the years went on. "I think there was some degree of media saturation involved. The first time a bunch of activists get naked in the middle of downtown Sioux Falls or wherever, it's big news; the fifth time … interest wanes. Maybe the takeaway message is that activists have to keep coming up with new things that the media have never seen before to really keep interest in demonstrations high."

Wendy Suares of ABC-TV affiliate WTOK in Mississippi is one of many reporters who acknowledge the power of sensational protest images. "In those cases," she says, "the issue isn't as controversial as the protesters' methods. Like getting nearly naked and locking themselves in a cage. That act alone guarantees publicity." But it wasn't sensationalism that motivated Wendy to report on a low-key demonstration in her state in 2007. Activists were gathered outside the University of Mississippi Medical Center to protest the cruel treatment of an eight-year-old rhesus macaque named Mowgli. Animal advocates from across the country had formed an alliance to save Mowgli from invasive experiments and certain death, and many of them stood quietly outside the center holding signs of protest. "That was a situation that not many people knew about," says Wendy, explaining her interest in the story. "It was something new and controversial – the idea that tax dollars were going to support such procedures on a monkey that had previously been abused. I also was interested because the effort behind the protest was coming from across the nation." (Although using tax dollars to fund animal abuse may be controversial, sadly, there's nothing new about it, and Wendy's remark highlights how much public education activists have yet to accomplish.)

"There are a number of factors that go into covering animal-rights protests," says Henry Lee, a reporter with the *San Francisco Chronicle*. "Are there multiple protesters? Is the protest affecting traffic or commerce? How unusual is the method of protest? Is there conflict between protesters and police or protesters and ordinary citizens or employees of targeted companies?" Henry covered the week-long UC Berkeley demonstration for the *Chronicle*, and he says reporters also take the length of a protest into consideration. "Is it a drawn-out demonstration, with an activist perched somewhere and vowing not to budge, eat or stop doing some other action until his or her goals are met? Or is it a quickly fizzling event that could potentially be missed by late-arriving media – or wasn't properly announced to the press beforehand? Having said that, there is a balance that must be considered. Some media outlets might tire of any protracted protest where nothing new occurs. In the news business, reporters look for unusual, novel things to cover."

Patty Mark says a good banner or protest sign can make all the difference. "I've never forgotten what a top journalist told me over a coffee in 1979: 'Patty, never look like Lucy's Lemonade Stand.' The more professional looking we present, the more professional our message appears." Patty also recommends that activists never exaggerate the message. "Always be honest to the public and the media," she says. "It is most important for the animals that we always maintain our credibility. Make sure the public and media always know they can trust what you say and that your facts are spot on. If you don't know something for sure, don't say it. The media will come back again to those groups and activists they know do their homework

There's nothing like a strange visual to gain attention: Activist Jamie Yew helps with ALV's "Milk Sucks" campaign.

and present well."

Many activists make the mistake of just emailing a press release or media advisory and hoping the news media shows up. (A press release includes more information than a media advisory, which is used when you want to keep the specifics secret until the actual event.) Erica Meier of Compassion Over Killing suggests that after activists send out their protest details, they should make a phone call or send an email to the reporter. "Media outlets get bombarded with contacts every day alerting them about different activities," she says. "You *have* to follow up, making personal contact. Figure out who has been focusing on animal issues within the community and target those journalists to make sure they know about your protest. Because even if your media advisory goes to the newsroom, it doesn't mean it's getting to their desk. I think personal follow-up is essential, and I don't think it happens often enough."

And don't overlook even the smallest neighborhood media outlets. "Little local papers are always good to contact when doing actions as these papers cover things that are happening in their area, and often a demo is a quite interesting and different story to what they normally may cover," says Suzanne Carey of Auckland Animal Action. Even a paper with a circulation of just ten thousand readers will reach one hundred times more people than you're likely to reach simply passing out leaflets for an hour.

Of course, media attention goes well beyond having a protest covered in the newspaper, large or small. Unfortunately, many of the animal-rights stories you see in the news perpetuate the view of activists as extremists or even "terrorists." Getting events that counter this misconception covered by the press can both disabuse people's negative perception of animal activism and foster compassion for animals. One example I will explore in Chapter 11 concerns a coalition of activists who rescued eighteen hundred hens from a battery-cage farm; the ensuing media exposure raised public awareness and even caused people to forgo eggs ("I had no idea hens lived like that," was a common refrain).

"We see the media as a vehicle to communicate," says SAFE's national director Anthony Terry, who estimates his New Zealand-based group has an eighty to ninety percent success rate for getting positive media coverage with their press releases. His secret is creating events that don't seem like protests. "We favor publicity stunts and actions that aren't immediately deemed as protests; therefore, we don't automatically get tagged as the troublemakers – both by the journalists doing the story and the viewer or reader of the story. That helps get the message out. Instead of [a headline reading] 'Activists mar local meat conference during scuffles with police,' you get 'Group warns public to the dangers of eating meat.'"

Anthony has also positioned SAFE as experts the media can turn to with questions about animal rights or welfare. "SAFE assesses the best way to communicate with every action or outreach event and looks at how to work with media agencies to get the right message delivered with maximum gain," he says. "While we do protest, we often see protesting isn't the best use of time, resources, the organization's reputation or for the issue to get the message across. We find society too judgmental over protests that they get too caught up in the actual action and merely see troublemakers. They can't relate and the issue is ignored."

Small Can Be Big News

"I think one of the main misconceptions many activists have is that you need significant numbers in order to have a successful protest, but that simply isn't the case," says activist Andrew Butler. "One outstanding and extraordinary example of that is Brian Haw, whose non-stop, one-man protest outside the British Houses of Parliament, which began on the second of June 2001, not only drew international attention to his anti-war message, it also won massive support for the right to protest in Britain. The government even enacted a new law to remove him from Parliament Square, but to no avail. He's still there – a constant reminder of what one person can do to educate others."

In February 2004, Andrew engaged in a similar, albeit shorter, protest. "I went to Stockholm to protest against an artist named Nathalia Edenmont, whose 'art' involved killing and then chopping off the heads, tails and paws of mice, cats and rabbits, arranging them on vases, her fingertips or flowers and then photographing them for exhibition," he explains. "I went to the gallery

Promote your campaign's Web site *everywhere.*

where the photographs were being shown, took out a sign reading 'Cruelty Is Not Art' and said I would remain there twenty-four hours a day until the exhibition was removed." After five snowy days and nights of Andrew speaking to everyone who came to the gallery and many people deciding not to patronize it, the exhibition was taken down. "I think you win support and sympathy simply by acting on what you hold to be morally right and true," he says.

Patty agrees that a small protest can have impact and stresses it can make for a great photograph, too: "For instance, we had an activist sit in a Perspex box filled with red seawater on the St. Kilda beach in January, which is summer in Australia, to protest Japanese whaling in Antarctica. It took only a few of us to get the box to the beach and fill it with water, but the photo-

graphic shot, which got a lot of media attention, was basically only *one woman activist* sitting in the red water holding a simple sign saying 'STOP WHALING' with the appropriate Web site on the sign. Photographers loved the image, and you don't even need an interview as long as the photo makes it in some papers with the Web site on the sign." PETA's Bruce Friedrich, meanwhile, observes: "We had one person dressed as Satan at a poultry convention with a sign reading 'See You in Hell, Chicken Abusers.' It made the front page of the *Atlanta Journal-Constitution.*"

Can a small demonstration be considered successful even if it garners no media attention? If it is benefiting animals, yes. Peter Milne, for example, turned a few slaughterhouse images into posters and asked his friend Mitchell Asquith to join him in regular low-key demonstrations on the streets of Brisbane, Australia. They couple this with some leafleting, and Peter reports they have changed a lot of hearts and minds. He recalls one woman who frequently walks by their display. "I offered her a leaflet," he says. "She looked at me and said, 'Since seeing these posters I don't eat meat anymore.'"

Tips for Effective Protesting

Before engaging in a protest, clearly understand the actions you want the organization or company you're targeting to take; contact them and see if your grievance can be settled without a demonstration. As we saw in Chapter 2, businesses that rely on good relations with the public may be inclined to resolve an issue without you even having to pick up a protest sign. If your opponent won't agree to end their abuse of animals, it's time to plan and carry out your protest.

Before the protest

- Pick a good day. Nick Cooney's foie gras demos are not media events, but they're very successful. If media is important to your effectiveness, avoid holding your protest when the media will likely be busy covering major stories, like elections or big events. Weekdays are ideal, and earlier in the week is generally better for media attention. If reaching the maximum number of people is your goal (such as at a restaurant that serves foie gras), go at a key time like Friday or Saturday night; the media will likely never come, but that's not important in this case.

- Pick a good location – one that is easily accessible to reporters and protesters. Consider traffic issues and work schedules.

- Once you've chosen a location, check with the local police to determine where private property stops and public property begins. You need to protest on public property, such as the public sidewalk along a city street. The police will sometimes tell you that you can't be in a public place; they often see themselves as guardians of business, rather than protectors of the First Amendment. If you believe your rights are being violated, contact PETA – they have an entire division (their largest) to work with grassroots activists.

- If appropriate, disseminate a well-written press release or media advisory (be sure to proofread it!) to the local newspapers and television news stations a day or two prior to the protest. This should briefly outline the issue you are protesting against and state where and when (the exact time) the protest will be. Include the name, phone number and email address of a contact (someone who can be reached during the event as well) in case the reporter has questions.

- The day of the event, issue a press release early in the morning that provides more information on the event and the reasons for it. Again, make sure to include a cell number of someone who will be accessible to media during the event. Print a few extra copies of the release, as well as any background material, that you can distribute to reporters who arrive.

- Ensure that all participants are familiar with the issue(s) you're protesting against. Brief everyone on your goals and main message points. Passersby and the media may direct questions to any activist, so everyone must be prepared!

• If you expect more than ten people, prepare a few simple chants; these will help keep the energy high and communicate your message. Weigh the value of chanting against the value of passing out literature, since chanting may cause passersby to avoid your event.

• Assign all protest participants a task. Ask someone to be in charge of taking photos, someone to wear the costume (if you will have one), people to hold your banner (if you will have one) and ask another person to keep the chants going. Ask everyone else to hold posters and/or pass out leaflets.

• Designate one spokesperson to talk to the media. This person should be well educated on the issues, prepared with brief statements to the press and able to stay on message. It's best if the media spokesperson doesn't have to worry about anything other than talking to and keeping track of the media. Use the media spokesperson's name as the contact on the press release or media advisory, and ensure everyone at the protest knows to tell the media to speak with the spokesperson; the media will usually honor that request.

• Dress conservatively: You want to appeal to the masses, so it's best if you look like them.

• Avoid wearing any clothing or accessories made from animals, such as leather shoes or belts, to the protest. If the public regards you as hypocritical about defending animals, it will detract from the message.

• To ensure everyone is present when the media arrives, ask all activists to be at the protest fifteen minutes before you've told the media that the protest will begin.

During the protest
• Be polite at all times. Some people would love to stereotype animal-rights activists as "radicals" so they can avoid the truth about animal exploitation. You're less likely to be typecast if the public perceives you as polite and rational.

- Concentrate on the protest. This should be about the animals; people can socialize after the event.
- Hold protest signs prominently.
- Double the chances that your signs will be seen by photographers and passersby: make them two-sided.
- If you have enough people, chant!
- Never say "We're disappointed by the low turnout" if fewer activists than you'd hoped for show up; instead, remain upbeat: "We're thrilled to be out here. Our costumed activist is really making the point that KFC tortures chickens!"
- If you are leafleting, look friendly and approach people. Make it easy for them to take a leaflet; don't expect them to ask for your literature.
- Body language is important: Do not to sit or lean.
- Activists should not be eating, smoking or chatting on mobiles/cell phones.
- The main organizer should always be stepping back to confirm everything is in place.
- Take down the names of the reporters who show up, along with their media affiliation.
- Take photos, especially shots of the group with signs visible. Deliver a few of the best images (along with a brief description of each) to the media that didn't attend.

After the protest
- Get the phone numbers of everyone who attended the demonstration and then call them later to thank them – and ask if they'd be interested in protesting again.
- Create a press release that recaps the protest and disseminate it to the media outlets or reporters who did not attend. Don't merely cover the same points as the pre-protest press release – include news about what happened, how the public was educated, etc. You want the reporter to know there's a story here!
- Better yet, call the media that weren't able to attend and discuss the high points of the protest. They may run a story even if they weren't

there.

- Follow up with reporters who showed interest in your protest, sending them any other information they may have requested.
- Write a letter to the editor. Pick up the newspaper the following day to see how your protest was covered; regardless, write a letter to the editor about the issue and thank the community for their support (even if they weren't very supportive).

When to Downsize

Prepare two banners for your protest – a large one (ten or more feet/3 meters long) and a small one (about six feet/1.8 meters long). Use the smaller banner if only three or four activists turn out for the protest – a few people holding a large banner emphasizes the low turnout.

Give Peas Some Chants

Chanting a slogan is a protest tradition and is perhaps epitomized by the ubiquitous anti-Vietnam War mantra "Hell no, we won't go!" It was catchy, it rhymed and it reflected the anger of the time. Animal-rights protests can also be enlivened by memorable, rousing chants that convey the message of the protest in a few words and gets activists energized. Often, one person leads the chant by calling out a question, and the rest of the group responds. An example is the standard chant that has been adapted for our movement, which is, alas, rather boring: "What do we want? Animal rights! When do we want them? NOW!" Some additional chants I've come across include:

- "Animal abusers: Total losers!"
- "Make compassion the fashion! Don't buy fur!"
- "One struggle, one fight! Human freedom, animal rights!"
- "Hey, hey, J. Lo! Animal abuse has got to go!" (targeting fur-loving fashion designer Jennifer Lopez)
- "Namibia, Namibia, you can't hide! Stop the seal pup genocide!"
- "KFC, what do you say? How many chickens have you killed today?"
- "Don't breed, don't buy – while shelter animals die!"

- "Fur trade! Death trade! Fur trade out!"
- And this succinct little ditty directed at the president of US poultry company Perdue Farms: "Cluck You, Frank Perdue!"

Brainstorm chants with fellow activists until you all agree on a few you like. The time-honored "Two, four, six, eight…" motif is a good start, provided you can come up with something suitable that rhymes with "eight," such as "tolerate" or "eliminate." Example: "Two, four, six, eight – rabbits we will liberate!" But a chant that states the issue and includes a call to action is best: "Vivisection is our foe! Let those helpless beagles go!" Envision your chant ending up on radio or television. What message do you want the public to remember?

Active Voice

Whether your protest is modest or dramatic, large or small, keep things professional. Create posters with messages and images that reflect the chant – and check your spelling! "Be creative and think visually," says Patty. "Always step back from your action and look at what you see, because what you see is what the media photographers will film and photograph. Even take a photograph of a mock-up of your action to see how it looks in a photo-graph – you'll be surprised how easy it is to pick up things doing this. 'Oh, dear, I didn't notice that we couldn't see the main sign or that so-and-so was standing in front of the cow's head.' Study your protest as you would a rough draft of an article you are writing."

"I know a lot of people don't like protesting, but I think it's an important act and an important experience for people to have," says long-time activist Mia MacDonald. "Yes, you can feel powerless out there, but you can also feel powerful. I look back on some of the small protests where I and others at times might have felt awkward, self-conscious, ineffectual, cold, strange or whatever, that I now think really had an impact or contributed to the reframing of animal issues and animal activism that's going on today. I don't think the increased media attention to the animal angle or to animal concerns and those promoting them is unrelated to all those protests in the 1980s and 1990s."

While it's true that some protests may require a lot of planning, the attention they garner can help put pressure on the organizations and companies you target – and animals will reap the benefits. "Whether it's getting a business to stop selling fur or the public to vote for an initiative to ban gestation crates, all protests should be focused on getting something done," advises Sarahjane Blum of GourmetCruelty.com. "It's paramount that you can give a concrete answer to anyone who asks 'what can I do?'"

Resources:

Animal Liberation Victoria
www.alv.org.au
Animal Rights Direct Action Coalition
www.bapd.org/gancon-1.html
Brian Haw
www.parliament-square.org.uk
Compassion Over Killing
www.cok.net
Farm Sanctuary
www.farmsanctuary.org
GourmetCruelty.com
Hugs for Puppies
www.hugsforpuppies.org
In Defense of Animals
www.idausa.org
Jill Phipps (memorial site)
www.jillphipps.org.uk
PETA
For young people: PETA2.com
For others: www.AnimalActivist.com
SAFE
www.safe.org.nz
Sonoma People for Animal Rights
www.sonomapeopleforanimalrights.org

CHAPTER 5

ANIMAL FRIENDLY:

FOOD AS OUTREACH

I have from an early age abjured the use of meat, and the time will come when people such as I will look upon the murder of animals as they now look upon the murder of humans.

Leonardo da Vinci

Thirty faces in the room suddenly look appalled. People who just a moment ago were laughing or whispering to the person seated beside them as they snacked on tempeh paté appetizers have soberly fixed their gaze upon Colleen Patrick-Goudreau as she lets the attendees of her vegan cooking class in on the dairy industry's dirty little secret: Cows must be continually impregnated to give milk and their offspring are taken away immediately after birth. As Colleen sets up a row of a dozen non-dairy milk options for everyone to sample, she explains that female calves go back into the dairy industry system, to spend their lives either pregnant or lactating, while the males calves are raised and slaughtered for their flesh; many of these babies are sold to the veal industry, where they will live in tiny crates for four to six months before they are killed. The revelation is horrible and yet so obvious – how else could it be? – and it creates a communal *Aha!* moment. A veil of ignorance is uneasily lifted from a meat-eater in the last row and the color drains from his cheeks. He had said he came to the class to learn to eat healthier; perhaps he realizes it's equally important to eat more compassionately.

Food is an incredibly powerful component in the activist's toolkit, which is one reason Colleen founded Compassionate Cooks. Whether it's through her cooking classes, "Vegetarian Food for Thought" podcasts or her writing, she uses our universal passion for cuisine as a key to shifting people's attitudes, empowering them with the facts about veganism. "With information and power, they will not only make changes in their behavior, but they will experience transformation in their heart, as well," she says. "I really believe positive reinforcement is better than anything that makes people feel bad."

When we speak of animal cruelty, the overwhelming majority of abuse is suffered by animals who are bred, raised and eventually slaughtered because humans happen to enjoy eating them. Not because we *need* to eat them, but because they taste good to us (cooked and seasoned, that is). This does not mean that other forms of exploitation are less deserving of the activist's attention – vivisection, circuses, blood sports and the fur industry, to name a few, all rightly attract the time and effort of countless animal advocates. But because most of the Earth's human inhabitants directly contribute to the needless cruelty suffered by so many billions of non-human animals each year simply by eating them, changing the hearts and minds of these people yields extraordinary benefits.

"There is no love sincerer than the love of food," wrote George Bernard Shaw, who understood that food is imbued with special meaning in the psyche of humanity. We need it to nourish our bodies, but we also look to food as the centerpiece of many of our rituals and ceremonies. For most people in the United States, Thanksgiving is synonymous with turkey flesh, as it is for Canadians on Christmas. Lamb chops are practically a point of national pride on Australia Day, while in Jewish households around the world the Passover Seder is celebrated with six specific foods, each symbolically linked to the Jews' Exodus from ancient Egypt. The birthday of Robert Burns, the bard of Scotland, is honored with a haggis supper by Scots at home and abroad. Eating is such an important aspect of culture that many religions proscribe certain foods and encourage fasting or not eating meat as a way of demonstrating devotion. Food or sources of food can even be an object of worship: the Mayans had a corn deity, for example, and Hindus revere Annapurna as the goddess of food and cooking. (And let's not forget Catholicism and its many "feast" days for saints.) Sitting across a table from each other, eating becomes an intimate act. We cook to demonstrate love, and we find comfort in certain foods.

Because of food's unique position in our lives, it also offers the promise of transformation, for what we place in our bellies can be the bridge to a higher level of compassion – a rich appreciation of life itself. The simple act of sharing a delicious plant-based meal with someone more accustomed to dining on dead animals may not inspire them to immediately embrace a cruelty-free lifestyle, but it removes another brick from the massive edifice built upon the myths of ethical eating: that vegan food is strange, that it is hard to prepare and, perhaps the biggest false premise, that a meat-based diet is ideal for optimum health.

Most of us were raised eating animals. Moreover, the meat, egg and dairy industries spend considerable time and money promoting this lifestyle to keep consumers hooked. The meat industry has been at it so long that even producers of non-meat foods have tried getting into the act. A certain maker of ketchup and tomato sauce in the US, for example, once advertised its products as "Made from the *meat* of the tomato." So it's little wonder that most people cling to the primacy of animal flesh. We are creatures of habit, and like any habit, a person's preference for eating animals and their secretions (eggs and dairy products) can be changed – sometimes gradually, sometimes quickly – and activists can play a critical role in making it happen.

Activist Mark Reinfeld witnesses plenty of habits being broken in his work as executive chef of the vegan restaurant Blossoming Lotus in Hawaii and as the author of the *Vegan World Fusion* cookbook. "We get many people who wander in, order off the menu and then realize there are no animal products," he says. "People are truly amazed. Many say that if they knew vegan food could taste this good, they would eat this way more often." Customers often tell Mark they're going to include more vegan food in their diet, and learning about animal abuse is frequently the reason. "I don't think most meat-eaters realize the connection between what they eat and the exploitation of animals until it's explained to them – usually when they ask 'Why is there no dairy or eggs in this, or why no animal products?'"

The Herbivore's Dilemma
If you're new to vegetarianism or veganism, or you've just never used your love of plant-based food in your activism, getting started can seem a bit

daunting. How does one begin? You needn't be a professional chef or cooking instructor to have an impact on another person. Erica Meier of Compassion Over Killing recommends starting with your immediate circle: friends, family and co-workers. "Bringing vegan treats to the office or hosting a vegan dinner party for your neighbors or meat-eating friends are two simple yet effective ways to introduce others to animal-friendly eating," she says.

One crucial point about using vegan food in your outreach: Make sure the food is *delicious*. "I will happily eat good vegan food, but I will never offer good vegan food to non-vegans," says Erik Marcus, author of *Vegan: The New Ethics of Eating*. "Any food I offer to non-vegans has to be *outstanding*, or I won't offer it at all. We don't want non-vegans to try vegan food and decide it's only okay. We need them to think this is some of the tastiest food they've ever eaten." This attitude applies not only to the food Erik offers, but to the food products he recommends, the cookbooks he suggests and the restaurants he takes his friends to. "Vegan food is indeed a powerful outreach tool, and that's why I make sure that non-vegetarians get only the very best of what the vegan world has to offer."

> **Food Fact: The Animals**
> The average meat-eater is responsible for the abuse and death of about one hundred animals each year.

Whether you're bringing in treats to the office or having friends over for dinner, if you're hoping to encourage someone's own vegan culinary adventures, don't start them off with anything too complicated or that contains hard-to-find ingredients. "The food must be easy to make, so that those eating might actually make it at home," advises activist Monica Engebretson. Chilled Avocado, Tomatillo and Cucumber Soup with Saffron-Lime Ice may be impressive and delicious, but any recipe that calls for saffron threads and toasted Hungarian paprika is not for beginners, and we want to emphasize that veganism is easy! Fortunately, one outreach effort that Monica and countless other activists have found particularly successful uses some of the easiest vegan foods you can find.

Feed-Ins

The idea is pretty simple: Hand out free vegan food to the public. After all, who doesn't like free food? For a feed-in, activists prepare some vegan versions of popular meat-based foods, such as veggie burgers and "chicken" nuggets, and pass out samples at a location with lots of foot traffic – like the front of a fast-food restaurant. Passersby get to try some tasty vegan treats, have a non-confrontational encounter with an animal activist and, we hope,

walk away feeling that veganism isn't that strange after all. Feed-ins can be as basic as one person with a platter of Tofurky sausage samples and some vegan literature or several activists going all out with a table, veggie dogs with condiments and a banner declaring "FREE Vegetarian Food!"

People love free vegan food at feed-ins.

"We *love* using food for outreach," says Dawn Moncrief of the Farm Animal Reform Movement (FARM). "It's friendly, so it's appealing to most activists, especially those who don't like to protest. It gives us the opportunity to not just say something or someone is 'bad,' but to provide a superior alternative, saying 'Try this – it's better.' Food draws people in and gives activists an excuse to approach others. It's very easy to approach people when you have something they'll probably be interested in and actually like. Of course, then we can talk with them and provide veg literature." Dawn also likes feed-ins because they promote makers of vegan food products. "If we create more demand and make the veg food profitable, we'll have more to choose from and more stores offering them."

"The challenge with feed-ins is that the food has to be *really* good," says Nora Kramer. "Plus, you need to present it in a way that looks good *and* tastes good at that moment, like on a street corner. Vegan chicken nuggets, for instance, taste really good, if they're hot, with ketchup or barbecue sauce. If they're cold? Um, not so good. You're really not helping any chickens. Same thing with giving out vegan ice cream – you've got to keep it cold. If it's a hot day, no one's going to want you're melted, liquidy ice cream. So, keeping things hot or cold and presenting it in a way that will make people want to try it is important."

Nora also notes that it's important people know why you're there. "It needs to be clear that you're not representing Soy Delicious or whatever," she says. "You're there volunteering your time because you care about animals and you want people to know that vegan food tastes really good."

While Dawn warns that "not all meat alternatives are the same" and recommends that activists "pay the extra money if needed to serve the best kind," Nathan Runkle of Mercy For Animals (MFA) advises getting the food donated, if possible. "When soliciting food donations," he says, "keep in mind what will be easiest to prepare and how you're going to distribute it. Soy ice cream in tubs, for example, is going to be more difficult to distribute than Tofutti Cuties, which come pre-wrapped."

Getting companies to donate food is not that difficult, according to Caroline McAleese of Vegan Campaigns, which organizes annual food fairs and monthly vegan food and information stalls in busy shopping areas. "If you do not already have a contact name at the company," she says, "I would send an email to the general address, then follow it up with a phone call and keep the contact name for next time. I normally write quite a detailed email about the event or stall. I would include how many people you would expect to come, the venue and the aim of the event." Caroline also recommends giving the company an incentive, such as adding their name to a flier for the event, offering to give out their leaflets at the event and posting a link on your Web site to theirs. "It's good to feed back to the companies afterwards, to show

> **Support Vegan Businesses**
>
> Help local vegetarian and vegan restaurants stay in business by patronizing them – and bring a friend. "We've really increased the demand for and supply of vegan products in our area," says Adam Durand of Compassionate Consumers. "A number of our members, for example, have a weekly get-together at a vegan-friendly restaurant as a way of thanking them for offering vegan options."

them photos and let them know how it went." If this all sounds like feed-ins are a complicated exercise demanding many people, relax. "Most of the feed-ins we do are just a couple people," Nathan says. "It's taken us a little while to master the marketing of feed-ins, because if you just go the street corner wearing regular clothes, and you're handing out food, it seems kind of sketchy, and people get a little nervous taking food from strangers." So now Nathan and his fellow activists don black aprons and plastic gloves, giving their feed-ins an air of professionalism. "We also have a large banner that reads 'For the Animals, Earth and Your Health – Enjoy a Free Vegan Sample.' This makes it look more like an event so people will come up to try the food." To really make an impact, MFA sometimes sets up a table with the dipping sauces, vegetarian starter kits and local veg guide. "The veg guide also lists health food stores, so we can tell people how to find specialty items," he says.

How to Conduct a Veggie Hot Dog Feed-In
Courtesy of Compassion Over Killing
Many animal advocates agree that distributing free vegetarian food with literature and recipes is a great idea, but they aren't sure how to hold feed-ins without the hassles of obtaining permits, grills and so on. Happily, organizing an effective feed-in is relatively simple. Once you have your location selected, all you need is some food to share, a bit of preparation time and plenty of energy to spread the animals' message.

Here are some suggestions to help you organize a successful hot dog feed-in:

What Do I Need?
- Veggie dogs
- Hot dog buns (save money by checking out bakeries that sell day-old bread)
- Condiments (ketchup, mustard, relish and/or sauerkraut)
- Several rags or hand towels
- Plastic bags (large enough to hold a towel)
- Paper towels/napkins

- Tin foil
- Coolers
- Cooking pot
- Tongs

Do I Need To Know How To Cook? Not Really

Getting food ready for a feed-in is fairly easy. Depending on the quantity of food and commute time, you'll need about two hours' preparation time. By cooking everything in advance and taking it to your chosen location (instead of setting up a grill and cooking on-site), you can bypass food preparation rules and regulations.

1. Cooking the food
   - Begin cooking the veggie dogs put by boiling them in water.
   - You can usually fit two packages (or twenty-four veggie dogs) in a medium-sized pot, or four packages (forty-eight dogs) in a large pot. Just make sure they all get cooked (check the directions on package for cooking time). Since veggie dogs tend to be small, you can cook lots of them quickly.
   - While the food is cooking, start step 2.

2. Keeping the food warm
   - Take several hand towels and soak them in hot water.
   - Microwave the wet towels for five to ten minutes – time may vary for microwaves. Alternatively, boil the towels in a pot of water.
   - Using tongs to protect your fingers, place these hot towels in plastic bags (if they melt the bags, don't heat them as long).
   - Seal or tie off the bag to prevent water from leaking out.
   - Line the bottom of an insulated cooler with a layer of hot, towel-filled bags. Save the rest for step 4.
   - While warming the towels, start step 3.

3. Getting the food ready to go
   - Cut several pieces of tin foil into large enough to individually wrap the

hot dogs in the buns.

- Set out several open hot dog buns, each on a piece of cut foil.
- When done cooking, remove the hot dogs from the water and let them dry for a few seconds so the buns don't get wet.
- Put one hot dog in each bun, and wrap them up with the foil. Option: to hand them out more quickly, put condiments on before wrapping.

4. Packing the cooler
- Place a layer of wrapped hot dogs on top of the hot, towel-filled bags.
- Put a second layer of hot, towel-filled bags directly over the hot dogs.
- Put another layer of wrapped hot dogs ... and so on.
- Grab your extra condiments and napkins, and now you're ready to go!

Tips:
- If possible, have relish and/or sauerkraut on hand. Remember, people rarely eat meat-based food plain, so they shouldn't be expected to eat plain veggie dogs, either.
- Bring an empty veggie dog wrapper so if people ask, you can show them what to look for when they go shopping.

Note: Great-tasting veggie dogs are critical to the success of a hot dog feed-in. Recommended brands include Yves Good Dogs, Lightlife Smart Dogs and Worthington Big Franks.

Food Fairs

Popular in the UK and catching on with activists elsewhere, food fairs (or "fayres") are a bit more elaborate than feed-ins, but the opportunities for vegan and animal advocacy are exponentially greater. Food fairs create a social context for your activism, attracting many attendees while giving you the chance to make a presentation to promote cruelty-free living. Not only do these events give attendees a better idea of what animal activists are like, but they showcase the amazing variety of plant-based food options and demonstrate that vegans do not live off of iceberg lettuce.

"All the food fairs I have been involved in have attracted lots of meat eaters, the majority of which have said they will reduce their meat consumption or go veggie or vegan," says Kelly Slade, campaigns officer with the UK's Animal Aid. "All the feedback is positive and people always comment about how good the food tasted and how they were surprised at how much variety there is."

Mercy For Animals, based in Ohio, sponsors a food fair once a month. "We reserve the main auditorium in the main libraries of the city, which is free of charge, and then we'll prepare a dinner," explains Nathan Runkle. "Sometimes the food will be donated by local veg-friendly businesses, sometimes MFA will pay for the food, or activists will bring a dish, so it's more like a potluck event." One element Nathan is sure to include each month is a guest speaker, which might be a dietician, a chef, a vegan philosopher or Howard Lyman, the former cattle rancher who now promotes veganism.

In addition to teaching the public about vegan-related issues, says Nathan, these dinners and lectures help train activists to be effective spokespeople. "We really want to build an army of activists here in Ohio – people who are really educated on all aspects of animal rights so that when we have tabling events and outreach events, people are comfortable talking about these issues – not just for outreach events, but for day-to-day life." He adds: "These are social events, so activists can network with other activists in their community, which I think is a huge part of building a base of activists."

Sarah's Maple Apple Dip

Sarah Kramer shares this simple recipe that can be used as a fruit dip or fruit salad topping. "It's high in protein because of the tofu and is one of those recipes that will convert any unsuspecting non-vegan into admitting that tofu can be yummy!"

1 cup soft silken tofu, drained

½ tsp cinnamon

½ tsp vanilla extract

¼ cup maple syrup

Blend all ingredients in a blender or food processor. Serve chilled with fruit slices.

Tips for a Successful Food Fair

Location

- Try to rent a large room in a busy area, such as a street with lots of shopping. This will increase the attendance.
- A room with a kitchen is ideal but not critical.
- Verify that the room will have tables and chairs; otherwise, you will have to rent them.
- Make sure you have a table cloth for every table.

Promotion

- Promote your fair with a press release to the local media and small posters around school campuses, health food stores and any shops that will grant you permission.
- If you have a Web site or MySpace page, include some details about your fair – then direct people to the site in other promotion (posters, letters, etc.).
- Invite the media – newspapers, local radio and television – to attend the food fair. Be sure to mention if you'll be giving a presentation, as that may entice the media outlet to send a reporter.
- Invite students from local schools to attend your fair via the post; don't email the invitation, as many schools' computer servers use filters that may block your message.
- Follow up with the media a couple of weeks prior to the fair. Try to speak with someone at the newspaper or television/radio station to determine if a reporter might be covering your event. Suggest they also bring a photographer.
- Also two weeks before your event, send letters to editors of local papers and mention your fair. Your letter will stand a better chance of being printed if you can tie it to a recent news event; there's so much happening in the world of vegetarianism that this shouldn't be a problem (see Chapter 2).
- Ask animal groups like PETA and Animal Aid to mail out details of your fair to their members.

Food

- Remember the importance of choosing delicious food for your event.
- Check with local vegan food companies to see if they might donate something. Some makers of vegan food products are happy to donate to pro-vegan or animal-rights events.
- Book any bulk items of food with your local health food shop or local wholesalers at least two weeks before the event.
- Remember to have drinks on hand: water, soft drinks, etc.

Your Fair

- Ensure you have plenty of literature on hand and arrange it on a table off to the side but in plain view.
- Consider having a speaker make a presentation relative to animal rights. They might also speak about health or the environment.

Cooking Classes & Workshops

"*Fervet olla, vivit amicitia,*" goes the Latin aphorism. "While the pot boils, friendship endures." In other words, knowing your way around the kitchen can feed your stomach *and* your heart. Being able to cook a delicious, nutritious meal is a valuable skill for anyone to have, but this becomes all the more important when you want to show meat-eaters the joys of ethical eating. There are a number of wonderful vegan and vegetarian cookbooks available, and Compassionate Cooks even offers a vegan cooking DVD, but if you're more comfortable with some hands-on experience, a cooking class will certainly give you some culinary confidence. Typing "vegetarian cooking class" into your favorite Internet search engine will point you to classes around the world.

> **Food Fact: The Environment**
> A vegetarian diet requires only half an acre of land – seven times less land than a meat-based diet.

The flip side for activists is, if you're good at cooking, consider sharing that talent. "I think, particularly when we are talking about animal activism as it relates to farmed animals raised and killed for human consumption, that cooking classes are such effective, vital aspects of activism that not many people do," says Colleen Patrick-Goudreau. "Giving people the tools and resources they need to eat healthfully empowers them to get away from the animal-based foods and embrace healthful plant foods." And teaching is not as scary as it might sound. A lack of any formal training did not stop Colleen from offering cooking classes, for instance; she simply saw it as a natural extension of her activism. "I realized that a huge gap needed to be filled – one that would provide resources, answers and empowerment to people who desperately wanted to make a change but just didn't have the tools," she says. "I think the fact that I'm self-taught is even more beneficial for those who attend my classes and follow my recipes. If I can do it, so can they."

But how does one go about teaching a veggie cooking class? If you feel you're ready to teach, you can begin by talking to a manager at your local health food store or someone in the activities department of your community college. Many markets and adult-learning centers will be happy to give you space in their facility to teach a vegetarian cooking course. Most will promote the class for you, and some natural-foods markets and co-ops will even donate the ingredients you'll need, since people will likely buy the ingredients from the store.

Colleen promotes her classes as vegetarian, even though she uses absolutely no animal products. "There are so many misconceptions and myths about veganism," she says, "some of which actually make people afraid of the whole concept. The word 'vegetarian' doesn't scare people as much, so they're at least open to it.

Colleen Patrick-Goudreau gets ready to teach a cooking class.

Once they attend the classes, they understand that what I'm really talking about is veganism, and they get it." In addition to giving students the straight scoop during her classes, Colleen sets up a table covered with literature

> I find a lot of times that when we tell people about issues affecting animals, they instinctively want to know what they can do. On some issues, such as research, there may not be something they can do directly, other than writing a letter. But by changing their eating habits, they can do something immediately, and by encouraging them to spread the word, they can also change other people.
>
> **lauren Ornelas**
> *Satya* magazine, October 2003

related to vegan living and animal rights.

You can also have much the same impact with cooking workshops: you organize the menu, charge a fee for ingredients and let the participants do the cooking while you monitor everyone's progress. PETA's Alka Chandna conducted vegan food workshops for years right in her apartment in Canada. She created a booklet, placed classified advertisements in the local paper and promoted the classes to the university community. Alka says, "The idea was to use great food as a way to bring people along – to acknowledge that food is important, but to also acknowledge that there are serious issues, such as animals, the environment and health, that we must consider when we make food choices. Although I didn't pull any punches or graphic details in painting the realities of factory farming, I also worked hard to keep the tone upbeat and non-judgmental." She says a number of people went vegan on the spot. "Most everyone else reduced their meat consumption, taking the recipes and incorporating them into their dietary rotations."

Alka's guide to conducting cooking workshops explains why and how to run a vegetarian workshop, complete with menus, recipes, sample public service announcements and suggested talking points. You can order her free booklet by sending an email to veginfo@peta.org.

Tips for a Successful Food Workshop

Preparation

- Promote it. Post your workshop announcement with all the details on craigslist.org and other free Internet sites, and post fliers in your neighborhood health food stores. Many newspapers will also print events and activities notices; check their Web sites.

- Charge a fee that covers your expenses. Asking for payment also helps motivate people to show up!
- Prepare a menu that demonstrates the wide variety of vegan eating. Alka recommends including a few entrées that are familiar to the Western palate like vegan shepherd's pie, vegetarian chili and vegan pot pie. She also suggests including some ethnic cuisine such as Indian and Chinese dishes. And don't forget dessert.
- Diversity is important, but don't attempt more entrées than your kitchen (oven, stove, countertops) can handle.
- Shop for ingredients the evening prior to your workshop.
- Set up your kitchen, tables, literature and food just before attendees are due to arrive.

Execution

- When all attendees have arrived, briefly introduce yourself and ask others to do the same.
- Divide everyone into small groups and give each group a good variety of three or four recipes to prepare.
- Let your workshop attendees prepare the meals while you observe, offer cooking guidance and answer questions.
- Use questions about unfamiliar ingredients, such as why they're using soy milk instead of cow's milk, to emphasize both the nutritional value of the plant-based food and the cruelty involved in their animal-based counterparts.
- When it's time to eat, ask participants to critique the meals and their preparation.

Vegetarian Starter Kits

As mentioned in Chapter 1, providing people with information about the source of meat, eggs and dairy foods is one of the most effective ways to promote a vegan or vegetarian diet. Vegetarian starter kits – full-color guides available from many animal-rights groups – explain where animal-based foods come from and demonstrate how easy it is to "go veggie" by offering simple recipes, nutritional information and advice on where to find plant-based convenience foods.

Tips for Using Vegetarian Starter Kits

- Order a supply of kits from an organization (see Resources at the end of this chapter) and hand them out in places with lots of foot traffic. See Chapter 1 for leafleting advice.

> **Food Fact: Human Health**
>
> "[T]he vast majority, perhaps 80 to 90%, of all cancers, cardiovascular diseases and other forms of degenerative illness can be prevented, at least until very old age, simply by adopting a plant-based diet."
>
> – Dr. T. Colin Campbell, Cornell University nutritional researcher and director of the largest epidemiological study in history

- Have a Web site? Post a link to one of the many vegetarian starter kits available for free from organizations like Action for Animals, PETA, Mercy For Animals, Vegan Outreach.
- Add this to your email signature: "Receive a FREE vegetarian starter kit and a FREE DVD at VegetarianStarterKit.com."
- Order small cards advertising kits from PETA; hand them out to friends or post them on message boards at school, the gym or other public places.
- Ask your local library, veg restaurant, health club, co-op or doctor's office if you can leave some veg starter kits on the counter. Remember to re-stock frequently!
- Ask PETA about adopting a vegetarian starter kit stand.

Tips for Using Food as Outreach

- Learn to prepare a variety of vegan foods: take a vegetarian cooking class, buy a vegan cookbook or DVD.
- Bring easy-to-prepare vegan dishes to potlucks and parties – and bring the recipe in case someone would like to prepare it at home.

Colleen's Sure-Fire Three-Bean Chili

Colleen Patrick-Goudreau describes this delicious entrée as an easy dish for anyone to prepare. "Don't be intimidated by the number of ingredients," she says. "Many of them are just spices."

1 orange bell pepper, seeded and cut into ½-inch squares

1 red bell pepper, seeded and cut into ½-inch squares

1 yellow bell pepper, seeded and cut into ½-inch squares

1 yellow onion, coarsely chopped

2-3 cloves garlic, finely chopped

3-4 tablespoons water for sautéing

¼ teaspoon cayenne pepper

1 teaspoon ground coriander

1 teaspoon ground cumin

1 teaspoon dried oregano

2 tablespoons chili powder

3 medium tomatoes, peeled and chopped (or one 16-ounce can diced tomatoes)

1 can kidney beans, drained and rinsed

1 can black beans, drained and rinsed

1 can pinto beans, drained and rinsed

1 can corn, drained (or 1½ cups frozen corn, thawed)

Salt and freshly ground pepper to taste

Water or tomato juice as needed

½ cup chopped fresh cilantro leaves or fresh parsley (optional)

1. Heat up a few tablespoons of water in a heavy 4-quart saucepan over medium heat. This is to replace the oil that is often used for sautéing.

2. Add the bell peppers, onion, garlic, oregano, and chili powder, cayenne, coriander and cumin and cook, stirring, for 5 minutes.

3. Stir in the tomatoes, the canned corn and all the beans and bring to a boil. Add a little water as needed.

4. Lower the heat and simmer for 30 minutes, adding water or tomato juice as needed if too much liquid evaporates. Season with salt and black pepper, and stir in the cilantro or parsley. Serve in shallow bowls. Serves 6.

Serving suggestions and variations:

*Add a dollop of non-dairy sour cream or guacamole on top of the chili once it's plated.

*You can obviously use any color variation of bell pepper; the more color variety, the prettier the dish is. Same goes for the beans. You can use all black or white (navy, Great Northern, etc.) instead of pinto. It's really up to you, your preferences and what you have on hand.

*Add more cayenne and chili powder to make it hotter.

*Serve with different color tortilla chips: white, red and black/blue.

*Sprinkle shredded non-dairy cheese over the chili.

*Add meatless crumbles, if you like.

- Offer to cook for holiday gatherings; make enough for everyone to sample it.
- Make sure you keep the wrappers of any product samples you want to recommend to people.
- Remember: taste buds are important – be sure the food is delicious!

Insights from Vegan Chefs

Eric Tucker, executive chef at Millennium, a gourmet vegan restaurant in San Francisco, does not necessarily see his work as activism, although he believes eating great animal-friendly food can lead to larger considerations. "Through what we do at the restaurant, the only thing we'd like to achieve through putting out some great vegetable-based chow is that people will eat more vegetables," he says. "Though through our support of local, sustainable produce – not just purchasing, but through cooking classes and demos, special events like our farmers market dinners – we will pique our diners' curiosity on where their food comes from and how it is produced, both veg- and animal-based. From there they can make choices on whether and how much they want to support animal welfare. Education is the key."

Jo Stepaniak, author of *Vegan Vittles, The Ultimate Uncheese Cookbook, Raising Vegetarian Children, The Vegan Sourcebook* and many other related books, observes that most people in the West are stuck in a "food rut" and are often suspicious of foods that are the least bit different from their normal fare. "When someone reaches out and helps them over that hurdle," she says, "they are able to discover that their initial fears were unfounded. Then they are more willing to keep exploring and learn more about other new foods and alternative ways of eating." She finds that being friendly and approachable makes her a better vegan advocate. "This may be a subtler and more moderate approach compared to conventional views of activism, but I have found that it is as effective and has greater 'sticking power' than forceful or antagonistic methods."

Writer and chef Tony Bishop-Weston (*Vegan: Over 90 Mouthwatering Recipes for All Occasions*) also runs Foods For Life, a nutrition and catering consultancy that emphasizes the health benefits vegans enjoy. "By pretending to be a mainstream health consultancy," he says, "we have managed to get vegan ideology into the mainstream media. We rarely tell people not to do things – we more often just focus on the solutions and the basic philosophy that eating more plant-based foods has positive repercussions to their health."

Beverly Lynn Bennett (*Eat Your Veggies!*) says she considers her writing and work as a chef to be animal activism. "The food choices that people make have a huge impact on animal suffering, and the bottom of the animal foods industry can fall out overnight if enough people wake up and go vegan. So those of us who advocate a plant-based diet, and try to show people how they can prepare plant-based foods in their own lives, are helping to strike a blow against the industries that are most directly responsible for most of the suffering that exists today."

Matthew Engelhart, co-founder of the Café Gratitude chain of vegan restaurants, reminds us that animal-based foods are the largest contribution to animal cruelty. "Being a

> **Food Fact: The Developing World**
>
> While an estimated seven hundred and fifty million people go to bed hungry every night, a third of the world's grain is fed to farmed animals. The typical Western meat-based diet can only feed two and a half billion people, but a plant-based diet will feed everyone on the planet.

vegan is the loudest vote for a humane relationship with the animal kingdom," he says, adding a familiar suggestion: "Serve delicious vegan food. Demonstrate that participating in animal justice and sustainability doesn't have to be a sacrifice."

Sarah Kramer, author of some of vegandom's most popular cookbooks, is another home-schooled cook. Her award-winning cookbook *How It All Vegan* started life as a modest zine created for family and friends, and its bestseller status quickly inspired *The Garden of Vegan* and *La Dolce Vegan*. "In my experience," she says, "you can really open the mind of a meat-eater by starting with their stomach. Putting delicious, nutritious and mouthwatering food in front of them speaks volumes to the kind of a glorious food-filled life a vegan can live. I find it also helps to lighten the conversation to a level where you can really intelligently discuss your vegan lifestyle and choices without it being a back-and-forth argument where you're not making any headway."

Resources

ActiVeg (offers suggestions on food events)
www.activeg.org
Animal Aid
www.animalaid.org.uk
Beverly Lynn Bennett
www.veganchef.com
Blossoming Lotus
www.blossominglotus.com
Café Gratitude
www.withthecurrent.com/cafe.html
Compassion Over Killing (guide to organizing feed-ins)
www.cok.net/lit/feed-ins.php
Compassionate Cooks
www.compassionatecooks.com
FARM
www.farmusa.org
Foods For Life

www.foodsforlife.org.uk

Mercy For Animals

www.mercyforanimals.org

Millennium

www.millenniumrestaurant.com

PETA

www.peta.org

PETA Veg Cards (UK)

www.peta.org.uk/cmp/vegcard.asp

PETA Veg Cards (US)

http://goveg.com/literature.asp

Sarah Kramer

http://govegan.net

Veg Cooking

www.vegcooking.com

Vegan Campaigns

http://vegancampaigns.org.uk

Vegan: The New Ethics of Eating

www.vegan.com

The Vegan Society (sponsors food events)

www.vegansociety.com

Vegetarian Starter Kits

www.afa-online.org/starterpack.html

www.mercyforanimals.org/vegan_starter_kit.asp

www.peta.org.uk/feat/UKvegkit

www.vegetarianstarterkit.com

www.vegkids.com/order.asp

www.vegkit.org

VegSource

www.vegsource.com

CHAPTER 6

ANIMAL PHARM:
CORPORATE CAMPAIGNING

Loyalty to a petrified opinion never yet broke a chain or freed
a human soul.

Mark Twain

You wouldn't know it now, but Java Green, in the heart of Washington, DC, was not always veg friendly. When it first opened, this café was like so many others offering a variety of meat-based entrées. Then Josh Balk walked through the door. "I went one day during the late afternoon when restaurants aren't as busy, hoping that the owner would spend some time speaking with me about adding mock meat dishes to the menu," he says. Josh showed the owner, DJ Kim, how delicious a meal can be made with soy rather than the flesh of chickens, cows or fish. "I figure that the best way to have more people eat vegetarian dishes is to offer them their favorite meat dishes; however, this time in its vegetarian counterpart." Not only did DJ like the mock meats, he started adding them to the menu almost immediately, and Java Green was soon a vegetarian restaurant attracting six hundred customers a day – eighty percent of whom are not vegetarian. Think about it: this transformation occurred because one person took the time to show a restaurant owner a more compassionate, and ultimately more successful, way of doing business.

Josh is among the most enthusiastic practitioners of the corporate campaigning model of activism, a strategy that, as implemented by animal advocates, encourages a business to adopt changes in the interest of animals. Although a protest, as outlined in Chapter 4, can play an important role in this type of outreach, full-scale corporate campaigning relies on a broader approach that may mobilize the pressure of consumer buying power and/or public opinion to create an atmosphere in which companies realize that addressing the changes activists are seeking on behalf of animals makes good business sense. (For the purposes of this chapter, we will consider restaurant outreach as a form of corporate outreach.)

Some examples of campaign targets include:

- Pharmaceutical companies that test on animals
- Corporations and medical schools that support vivisection
- Manufacturers that subject animals to product safety tests
- Companies that sponsor events, such as rodeos, that abuse animals
- Agribusiness
- Retail shops that sell fur
- Restaurants (persuading them to offer vegan options)
- Corporate and college dining halls
- Local and national governments that support animal abuse
- The military, which often tests lethal weapons on animals.

The circumstances of each corporate campaign will dictate what tactics to use. Friendly persuasion and some face time with a local business owner may be just the thing, as Josh's example illustrates; persuading a multinational corporation to end an abusive business practice, on the other hand, may require more effort and creativity. Henry Spira, described by Peter Singer as "the most effective activist of the modern animal rights movement,"[1] used advertising campaigns and letters directly to corporate heads. Many of his successes were the result of companies not wanting the negative publicity Henry's tenacious tactics would surely generate: print ads exposing deceptive marketing, horrific cruelty and corporate malfeasance aimed to shock the public and shame animal abusers.

His first campaign for animals targeted the American Museum of Natural History, which was researching the impact that castration and other mutilation had on the sexual behavior of cats. A full-page ad in *The New York Times*, funded by a local vegetarian group called the Millennium Guild, produced so much bad press that the museum was forced to stop the experiments in 1977. Animal activists praised Henry for spearheading the first campaign in more than one hundred years of anti-vivisection outreach in the US and Europe to bring an end to any animal testing.

Corporate Campaigning Today

"The world of corporate campaigns has changed drastically since Henry Spira's day," says David Benjamin, director of corporate affairs for PETA. "Today, we push companies to make changes by using the Internet to disseminate information – including graphic cruelty videos that TV stations won't play – to millions of people. We incorporate cutting-edge marketing and branding strategies, use celebrity support to draw attention to a company's cruel practices, work with the media to expose cruelty, and encourage activists across the nation to boycott companies, hold demonstrations and speak out against cruelty in their own communities."

An activist need not have the financial backing of sympathetic supporters like Henry Spira did or even be part of a large organization to engage in corporate campaigning. "The easiest way to help stop cruelty to animals is simply to stop supporting cruel companies," says David. "Go vegetarian, buy cruelty-free cosmetics and household products and don't patronize entertainment venues that use live animals." He recommends contacting companies directly to encourage them to make improvements, such as insisting that animal welfare be included in the scope of its corporate social responsibility. "Nearly all products list a toll-free number on the packaging for consumers to call and register complaints or comments. The bottom line is that companies need to hear from consumers. If a company does not respond to your complaints, get some friends together and hold a demonstration, write letters to the

> Let's get out of the past and stop ignoring the vast majority of animal misery. We activists need to remember our objectives and why we're doing what we're doing. This involves a realistic recognition of the problems, a sense of what's possible, the ability to search out and seize opportunities as they appear and, whenever necessary, to switch gears.
>
> **Henry Spira**
> *Satya* magazine, June 1996

editors of local newspapers and distribute leaflets and information about the company to anyone who will listen. Individuals can also donate stock to PETA so that we can attend annual meetings and present shareholder's resolutions." But there's still room for some Henry Spira-style tactics today. Although she campaigns against the battery egg industry and other animal exploiters, Wendy Parsons is passionate about rabbits. Armed with a ream of paper and a stack of images depicting bunny slaughter in China, Wendy uses her free time to wage a crusade against businesses throughout Australia that sell products using rabbit fur – and she's winning a number of important battles. "I write a letter enclosing the pictures," she says. "If it's a chain of shops, I send the letter to the head office with a copy to all their individual shops so that their staff knows how brutal the fur industry is. Australia's three largest department stores have stopped selling fur as a result of this, and Woolworths supermarkets and a swag of smaller shops and retail chains have stopped selling fur cat toys across Australia."

Wendy often encloses a three-minute video disc showing the inhumane treatment of rabbits during handling and transport from fur farms to slaughterhouses, but she stresses that it's important to include evidence that cannot be avoided. "CDs and DVDs are too easy to throw in the trash without watching," she says. "I enclose six pages of photos with only a small amount of text as a caption. When people open the letter they cannot avoid looking at the photos, which speak a thousand words. People always have a definite reaction – sometimes defensive, sometimes horrified – and on one occasion a sales assistant from a dress shop had to go home because she was so upset. After contacting a chain of more than sixty pharmacies that also sell gift items, they now invite me to check any 'suspect' stock [products possibly made of fur] they are thinking of buying." Wendy says the strategy is effective but patience and tenacity are definitely keys to success.

"Animal abuse is often about corporate abuse," says Camilla Fox, an activist with many years of corporate outreach experience, "so we can't *not* conduct corporate campaigns." She believes it is crucial that activists know how to organize and run effective, politically savvy corporate campaigns. "That means doing the hardest thing for some activists, which is actually learning how to sit down and have conversations with corporate CEOs and figuring out how to appeal to them, generally from an economic stand-point." Camilla recommends activists always have something to trade in exchange for what they want – something worthwhile. "We live in a capitalist society," she says, "so we have to think about the incentive we are going to offer to a corporation. If our position is 'Don't sell fur,' what are we going to advocate in place of that? What is going to appeal to a CEO?" She uses as one example the "leaping bunny" label for cruelty-free cosmetics. "That logo has become something that corporations and businesses and retailers *want* to have on their products because they saw that customers were seeking it. So the incentive was that there is a demand for this."

Grassroots Activism

To underscore the profound role individual activism can play in convincing businesses to stop carrying fur, Fiona Pereira of Animal Aid explains that UK-based activists have been voicing their objection to department stores across the country, forcing these companies to confront some brutal realities. Fiona reports that such stores as Liberty, Harvey Nichols and the Zara clothing chain have all stopped selling fur. And while many businesses are reluctant to admit the power activists can have in influencing corporate policy, "Selfridges cited this as the primary reason they adopted a fur-free policy," she says.

Other UK businesses are also feeling the pressure from corporate campaigns. Although foie gras production is essentially banned in Britain, the country still imports more than four thousand tons a year, making it one of the world's largest consumers of this "fatty liver." Grassroots activists have helped Viva! halt the sale of foie gras in supermarkets, and they're working hard to eliminate this brutal delicacy – what they call "torture in a tin" – from restaurants as well. "With foie gras and so-called 'exotic' meats, such as kangaroo, crocodile and ostrich, Viva! initially presumes that businesses may not be aware of all the cruelty inherent in its production," says campaigns manager Justin Kerswell. "In the case of foie gras, each business receives an information pack, which details how the meat is produced and the major welfare implications resulting from force feeding."

Justin says that local activists are critical to the success of such campaigns, since they can fill out customer feedback cards and ask restaurants to remove foie gras. Viva! will also send activists foie gras leaflets, stickers and large posters to help educate restaurant owners and patrons. "If these measures do not work, Viva! contacts local media – to put pressure on the business and to raise awareness of the issue with the public at large – and we step up local actions such as protests and leafleting. These campaigns have received widespread media coverage at both the local and national level."

On the importance of working with small activist groups, Juliet Gellatley, the founder and director of Viva!, adds: "We need local groups to provide numbers, and local groups need us as big corporations are unlikely to react to a solitary local demo."

Campaigning Against a Government

With its ivory trade, trophy hunting, live-animal export, elephant-back safaris and other abuses, South Africa has some of the worst exploitation of wild animals in the world. Moreover, the government considers the elephant, the quintessential symbol of Africa, to be a nuisance and threat to the country's biodiversity; as a result, these majestic creatures are regarded merely as economic opportunities. Many animal and environmental advocates in South Africa believe their nation's heritage is being destroyed, and they are urging people, both inside and outside the country, to become involved.

"The government keeps saying there are too many elephants in South Africa," says Michele Pickover of Animal Rights Africa (ARA). "But of course it's not about that at all. It's really about the ivory trade, and local people don't know that. Most people, if you stop them in the street, will say there are too many elephants. We're fighting a huge propaganda machine here."

ARA is also working to convince the government to end the export of animals and the practice of sport hunting – both of which are lucrative markets for the country. "Live wild animals are being exported from South Africa to the US, Europe, South America, Asia – everywhere," says Michele.

"They're going to safari parks and zoos. We're talking about half a million live wild animals being exported every year." As for the hunting of big game animals like the buffalo, elephant, leopard, lion and rhinoceros (known collectively as Africa's "Big Five"), Michele says "We're the biggest trophy hunting country in Africa. Eighty percent of the trophies come from South Africa." South Africa is also where Gandhi spent twenty years honing the use of non-violent protest to create social and political reform.

Convincing the South African government to protect the country's wildlife is a vast campaign that any concerned individual can engage in. It involves more than communicating with legislators; it requires outreach to community leaders, companies and the general public. Here are some suggestions for taking action:

Do's:

- Educate yourself on the issues: Review the information provided by Animal Rights Africa.

- Contact the Minister of Environmental Affairs and Tourism, Martinus van Schalkwyk, and voice your concerns about the ivory trade, hunting, the export of live animals and other exploitation:

Fedsure Forum Building, 10th Floor, North Tower, 315 Pretorius Street, Pretoria

Tel: +27 21 465 7250/1/2

Fax: +27 21 465 3216

Email (in care of his secretary): mwillemse@deat.gov.za

- Write to provincial and national conservation authorities and object to the opening of conservation areas to hunters.

- Write letters to editors of newspapers and magazines expressing your views.

- Let hunters know that you are opposed to their violent pastime.

- Support campaigns to end hunting, elephant-back safaris, the ivory trade, etc.

- Write to or speak with travel agents and tour operators asking them not to support elephant-back safaris. Also ask them to approach the government through their tourism bodies to identify reserves and resorts, such as Kruger and Pilanesburg, where hunting is allowed so that ethical tourists may choose to avoid such facilities.

• Only support tour operators and destinations that do not support elephant-back safaris.

Don'ts:

• Don't visit reserves, resorts or conservation areas that allow hunting.
• Don't purchase ivory or products made from ivory.
• Don't purchase the byproducts of hunting, such as venison, biltong, animal skins or curios from hunted animals.
• Don't patronize stores that sell hunting equipment and promote hunting.
• Don't join or support conservation organizations that promote or tolerate hunting as an acceptable component of "sustainable use."
• Don't patronize zoos or circuses that use animals.

Animal Testing

Among the most egregious abusers of animals outside agribusiness are those who test on them: vivisectionists and manufacturers of pharmaceutical and consumer products. Despite studies that show that the physiological differences between humans and other animal species cause our bodies to react differently to drugs and diseases, millions of animals suffer and die in the name of "medical progress." Moreover, modern humane, non-animal research is more accurate and less expensive than its cruel counterpart. Still more animals are subjected to torture in the course of testing beauty and household products such as cosmetics, soaps, shampoos, lotions, cleaners and, ironically, food for companion animals. Fortunately, many companies understand that animal testing is unnecessary and inhumane – and they even engage in their own corporate campaigning.

Andrew Butler is the campaigns manager for Lush, a natural-cosmetics company based in the UK. The mostly vegan company is working to make all its products animal-friendly and hired Andrew, a long-time activist, to advise Lush on animal-related issues. The company has launched its Supplier Specific Boycott Policy, which means it refuses to do business with any supplier still carrying out chemical testing on animals. "However," Andrew says, "as soon as a manufacturer commits to stopping *all* animal testing, they immediately become eligible to supply Lush, regardless of when they were last engaged in animal testing." This gives an incentive to ingredients manufacturers to stop all testing in order to get more business. "And the more companies that adopt this policy, the more pressure there is on manufacturers to divest themselves of animal testing."

Andrew observes that financial incentives are a key ingredient to successful campaigns. "I think the thing people should remember – and thankfully most activists do – is to not only put pressure on those companies that are involved in bad practices, but also to congratulate and reward companies that are doing good."

What You Can Do to Combat Animal Testing

• Educate yourself. Few people, activists included, realize the massive scale of animal testing; read the literature available from groups working to eliminate this abuse, such as the American Anti-Vivisection Society, Animal Aid, Anti Vivisection Western Australia, the British Union for the Abolition of Vivisection, the Coalition to Abolish Animal Testing and PETA.

• Educate others. Armed with what you know, talk to family, friends and co-workers about the suffering animals endure in testing labs.

• Write letters – to editors, legislators and the companies that test on animals – expressing your position against this form of senseless abuse. It's crucial that your opinions are heard and that offending companies know you are boycotting their products because they test them on animals.

• Contact medical schools that still abuse animals in the name of education and ask them to eliminate live-animal labs from their curricula. (See the Resources section at the end of the chapter for a link to more information.)

• Make ethical choices when you shop: purchase cruelty-free products that have not been tested on animals.

• Call or send an email to companies *not* testing on animals: tell them

their no-animal-testing policy is why you buy their products.
• If you're a student, give a presentation to your class that makes a compelling argument against animal testing.
• If you're a biology student, don't dissect animals – and let your teacher, fellow students and school administrators know why you refuse to participate in this callous and archaic practice. (See the Resources section at the end of the chapter for links to more information.)
• Contact an animal-rights organization that campaigns against animal testing; volunteer to table for them or participate in demonstrations.
• Go undercover. Photographic and video documentation, usually obtained covertly, is incredibly powerful evidence against those who test on animals. Large animal-rights groups like PETA are always looking for people to engage in undercover investigations. (See Chapter 9.)

Even Big Companies Sometimes Listen
Rodeo is to the Australian city of Warwick what pigeon shoots are to the US state of Pennsylvania: a callous blood sport dressed up by their supporters as tradition. The Warwick Rodeo is billed as "Australia's most famous" and attracts thousands of people from around the country. It also attracts sponsors keen to capitalize on the rodeo's popularity. So when Wendy began writing to sponsors, asking them to end their support of the Warwick Rodeo, she wasn't discouraged by their initial resistance. With each letter she enclosed a video showing the abusive treatment suffered by horses, cows and other animals at the event. (In the case of rodeos, video is more compelling than still images, which don't always adequately depict the cruelty involved.)

"It took two years, but tenacity won in the end," she says. Telstra (Australia's leading communications corporation), withdrew its support – and then so did McDonald's, which surprised Wendy, especially since they ended their sponsorship after just one letter. "I have not been made aware of McDonald's sponsoring any other rodeos since this happened." Inspired by these victories, Wendy is lobbying the Victorian and Tasmanian governments on rodeo issues, and she's working to get rodeos banned from the sports curriculum in Queensland high schools.

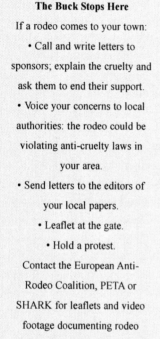

The Buck Stops Here

If a rodeo comes to your town:

• Call and write letters to sponsors; explain the cruelty and ask them to end their support.

• Voice your concerns to local authorities: the rodeo could be violating anti-cruelty laws in your area.

• Send letters to the editors of your local papers.

• Leaflet at the gate.

• Hold a protest.

Contact the European Anti-Rodeo Coalition, PETA or SHARK for leaflets and video footage documenting rodeo cruelty.

And speaking of big companies, the massive online auction site eBay has raised the ire of activists in the UK troubled over sellers auctioning wild-animal hunts. "This contravenes their regulations on the selling of animals," says Jenny Barsby of the League Against Cruel Sports. "But despite complaining a number of times through the usual channels, nothing was done." After learning of one particular hunt up for bid, Jenny alerted the media, which ran several stories on the issue, and eBay took the auction down. "Within twenty-four hours, it was back up," she says. "We went straight back to the media, got another hit, and it was taken down again. After all the bad press we'd managed to bring to bear, they were quite happy to listen to our complaints and agreed to police their site more effectively as well as take complaints more seriously." Jenny occasionally checks eBay UK and believes the company is working harder to exclude auctions of animal hunts. "Of course, some do slip through the net, but once complaints are made, they're normally taken down." (Auctions for animal hunts are allowed on eBay in the US, except auctions that guarantee an animal will be killed.)

Hit 'em in the Stomach

Just as protesting can be seen as corporate campaigning, there are occasions when corporate campaigning can overlap into the model from our previous chapter: using food in your outreach efforts. Activist Nora Kramer says ice cream works especially well. "There are some vegan foods that just aren't quite there yet," she says, "but a lot of vegan ice cream tastes just as good as dairy ice cream. It really busts the stereotype that vegans can't eat decadent food."

Every spring, Ben & Jerry's, the purveyor of frozen desserts that prides itself on socially responsible business practices, holds a "Free Cone Day" at its retail stores around the world. Eager customers form long lines out the door and down the block, which is about as captive an audience as you're likely to find. Nora regards this captive audience as an ideal opportunity for activism.

"VivaUSA had a campaign to try to get Ben & Jerry's to carry a vegan ice cream," says Nora. "So I'd go out on Free Cone Days with all these containers of Soy Delicious and a big box of plastic spoons. I would give each person a spoon and a choice of flavors and say, 'We're here today because we're trying to convince Ben & Jerry's to carry a vegan ice cream, and we want people to know that soy ice cream tastes really good; would you like to try some?' When people try it they go, 'Wow, this is really good.' We say, 'Yes, it's really good, there's no cholesterol, there's less fat and it really makes a difference for the animals.' We give them a flier about the dairy industry and ask them to sign a petition. If someone seems really interested, I'll ask them to request the sorbet when they get to the counter, but only if they are truly interested. And maybe when someone gets to the front of the line they'll ask themselves if they should really be getting dairy ice cream at all."

Restaurant Outreach

Vegetarian eating is becoming more mainstream every day, so asking a local eatery – or your campus cafeteria – to carry more vegan options is not the challenge it might have been even a couple of years ago. Independent restaurants are likely to be more receptive to meeting with you, as they have much more freedom to alter their menus than a franchisee or a national restaurant operated by a large company like McDonald's. Your local, family-owned restaurant is also able to make changes rapidly: DJ Kim of Java Green, for example, was adding vegan options to his menu one month after meeting with Josh, while it likely took fast-food giant Burger King a couple of years of market research, in addition to years of lobbying by activists, before it introduced its BK Veggie burger.

Clearly, convincing a restaurant to adopt a veg-friendly menu calls for a one-on-one meeting with a decision-maker. If this is a new model of activism for you, start off with an eatery you've been to at least a few times: you're a familiar, friendly face, and they want to keep their customers happy. (If your favorite restaurants are all vegan or vegetarian, pick a place you go to with non-vegetarian friends or family.) Ask to speak with the owner or manager and then schedule a brief meeting. Tell him or her that you would like to come back during off-peak hours and bring some samples of delicious, vegetarian foods for them to try. Assuming they are receptive to your suggestion, there are two things you will need to bring:

1. Food. Well, not just food – *delicious* food free of animal ingredients. Mock meats (also called "meat analogs") are becoming more popular every day, making it easy to turn common meat-based entrées like spaghetti with meatballs or a turkey club sandwich into a cruelty-free meal. The common mock meats we enjoy today have their origins in centuries-old recipes for seitan (wheat gluten), tempeh (fermented whole soy beans), tofu, rice, mushrooms, legumes and other plants seasoned and prepared to make the meat analog taste (and often look) like a wide variety of animal-based foods. More recent mock meats use a soy-based textured vegetable protein (TVP).

The owner has probably already heard of veggie burgers or veggie hot dogs, but these analogs may come as a surprise:

- "Chicken" made from soy
- "Beef" made from seitan
- Tempeh "bacon"
- Meatless pepperoni and sausages in many flavors
- "Chicken" nuggets made from soy
- Ground "beef" made from soy (delicious in tacos and burritos)
- Soy ice cream
- Dairy-free cheeses and yoghurts
- Chocolate soy milk
- Vegan cookies

- Earth Balance margarine-style spread
- Egg- and dairy-free mayo (such as Vegenaise)

You'll find these items in just about any health- or natural-food store, and even the larger grocery chains are carrying them now. Choose the foods that will be most appropriate for the business. A Thai restaurant with lots of chicken dishes on its menu may be interested in trying soy-based foods, for example, while veggie deli slices will be right at home in a sandwich shop. Also, remind the restaurant owner or manager that they can promote these items as not just vegan or vegetarian, but cholesterol-free and usually lower in fat than their animal-based counterparts. The Physicians Committee for Responsible Medicine recommends that restaurants adapt their existing menu items to offer familiar dishes, such as pancakes with veggie sausage, scrambled tofu, vegetable lasagna, Thai burritos, fruit smoothies and fresh fruit salad.

2. Information. An important part of this outreach effort will be to educate your audience. Take the soft-sell approach: you're not necessarily trying to make the owner go veggie (though that could be a consequence of your efforts), so bring literature that helps decision-makers understand the health benefits of a vegetarian diet and the increasing desire for these foods among restaurant patrons. Indeed, whether diners are fighting the battle of bulge, trying to lower their blood pressure and cholesterol or looking to eat more ethically to benefit animals and the planet, vegetarian foods are in demand. Be sure to:

- Tell them about Veg Advantage, a non-profit group of chefs helping other chefs and food-service professionals add vegetarian dining options to their menus. This is one of the most important resources you'll find for restaurant outreach, and they will be happy to assist you.
- Bring along some of your favorite veg recipes.
- Order vegetarian starter kits, available from many groups promoting a vegetarian or vegan lifestyle: Animal Liberation Victoria, Compassion Over Killing, PETA, the Toronto Vegetarian Association and Viva!, to

name a few.

- Visit the Physicians Committee for Responsible Medicine online (pcrm.org) and read their *Vegetarian Starter Kit for Restaurants* for more great advice.

Tips for Successful Restaurant Outreach

Courtesy of Compassion Over Killing, a group with a lot of experience in restaurant outreach, here are some suggestions to help make the most of your meeting:

- Dress professionally. First impressions are extremely important, especially when you are presenting an unfamiliar concept to someone. Dressing as you would at a job interview helps boost your credibility enormously. Remember, you are not just endorsing vegetarian products; you are also representing the vegetarian movement.
- Be organized. Having all of your literature and food samples ready to be displayed furthers your professional approach.
- Be appreciative and friendly. As soon as you meet the owner, introduce yourself and thank her or him for allowing you the opportunity to meet. And throughout the course of the meeting, don't forget to smile!
- Start at the beginning. Before offering the food samples, show the literature you brought so the owner has some background information on vegetarian eating.
- Appeal to the owner's taste buds. Following up with the food samples, attractively laid out, brings home the appeal of adding more animal-friendly fare to answer customer demand.
- Be honest. Chances are, the owner will have a string of questions (see below). Answer truthfully. If you aren't sure of a response, simply tell the owner you will research the question and provide an answer within a specified time period.
- Explain the appeal of vegan items. For many people, there is no difference between "vegetarian" and "vegan" fare. Explain that vegans opt not to consume any animal products, including whey and casein, and that adding completely animal-free items to menus will appeal to vegetarians, those with lactose-intolerance or health concerns, as well as

vegans, whereas dishes with eggs or dairy products won't.

• Be helpful. Even if the restaurant owner is enthusiastic about adding more animal-friendly menu items, the next step in actually doing so may be daunting. Offering your help in any capacity – from developing menu ideas to taste testing to promoting its new vegetarian options – shows your commitment to the campaign and your follow-through proves your professionalism.

• Be appreciative. At the meeting's end, thank the owner again for taking the time in a busy day to meet with you.

• Schedule a follow-up date. Giving the restaurant owner time to mull over ideas and talk with the chef is helpful, so suggest that you'll check back in – via phone or a meeting – to see if you can do anything to help with the process.

Frequently Asked Questions

In general, try to keep your conversation and any responses to questions focused on the growing popularity and appeal of vegetarian eating, rather than the ethical reasons you are vegetarian or vegan. You're there to encourage a restaurant owner to offer more animal-friendly items, not to explain your philosophical beliefs. If the owner feels judged or lectured to, chances are good the meeting will not be productive and, of course, not in the animals' best interest.

Some frequently-asked questions and possible responses include:

Q: Why are you doing this?

A: For a variety of reasons, more and more people are choosing to eat vegetarian foods than ever before. I'm just helping to make it more convenient for them.

Q: Why are you vegetarian?

A: Like so many people, I chose to be vegetarian for many reasons: to improve my health, to avoid supporting cruelty to animals and to help the environment.

Q: I offer salads and vegetable sandwiches. Isn't that enough?
A: The majority of people who are now vegetarian didn't give up meat and other animal products because they didn't like the taste. They gave them up because of health, ethical or ecological reasons. And many people who do eat meat are interested in cholesterol-free foods, which all vegan fare is, or lighter dishes that are commonly found in vegetarian options. So, offering pure vegetarian items – or going even further with mock meat and mock dairy items – will definitely diversify your menu while attracting new customers.

Once you've had success with one restaurant owner, ask for recommendations of other establishments that would be interested in creating or expanding their vegetarian options. Many times, owners associate with others in the restaurant business, and their connections and suggestions can be valuable to your outreach efforts.

Dining Halls

If you eat at a school cafeteria or corporate dining hall, you can engage in a variation of the restaurant outreach strategy and meet with your food services representative. You can ask that your dining hall carry more vegetarian or vegan entrées, or you can persuade them to eliminate the most egregious forms of cruelty to animals raised for food production: veal, pig meat from crated sows, chicken meat from typically raised "broiler" chickens and eggs from battery-caged hens. The Humane Society of the United States (HSUS) has been helping students make changes in their campus dining halls.

Tips for Successful Dining Hall Outreach

- Schedule a meeting with the director of dining services.
- Contact HSUS (jbalk@hsus.org) and ask for materials to bring to the meeting.
- Make sure the director and school officials know that you want to work with them, not against them.
- Talk about nutrition and health: vegans live longer, healthier lives than

meat-eaters. Citing nutritional studies helps.
• The food service staff may not know where to begin, so share some meat and dairy alternatives and your favorite recipes.
• Be polite yet persistent when following up to ensure that action is being taken.
• If dining services doesn't change its purchasing, get the student government involved – they can pass a resolution on this issue. You can also approach your school's newspaper for an editorial-board endorsement and collect student signatures on petitions.

Another tactic for nudging a restaurant over the veggie line is to fill their business with patrons eating vegan entrées, explains activist Liberty Mulkani, who organizes dine-out events for EarthSave Canada at least once a month. "Dine-outs are social dinner events that take place at restaurants around Vancouver," she says, adding that all the dine-out events are vegan. "I approach restaurants – usually not vegetarian restaurants – and plan a set vegan menu with tax and tip included. Once the menu, price and date have been agreed to we advertise the event to the EarthSave Canada email list of more than two thousand people, as well as to local activity groups in the city. While many diners who attend are vegetarian or vegan, a large percentage of the attendees are meat-eaters. The point of the dine-outs is to promote a healthy, veggie lifestyle and encourage restaurants to add more veggie options to their menus."

Although this may seem to be an ambitious approach for a grassroots activist, you can still do something like it on a smaller scale. "I definitely think an individual could call a restaurant and plan a similar vegan event for a group of friends," says Liberty. "Even without pre-planning the menu, this would be effective outreach." She advises making a call to the chef or manager, or visiting the restaurant in person during their slower business hours. "I try to do my research on the menu first so I know what things might already be vegan or which menu items could easily be made vegan with minor alterations. I also try to suggest good brands of soy milk, soy cheese, margarine and such in case the chef doesn't know how something could be made vegan. I would hate to have a chef go out of their way to

> We can't begin to imagine what it's like to be a battery hen or a pig in a gestation crate; the suffering of animals on factory farms and in slaughterhouses is beyond our worst nightmares. So yes, there is ample reason to become dispirited, misanthropic and generally unhappy. But that won't help animals, and really, we have come a remarkably long way in, historically speaking, almost no time at all.
>
> **Bruce Friedrich**
>
> *Satya* magazine,
>
> January/February 2004

veganize a menu item but choose an inferior brand of soy cheese or soy milk then be turned off of the idea of vegan food because of a bad result."

Don't be surprised to have a restaurant adopt some animal-friendly changes in response to your efforts. The first dine-out Liberty organized was at a Greek restaurant, and the chef prepared a vegan moussaka dish, replacing the cream in the béchamel sauce. "After the event," says Liberty, "the restaurant decided to make the veggie moussaka permanently vegan on their menu, as the result tasted the same and was a big hit with everyone." A Caribbean restaurant she worked with, meanwhile, was so impressed they "expressed an interest in having a weekly or monthly vegetarian buffet night and possibly eventually going completely veggie with their restaurant. These same things could certainly be accomplished by individuals who were willing to take the time to speak with restaurants about vegan menu options."

Targeting the Food Industry

As the largest abusers of animals, the corporations that produce meat, eggs and dairy foods are a prime target for campaigning. Recent improvements in the lives of confined animals are clear indications that such outreach is working, according to activist Lisa Franzetta. "I think a lot of the campaigns that are currently being done to put pressure on the big corporate players with deep pockets – and actually sitting down around negotiating tables with the executives behind multi-billion-dollar organizations like McDonald's to discuss animal welfare initiatives – have proven to be extremely effective," she says. "Take the example of Smithfield Foods agreeing to phase out gestation crates as an admitted result of their consumers leaning on them to provide improved welfare standards – and by 'consumers,' they mean massive corporate purchasers like McDonald's and Wal-Mart. In order to achieve small improvements in the treatment of animals raised in abusive industries, especially factory farms, I think this model is proving extremely effective. Money talks, so if we can make compelling arguments to the people behind the paychecks, I think we're using our time very effectively."

Lisa raises an important point. When lobbying a company to make changes, think not only in terms of what's best for animals – keep in mind that a financial return (and the bigger the better) is what motivates corporations. That's why boycotts are effective: they impact buying habits and thus a company's bottom line.

"A corporate policy-maker is, for the most part, concerned with the profits of the company and its shareholders," says activist Michael Hayward. "If you, as an animal advocate, are able to illustrate to these companies and policy-makers that improved animal welfare, or whatever, will profitably improve their perceived image in the public eye or their corporate efficiency, they may be motivated to pursue your ideas strictly for monetary reasons."

And the impact of a shift in corporate policy can have enormous ramifications for animals who are raised for food. Although we realize the ideal solution for everyone would be the total liberation of animals, improvements that can be implemented before that happens will help alleviate suffering.

"Most of HSUS' corporate outreach efforts are designed to get companies to stop using the cruelest and most inhumane factory farming products," says Paul Shapiro, director of the Factory Farming Campaign for HSUS. "To get companies to stop using battery cage eggs, pork from producers who use gestation crates, crated veal, foie gras and so on. Sometimes our campaigning has been to stop companies from using a certain animal product. For example, we worked with Gardenburger to eliminate eggs from its products, with just one exception, and for the one product they felt they had to have eggs they converted from battery cage eggs to cage-free eggs."

Josh Balk, now outreach coordinator for HSUS, agrees. "Since these animals represent the overwhelming majority of animals we use in our society," he says, "changes in purchasing by major food buyers and sellers can reduce animal suffering even faster than individual purchasing decisions."

Even small outreach efforts to the food industry can have an impact, as Joyce D'Silva of Compassion in World Farming has discovered. Because of the recent growth of the European Union, it has become more difficult for animal advocates to get reforms passed in the EU. So Joyce and other activists have started lobbying the food industry, in particular the grocery stores and retail outlets that buy from agribusiness. She's quickly learned the value of media coverage in these efforts.

Recently, Joyce's group tried to get Tesco (which she calls "the Wal-Mart of the UK") to label their battery eggs as being from hens confined to cages, but the chain's executives told them their focus-group studies showed Tesco customers did not want to feel guilty when buying battery eggs (Tesco needed market research for that?). "We organized a tour of eighteen major Tesco supermarkets in good media centers throughout the country – where there would be regional television and radio," Joyce says. "We had a big model of a de-feathered battery hen. On the morning we started the tour, my colleague was on one of the big radio programs with someone from Tesco. The Tesco representative repeated that people don't want to know where their eggs come from. At ten-thirty, Tesco faxed us to say they were considering our position. At eleven-thirty, another fax came through saying 'We've decided to label all our battery eggs as being from caged hens.' It just shows the power of the media. So we called off the rest of the tour and celebrated."

Joyce advises other activists who want to go after grocery stores to first speak with the manager, explain the issue you want addressed and suggest how it might be rectified. "If that fails, you might have a little demo outside the store, call the local press, hand out leaflets, talk to shoppers and ask them to sign petitions." And making it easier for the public to participate always helps. "One thing we did once was to print customer-comment cards that looked quite like the cards the stores use, only we printed ours with information about battery eggs and left room for customers to write their own bit," she says. "It helped build awareness at the top levels."

Whether it's doing food industry outreach or any campaign, remember your audience, advises Charles Stahler, co-founder of the Vegetarian Resource Group. "When working with the mainstream, you may have to change your tactics somewhat," he says. "You can't always say what you would say when talking to other activists." Charles recommends that activists trust their own voice. "People should appreciate and understand each other's role, not feel they have to replicate what others are doing or that everyone has to be like you. Each activist should work in a way they feel comfortable without feeling other activists have to be like them."

More Tips for Effective Corporate Campaigning

• Before beginning any campaign, clearly understand what it is you want to achieve for animals – and what compromises you're willing to accept from the target company.

• Do your corporate research: Find out what your target's corporate strategy is, profile the people that you will be contacting and frame your message to your audience and to their corporate culture.

• If you get a face-to-face meeting, dress appropriately. Your target will look for ways to dismiss you and your message – don't give them one.

• Before any communication, write out your talking points or draft an agenda so that you are organized and able to get convey your message.

• Frame dialog as a joint problem-solving session where you are looking for mutually advantageous solutions, rather than: "You have to do what I say because I say so!"

• Find support from other activists and groups. These need not be animal-rights groups, either; indeed, expanding your efforts to include people and businesses outside the movement demonstrates your issue is important to the entire community – or beyond – and not just "animal people." For example, if you're targeting a local government that plans to use a toxic poison to kill predators, you could enlist support from environmental and conservation groups.

• Boycott companies that are not animal-friendly, but don't keep it to yourself: Write letters, send emails and make phone calls to the target companies telling them why you are boycotting them. Stage protests outside their stores and offices, too.

- Contact the media – they can be a powerful ally. Send press releases to local and, if applicable, national news outlets telling them about your campaign.

- Don't forget to be positive: Always let target companies know that you will patronize them again once they make the animal-friendly change you're asking of them. (Without an economic incentive, most companies will not acquiesce.)

- Collect petition signatures to demonstrate support for your viewpoint.

- Don't be intimidated by big talk. Companies or other entities may say you haven't the support – or the right – to stand against them.

- Use the Internet: Add details about your corporate campaign on your MySpace page and any other Web sites you can. If there's a video available that addresses your position, post in on video-sharing sites like YouTube and Google Video.

- Add an action item to your email signature, asking recipients to take action in support of your campaign. Be specific: Tell them what you want them to do and provide links, if any.

- The larger animal-rights organizations have plenty of experience assisting activists. Try contacting PETA, which has people around the world ready to help.

"I think corporate outreach is a lot more efficient than going person to person," says Paul Shapiro. "It's great to be able to persuade your friends and family to change their eating habits – we should all act as ambassadors for the animal movement at all times and help persuade people to live in a more compassionate manner – but we can all have an even greater impact if we can also persuade the major food buyers to change the type of products they buy. Whether it's to stop buying the cruelest and most inhumane factory farming products, to get them to stop using certain animal products or to get them to serve more vegetarian options. It's just a whole lot more efficient."

"Long story short," adds Andrew Butler, "pick your corporate targets with care, go after the companies that can make the biggest influence in their field and don't let up until they do the right thing. When they do, *reward* them. Also make sure that the companies you support are the ones really doing something positive, not simply using it as a marketing tool."

[1] *Satya* magazine, October 1998

Resources:

American Anti-Vivisection Society
www.aavs.org
Animal Aid
www.animalaid.org.uk
Animal Liberation Victoria
www.alv.org.au
Animal Rights Africa
www.animalrightsafrica.org
Anti Vivisection Western Australia
www.avwa.com.au
British Union for the Abolition of Vivisection
www.buav.org
Coalition to Abolish Animal Testing
www.ohsukillsprimates.com
Compassion Over Killing
www.cok.net
Cruelty-free products
www.compassionateconsumer.com
EarthSave Canada
www.earthsave.ca
European Anti-Rodeo Coalition
www.anti-rodeo.org
European Coalition to End Animal Experiments
www.eceae.org
Google Video
http://video.google.com
HSUS
www.hsus.org
League Against Cruel Sports

www.league.org.uk

Lush

www.lush.com

Medical schools that use vivisection

www.peta.org/feat/medicalschools

PETA

www.peta.org

Refusing to dissect

www.arrc.org.au/dissection.htm

www.buav.org/pdf/Dissection.pdf

www.janewrdh.com/students/college.htm

www.petakids.com/disindex.html

Restaurant Vegetarian Starter Kit (online only - from the Physicians
Committee for Responsible Medicine)

www.pcrm.org/health/rvsk/index.html

SHARK (rodeo footage)

www.rodeocruelty.com

Soy Delicious

www.purelydecadent.com

Toronto Vegetarian Association

www.veg.ca

Veg Advantage

www.vegadvantage.com

Vegetarian Resource Group

www.vrg.org

Viva!

www.viva.org.uk

VivaUSA (soy ice cream campaign)

www.vivausa.org/campaigns/dairy/servingicecream.html

YouTube

www.youtube.com

CHAPTER 7

ANIMAL HOUSE: SANCTUARIES, SHELTERS & RESCUE CENTERS

Never doubt that a small group of thoughtful, committed, citizens can change the world. Indeed, it is the only thing that ever has.

Margaret Mead

Pam Ahern remembers the moment volunteer Sue Werrett became a hero. Pam, founder of Edgar's Mission animal sanctuary in Australia, says an epic drought in 2006-2007 had left livestock paddocks dry on farms across the country. "Sadly, another sight that was becoming all too familiar to us was of pathetically thin sheep stuck in the quagmire of mud that was once a dam," she says. One particular farm with a muddy dam (reservoir) and negligent farmer had been the scene of many tragedies as animals, drawn to the last vestiges of water, perished in the deep sludge. But luckily for one trapped sheep, Sue happened to drive by.

"I did a double take when I spotted what appeared to be a large rock in the mud," says Sue. Her heart sank when she realized the "rock" was a full-grown ewe. She immediately called Pam, who started off for the farm as quickly as she could – but Sue was not about to let the sheep languish. "She was wedged up to her shoulders in muddy water infested with mozzies [mosquitoes] and other flying things," says Sue. "I cleaned the mud out of her eyes as best I could and talked to her; I wanted her to know I was not going to let her die."

Sinking into the mud herself, Sue slipped her arms beneath the ewe's chest and pulled. Nothing. She pulled once more, straining against both gravity and the turbid suction. The sheep would not budge from her mucky trap. "I pulled again and again and again," Sue says. At last she felt movement – just an inch or two, but it was something. Bolstered by compassion for the ewe and anger at the farmer for his neglect, Sue at last pulled the animal free. "I lost one boot and my mobile phone, and my jeans were very low slung by this stage!"

The ewe, exhausted and unable to stand, lay on firm ground beside her liberator. "I will never forget the look in her eye as she gazed towards me, just lying there," says Sue. "I sat beside her and started to gather my thoughts as well as my jeans." The farmer, alerted by Pam, was now racing over the hill, and Sue, assuming he'd press trespassing charges, primed herself for a confrontation. "I was ready for a showdown. Yes, I was trespassing, but I trespassed to save one of his sheep! What could he say? Would he have a go at me, a member of the community, for caring? I was doing his job!"

Sue Werrett with Whoopi, whom she rescued from certain death.

Sue knew the sheep would not survive without proper medical attention. "I offered to take the ewe off his hands as he obviously had a lot on his plate," she says. Eyeing the dam bank, and clearly struggling to keep his animals watered during drought conditions, the farmer agreed; he even helped maneuver the mud-encrusted sheep into Sue's car.

"This is your lucky day," Sue said, patting her new friend, now christened Whoopi, on the head and driving them to her new home at Edgar's Mission.

Sanctuaries

Animal sanctuaries around the world rely on volunteers. The work may not be glamorous, but it is among the most rewarding work you will ever do as an activist. There's just nothing quite like seeing hens, pigs, cows and other animals able to indulge in their natural behaviors, or whistling to a turkey and having him gobble in reply.

"I find volunteering at a farmed animal sanctuary occasionally to be an effective way to put me back into contact with the animals I am advocating for, as well as to help an organization that needs people almost as much as it needs money," says Eric Prescott. "Some of these organizations also do humane education for children and even adults. I have participated in this before, and I am strongly encouraged by the potential impact this outreach has on people."

Following is just a sampling of sanctuaries that encourage volunteers and in some cases offer internship programs for people planning a career in animal protection or simply looking to enhance their effectiveness as activists.

Animal Place (US)

You'd never suspect that the long road in a quiet neighborhood forty minutes from San Francisco leads to a sixty-acre farm with forest, meadow, pasture, hills and a lake. This is Animal Place, where such residents as Howie the cow, Leland the turkey, Owen the pig and Jeffrey the goat are among more than three hundred animals who have been rescued from stockyards or neglect cases and are now peacefully living out the remainder of their lives.

Animal Place volunteer work includes just about everything that goes into running the sanctuary, from health checks for poultry and rabbits to cleaning and building projects. There are opportunities to get involved with other activism work such as letter writing, community outreach, collecting signatures for legislative initiatives and hands-on rescue efforts. Activists can also help with Animal Place's Food for Thought campaign, a national outreach effort that encourages humane societies and other shelters to demonstrate a consistent animal-friendly policy by not serving animals at shelter-sponsored events.

"The enthusiasm and vitality volunteers bring to a sanctuary is immense," says Kim Sturla, who co-founded Animal Place as a non-profit sanctuary with veterinarian Ned Buyukmihci in 1989. "They spread the word of what they learn here, so they are the ripple to the splash that we make. They tell their circle of friends, their circle of work mates, their circle of family – their whole community. I think those benefits are even greater than helping with the health checks and mucking out stalls."

Activists interested in learning even more can participate in Animal

Place's internship programs, which include animal work and marketing.

Eastern Shore Sanctuary and Education Center (US)

Anyone who questions the sentience of chickens would do well to spend some time at Eastern Shore Sanctuary. Here hundreds of hens and roosters, most of them former inmates from the egg and chicken-meat industries, have the freedom to indulge their natural behaviors and display rich emotional lives. Watch them preen and dust bathe and forage. Notice how the birds interact with one another – and with you. Ask pattrice jones, the sanctuary's co-founder, about a certain rooster named Viktor.

Discovered in a ditch on the side of the road, Viktor had probably jumped

Future sanctuary volunteers attend orientation class at Animal Place.

or fallen from a truck taking him to one of the many nearby slaughterhouses. He was the first bird pattrice and miriam jones brought home. Because the early months of his life were spent in the alien environment of a factory farm, Viktor was unsure how to socialize as more chickens arrived at what would become Eastern Shore Sanctuary. A pair of young chickens, Violet and Chickweed, perplexed him. Viktor didn't know if he should be a father to them or a peer; or perhaps he should court the hen and mentor the younger rooster. He tried each role, says pattrice, finally deciding everyone was happiest with him as a very devoted single parent. Viktor also fell in love. When Rosa, his first love, died, Viktor spent months mourning her. He eventually found love again, courting a new arrival named Ellie Mae. As the sanctuary's elder rooster, Viktor was vigilant and protective, even at the risk of his own safety: When he spotted two hawks circling overhead one day, Viktor stood in front of two chicks who hadn't taken cover. But it was agribusiness that would take Viktor's life. He died of a heart attack at about eighteen months of age, his body unable to cope with the rapid growth that "broiler" chickens are bred for by the billions each year.

Located in Maryland, Eastern Shore Sanctuary would love to have volunteers assist with writing and research for educational materials, and there's always a need for activists to come to protests or join in letter-writing campaigns and other efforts that can be done from home. "People who live nearby can come and help out with the birds on a regular basis," says pattrice. "And, some people who live a few hours away come for a work day every now and then to help out with big projects in the barns or yards."

pattrice jones with Franny the hen and cats Pearl and Pyjama.

Edgar's Mission (Australia)

Pam Ahern, founder of Edgar's Mission, believes in the power of "meeting your meat" face to face. Once people understand that farmed animals have personalities, needs and desires – and that they feel emotions like happiness, sorrow and fear – they can make more informed and compassionate lifestyle choices. Volunteers can assist with work around the sanctuary, outreach programs such as leafleting and administrative tasks. "I also manage to rope in a few people now and then when I drive the van around Melbourne showing video footage of a particular animal issue such as live export," says Pam.

Farm Sanctuary (US)

Shortly after their humble beginnings in a Delaware backyard, Farm Sanctuary opened the first shelter in the United States for victims of food animal production in 1986. Today they operate sanctuaries in New York and California. In addition to their animal-rescue work, Farm Sanctuary engages in legislative and humane education campaigns, and Gene Baur, the organization's president and co-founder, is one of the most visible farmed animal advocates in the world. "We have events around the country," says Gene. "Our annual forum, for example, is designed to give people skills and suggestions for activism in their own community."

Don Walker is Farm Sanctuary's intern coordinator. "Interns at our Watkins Glen and Orland shelters live at the farm and get daily hands-on experience with the animals," he says. "Our internship program offers many educational opportunities on a variety of topics, from an overview of factory farming to the basics of starting a sanctuary. Interns visit a working stockyard to see what it is like and how animals in a production environment are not only in visibly poorer physical condition than our animals, but also behave much differently because they are not treated with kindness and respect." Don says interns, who are at Farm Sanctuary from one to three months, have the option of working directly with the animals or working in one of their other departments to assist with campaigns, communications, education or other efforts. "We have many former interns working for us now, myself included."

Activists interested in becoming a Farm Sanctuary intern are advised to be prepared for hard and sometimes mundane work: interns may be shoveling manure one day and stuffing envelopes the next. "At the end of the day and the end of their internship," Don says, "there's a sure sense of accomplishment and encouragement that they made a difference in the lives of animals here and animals everywhere." Moreover, interns gain the knowledge and skills that make them better advocates for animals when they leave.

"Being able to spend time with the animals was really valuable," says former intern Nora Kramer. "I don't think I'd ever seen a chicken in person before I went to Farm Sanctuary. But the most important thing is that for the first time I was spending time with other people who felt exactly the same way I did. And I became such a better cook just by living with people who had also been experimenting with vegan cooking."

Hillside Animal Sanctuary (UK)

As with any sanctuary, each of Hillside's residents comes with a story. There's Matilda, for example, a breeding sow who attacked her owner as he handled one of her screaming piglets. Rather than slaughter her, the farmer released Matilda – and her piglet, Sugar Plum – to Hillside. Alice the camel was likely destined for a circus when a Hillside supporter donated the money to buy her at auction. A duck named Lucky escaped a processing plant and was discovered by a Hillside investigator wandering outside. And national publicity helped win the life of Spot, a wild baby rabbit who had journeyed across the sea from Holland amid a delivery of Chrysanthemums. When the media announced authorities planned to euthanize Spot because her six-month quarantine would cost seven hundred pounds, a public appeal quickly raised the funds and this long-eared stowaway now lives with Hillside's other rescued rabbits.

"The only volunteers we have at the sanctuary are those who help with the animals," says Pauline Lynch. "Because of health and safety regulations, anyone coming to work at the sanctuary has to undergo training and therefore we prefer to take on volunteers who are able to work with us on a fairly long-term basis, even though it may only be for a couple of days a week." In addition to its rescue work, Hillside, located in Norwich, England, engages in undercover investigations and public outreach.

> I regularly visit this wonderful park in the middle of the city and right now there's a whole bunch of baby ducks there. I've been walking there throughout the winter and now the ducks have been born, and I thought, "Everything renews itself – everything." The opposite of burnout, really, is renewal, and to renew ourselves really takes just slowing down and stopping and saying "Okay, I can turn this corner."
>
> **Carol J. Adams**
> *Satya* magazine, July/August 2001

Performing Animal Welfare Society (US)

Circuses, zoos, traveling shows, safari parks and other places of "entertainment" are anything but amusing to the elephants, monkeys, bears, tigers and lions who are often taken from the wild, cruelly trained to perform tricks and forced to live in lonely, unnatural conditions. The Performing Animal

Welfare Society (PAWS) is home to many of these animals, as well as victims of the exotic animal trade, who have been rescued and can now live in peace and contentment. PAWS operates three sanctuaries in California (none of which is open to the public), and they need many volunteers to assist with special events, grounds keeping, clerical support, supply transport, fundraising, fence building and many other jobs. "We have an enriching, learning environment, and we encourage new volunteers and interns," says Kim Gardner of PAWS, who adds some volunteers have been with them for twenty years.

Woodstock Farm Sanctuary (US)

It might seem like a long road from attending film school to running a sanctuary, but Jenny Brown has always put her talents to work for animals. Her video skills, for example, went into undercover documentaries for PETA, but her passion is working directly with animals.

"If you work or volunteer at a sanctuary and talk to people who are there visiting, you have the *best* opportunity to get your message out because you have a captive audience," says Jenny, who co-founded Woodstock Farm Sanctuary, just two hours from New York City, with her husband, Doug. "They have come to *you*, and so while they happily stroke the adorable pig or cow in front of them, you can tell them where that animal came from and how billions of others are systemically exploited and abused until death in modern-day agribusiness." Jenny, who interned at Farm Sanctuary, says most activists are shocked by how many people are unaware of the moral issues of modern-day farming, but she sees hope in every public tour she conducts and recommends that those in the animal-rights movement volunteer at a sanctuary. "As an activist fighting for the rights of animals, your resolve is strengthened by simply spending time with the animals you are fighting to protect."

Wildlife Rescue

No matter where you call home, living in harmony with wildlife is crucial to sustaining the delicate balance of nature. But if you live near an urban area, you probably know that the encroachment of humanity can kill or injure animals and threaten habitats. Even animals far from civilization may suffer the consequences of pollution, oil spills, hunters, motor vehicles, predatory animals and much more. Helping to educate the public and protect animals, wildlife centers around the world rescue and rehabilitate animals in need, releasing them back into the wild. Many wildlife centers also serve as advocacy groups, doing outreach and humane education. Although a wildlife rescue organization may have a paid staff, they rely on volunteers to assist with the thousands of animals they may help throughout the year. Here are just a few.

Center for Animal Rehabilitation and Education (South Africa)

On the banks of the Olifants River, along the western edge of Kruger National Park, the Center for Animal Rehabilitation and Education (CARE) began in 1989 as a facility to treat small mammals, reptiles and birds who had been injured or orphaned. But as CARE grew, founder Rita Miljo welcomed larger animals, and now baboons are the center's main focus. Most of the baboons Rita and her team rescue have been orphaned by hunting, road accidents, poaching or fire, or they are the traumatized victims of medical experimentation, habitat destruction or other abuses at the hands of humans. Once integrated into new troops, the animals are successfully released back into the wild.

Volunteers are needed to care for and socialize orphaned baby baboons, as well as to assist in CARE's daily operation. The Center appreciates compassionate, patient volunteers who have experience working with animals, a positive attitude, a love of nature, a sense of humor and a desire to ensure the survival of South Africa's natural heritage.

"Our minimum age requirement for volunteers is eighteen years, and we ask that you commit to stay for a minimum of four weeks," says Karen Pilling, who coordinates CARE's volunteer program. "We have found that a shorter stay will not give you time to become involved in the Center, to learn the names and needs of the individual animals that you are caring for or to really feel useful."

The Fox Project (UK)

The fox has certainly had a rough time in the UK. Characterized in folklore as one of nature's tricksters and hunted for thousands of years throughout Great Britain, the fox is also revered by many. Trevor Williams is among those working to aid these animals through his organization. Based in Kent, the Fox Project rescues sick and injured foxes and abandoned fox cubs, providing for their care, treatment and rehabilitation back into the wild. Because some householders still regard the fox as a villain, the Fox Project offers a humane fox deterrence and advice service.

"We operate with around seventy-five volunteers," says Trevor, a former hunt saboteur. "There are rescuers, fosterers, rehabbers, cleaners and fundraisers. Rescuers are simply folk who we call when an incident occurs near to them so that they can get hold of the animal more quickly than our duty wildlife ambulance. Fosterers look after healthy cubs, post-weaning, or convalescent adults prior to release, in cages on their own properties, thereby alleviating pressure on our central treatment facilities. The rehabbers' job is to release a group of five hand-raised cubs from a rehab cage on their property at end of summer when natural dispersal would be taking place. Cleaners speaks for itself, really. Their job is to keep cage areas on main facilities clean and tidy and to administer medication. Fundraisers carry out all the usual can shaking, sponsored events, raffles and such on our behalf."

(Though fox hunting with hounds is now officially banned in England and Wales, enthusiasts of this blood sport are working to overturn the law and, as Trevor observes, "It was never carried out by a particularly law-abiding section of society, so it still continues in most areas of the country with no real policing to curb it.")

Kingbilli Wildlife Rescue (Australia)

Georgina Beach was twenty-three feet (7 meters) up a tree, face to face with an injured koala, when she lost her footing. Fortunately for Georgina, who runs Kingbilli Wildlife Rescue, and for the elderly marsupial, who also became dislodged from the tree, a Dutch couple volunteering for Kingbilli were waiting below. "This was the best advertisement for having two volunteers present on a wildlife rescue," she says. "One volunteer to catch the koala – and the other to catch me!"

Most volunteers at this busy wildlife refuge and rehabilitation center in the central highlands of Victoria, however, don't have direct contact with the animals. It's a matter of not having proper training, Georgina explains. "The biology, ecology and behavior of native wildlife are a world apart from those animals with whom most humans are familiar, and at least a basic understanding of these areas is required before people can work hands-on with them." Volunteers are more likely to be helping with manual labor at the refuge or crowd control during rescues.

In addition to koalas, Kingbilli rescues a veritable roll call of outback critters, including kangaroos, wallabies, wombats, possums, Phascogales and Agile Antechinus. "Wildlife rehabilitation is not all cute and cuddly," says Georgina. "It involves considerable hard work – and much more than its fair share of heartache." Although she says the work is difficult, "the most mundane, boring or back-breaking tasks are just as important as bottle-feeding a cute and cuddly baby."

WildCare (US)

WildCare is one of the few truly urban wildlife rehabilitation centers, located near a thriving downtown area in Marin County, California. The organization pursues its advocacy through nature education, wildlife rehabilitation and community outreach, and it relies heavily on volunteers.

"Each year our incredibly dedicated volunteers reach and teach more than forty thousand Bay Area children and adults, encouraging an awareness of the need for sustainability and a love of nature," says Alison Hermance, WildCare's volunteer manager. "Our wildlife hospital is ninety-five percent run by volunteers, so we couldn't treat the more than three thousand animals we take in every year without their help. Volunteers handle the majority of the feeding, medicating, cleaning and caring for our patients. Our goal is to rehabilitate animals and then release them back into the wild, and we absolutely could not provide such quality care for the more than two hundred different species of animals we treat without our volunteers."

WildCare also welcomes people to work on their wildlife hotline, fielding calls from the public regarding the many issues involved in sharing the region with wild animals, and for the foster care of baby wild patients and to represent WildCare at fairs and other outreach events.

"WildCare's volunteers come from all walks of life and all ages," says Alison. "Volunteering has given them the opportunity to come face to face with amazing wild animals, participate in their healing and share a love and respect for the natural world with the next generation."

Wildlife Rescue Association (Canada)

Located in British Columbia, Wildlife Rescue Association (WRA) cares for thousands of injured, orphaned and pollution-damaged wild animals every year. Upon completing a hands-on training program, volunteers work directly with animals, returning them to their natural habitats as soon as they are healthy and able to live independently in the wild.

> How often do we take the time to look at ourselves? Can we even allow ourselves a moment to put ourselves first? Or would that be selfish – are we too busy, can't say no to helping out, who else is going to take care of my critters, the homeless, the environment?
>
> **Kymberlie Adams Matthews**
> *Satya* magazine, April 2005

"WRA volunteers begin with the pigeon cages, as pigeons are the gentlest birds to work with," says Liberty Mulkani, a former volunteer. "To clean a bird's habitat you first have to carefully wrap the bird in a towel and transfer him or her to a cardboard cat carrier. This can be quite intimidating as you want to be as gentle as possible without letting them escape, which could lead to further injury." Liberty says one of the most challenging aspects of the job is not speaking to the animals. "As the patients at WRA are all wild animals, the staff is very strict about the importance of not allowing them to imprint on humans, as this would detract from their survival chances once re-released." As volunteers become more comfortable with pigeons, they're moved to other birds such as gulls, crows, ducks, geese, swans, starlings and hawks. WRA also assists the occasional chipmunk, beaver, raccoon, deer and bat.

Shelters

Unlike most animal sanctuaries at which animals spend the rest of their lives, shelters offer animals for adoption to members of the public. Overpopulation of dogs, cats, rabbits and other domestic animals forces shelters to euthanize about half of the millions of animals who end up in shelters each year. Although "no kill" shelters may seem like a wonderful solution, the reality is these facilities only accept the most "adoptable" animals (who may spend years in a cage), while the animals turned away likely end up in an open-admission shelter down the road – or simply abandoned to fend for themselves on the street.

"We need more animal-rights activists working in shelters," says Kim Sturla, who for more than a decade served as executive director of the Peninsula Humane Society in northern California. "Activists can help shelters have a broader perspective of who they think needs protecting and who doesn't – and not to serve animals at their events."

Shelters need activists willing to donate their time and energy, and such volunteer work might include:

- Exercising, grooming and socializing animals while they wait for loving homes
- Cleaning cages, the backyard or the shelter's office
- Helping to reunite animal guardians with their lost companions
- Participating in community outreach activities to educate the public about the need for humane treatment of all animals
- Helping with shelter events and fundraising.

Don't be afraid to suggest your own ways to help. For example, if you're computer literate, you could offer to maintain a shelter's Web site or create a MySpace page for them and keep it current with information on the animals available for adoption.

Because most cities have an animal shelter, all of which need volunteers, a list of suggested places to start is not necessary. You will need to contact each shelter directly to learn about volunteer needs and opportunities. Check the telephone directory under the headings "animal shelter," "humane society" and "animal control," or type those words plus your city into your favorite search engine online. You can also try these Web sites:

- In Australia: www.govolunteer.com.au or http://volunteersearch.gov.au
- In Canada: www.animalinks.com
- In South Africa: www.animalrescue.org.za
- In the UK: www.timebank.org.uk or www.animalrescuers.co.uk
- In the US: www.volunteermatch.org or www.petfinder.com

Unfortunately, not all shelters are clean, safe havens for animals. Some shelters, for example, knowingly turn animals over to vivisectionists – a practice known as "pound seizure." "Activists can play a vital role in identifying and ending abuse and neglect at animal shelters," says PETA's Megan Hartman. "To assist activists, PETA offers materials including a 'How Does Your Shelter Measure Up?' checklist, which lists basic guidelines for humane housing and treatment of homeless animals; a sample 'Animal Shelter Inspection Form,' which activists can use to document conditions at the shelter and present their findings to officials as they discuss problems and solutions; and a 'Step-by-Step Guide to Campaigning,' which offers detailed advice for making positive changes at animal shelters."

Due to severe crowding, most shelters are forced to kill animals who are considered "unadoptable" because of their age, illness or aggressive personalities. Even animals who are in perfect health and have friendly temperaments may be killed if they have remained at the shelter for too long, thus making room for another animal. This heartbreaking reality is the result of animal overpopulation, caused in large part by businesses that continue to breed companion animals and guardians who fail to spay or neuter their animals. It is also very stressful for shelter workers, even those who work in so-called "no kill" shelters.

"In my previous animal rescue work, I had to regularly make decisions to refuse animals from open-admission facilities when our shelter was beyond capacity," says Erin Williams, who now works for the Humane Society of the United States. "It was tough not to feel that I had failed those animals who were euthanized after we could not accept them."

Improving a Shelter

If your local shelter needs reform, take action by launching a campaign. PETA recommends these steps:

- At all times, maintain a positive attitude. For each problem that you encounter, offer a solution, along with assistance in implementing your suggestions.
- Focus on specific problems. And don't expect to get everything that you ask for all at once.
- Thoroughly document the abuses. Common problems include cruel killing methods (such as shooting or electrocution), dirty conditions, lack of veterinary care, lack of adequate food and water, poor record-keeping that results in animals being "accidentally" destroyed, lack of spay/neuter requirements or programs, turning animals over to experimenters, inadequate screening procedures for adoption applicants, and callous, untrained or unthinking staff. (According to the American Veterinary Medical Association and other animal advocates, the most compassionate method of euthanizing animals is an intravenous injection of sodium pentobarbital administered by a trained professional.)
- To effectively document abuses, volunteer at the facility or visit it frequently. Compile photographs, written statements, and observations about specific incidents and conditions. Record all pertinent information (date, time, people involved, weather conditions, etc.). Label each photo and get statements notarized. Have as many people as possible visit the shelter and document their experiences. Be sure to keep copies of all your documents and correspondence.
- Organize a group. After you have collected concrete evidence indicating that there are poor conditions at the shelter, enlist others to work with you. Not only will you need help with your campaign, you'll also find that public officials tend to be more receptive to groups than to individuals. You might want to run an advertisement – use an address with a post office box – in your local newspaper, asking people who have complaints about the shelter to write to you. For instance: "Do you think that our animal shelter needs improvement? If you have experienced

problems with the shelter or want to get involved in efforts to improve it, write to ..." In your ad, be careful not to target any individual, such as the shelter director.

• Organize a meeting with other interested people and set goals. Address the most serious problems first. Group members should be familiar with local anti-cruelty statutes, local animal ordinances and the specifics of animal behavior and care. Your efforts will be more productive if each member has clearly defined responsibilities.

• Present your case. Depending on the problems that you have observed, you may want to start by meeting with the shelter director to discuss how you might help improve the facility. If this approach fails or is not feasible, request a hearing before the agency that oversees the shelter – the city council, board of county commissioners or the humane society's board of directors. Attend the hearing with members of your group and as many other supporters as possible. Present your documentation in an organized way, and be specific. To maintain a high profile in local politics, have several of your group's members regularly attend these public meetings. This is essential to monitor progress and show officials that your group is serious about reaching its goals.

• Launch letter-writing campaigns to contact local officials. Be sure to write letters of thanks when improvements are made. Develop media contacts so that the entire community gets up-to-date information. Local newspaper and TV reporters who are sympathetic to your concerns can be valuable allies.

• Write letters to the editor (see Chapter 2).

• Get involved in local politics. If there is an upcoming election, you may want to meet with one or more candidates. Schedule your meetings early in the race, dress professionally and keep your presentations short and concise. Emphasize votes first, and if the candidate is sympathetic to your concern for animals, you may want to offer your group's endorsement and active support. You will be in a good position to influence your candidate if you have helped get him or her into office.

Rabbit Rescue

As the third most popular companion animal in the UK, US and other countries, rabbits have a devout following. Humans who live with them are usually amazed by the rabbit's intelligence, beguiled by their gentle natures and captivated by their lively personalities. Sadly, domestic bunnies are also some of the most abused creatures in the world. They are slaughtered for their flesh, skinned for their fur, used in entertainment, blinded to test cosmetics, bred for show, drugged in the name of science, exhibited in zoos, clipped for wool products, killed in vivisection labs, sold as food for pet snakes, shipped by breeders and imprisoned in small cages by guardians who haven't learned about proper bunny care. To add insult to all this injury, we chop off their paws and tout the rabbit's foot as a "good luck" charm.

Too often people give little thought before bringing home a rabbit, impulsively buying them at pet stores (especially during Easter season) and then, when the novelty has worn off, discarding the bunnies at shelters or dumping them in a park, where they are usually unable to survive. Responsible rabbit guardians take the time to learn about bunnies before rescuing one (or two!) from a shelter and then spaying or neutering their new companions.

Because of the rabbit's unique position as perhaps the only companion animal humans abuse to such a vast extent, I wanted to provide information on a few organizations that shelter bunnies and find new homes for them. This is by no means a comprehensive list, and I have tried to include only organizations that do not support any rabbit exploitation, such as breeding and rabbit shows, and that advocate rabbits living indoors as part of the family, not in backyard hutches. All of these organizations count on volunteers.

Bunderground Railroad (US)

Matching a rabbit with a good home got a little easier in 2004 when RabbitWise, a Maryland-based non-profit, launched the Bunderground Railroad. This growing network of shelters and rescue organizations is linked by drivers who transport rabbits between "conductors" – volunteers who house and handle the rabbits along the way – finally delivering them to their permanent homes. "Volunteers can live anywhere in the US, although we do have a conductor in Canada in case the need ever arises," says Lana Lehr, the organization's managing director. Lana estimates conductors handle about one rescue a month.

House Rabbit Society (US)

With chapters across the United States, the House Rabbit Society (HRS) rescues thousands of rabbits every year. The majority of these rabbits come from shelters where they have yet to find a permanent home and are thus facing euthanasia. HRS also takes in bunnies saved from neglect and abuse cases.

"Activists can help most easily by downloading HRS materials off of our Web site and educating the public at veterinary offices, pet stores, special events and at other places by handing out or putting up materials," says Margo DeMello, administrative director for HRS. Margo encourages activists to also get involved at their local shelters by socializing and grooming the rabbits, bringing in hay or toys and helping with adoptions. HRS is always looking for responsible people to foster one or more rabbits as well. "If they really want to be involved as an HRS volunteer," she says, "they can apply to be an educator, or, if they already are fostering and educating and have a non-profit group formed, they can apply to be a chapter." As part of their ongoing outreach, HRS also invites activists to help with tabling at events.

Rabbit Rescue (Canada)

For as long as she can remember, Haviva Lush has been devoted to animals. She went vegetarian at age five and has pursued animal rights and environmental issues ever since, attending and organizing protests, doing outreach and rescuing animals. As the founder of Rabbit Rescue, she now finds loving homes for domestic rabbits who have been abandoned, abused or neglected.

Rabbit Rescue is currently the only rabbit rescue organization in Ontario and the largest in Canada. They work with shelters across the province, taking in about three hundred animals a year who would otherwise be euthanized and helping those organizations in adopting rabbits. Rabbit Rescue spays and neuters every rabbit who comes into their care, and they are dedicated to special-needs rabbits who require ongoing medical treatment. "The biggest way to help us is by becoming a foster parent," Haviva says. "We work with the highest kill shelters in Ontario, and as soon as we have another foster home, it's another bunny saved."

SaveABunny (US)

SaveABunny is a volunteer-run organization where people can bring their passion, commitment, creativity and talent to directly help save the lives of animals. "We genuinely believe that anything people enjoy doing – whether it be cleaning bunny pens, designing a t-shirt, transporting animals and supplies, creating artwork or whatever – they can apply these interests in a fun and meaningful way to help animals in need," says Marcy Schaaf, who founded SaveABunny in 1999. The organization assists northern California shelters find loving homes for more than three hundred domestic rabbits every year, including many special-needs bunnies who were abused, neglected or have health issues.

"SaveABunny is a proactive and progressive group that deeply values our members and supporters," says Marcy. "Many long-lasting friendships have been made while caring for the rabbits, and our events are notoriously fun." In addition to disseminating informative educational materials, conducting community outreach and providing hands-on grassroots rescue work, SaveABunny has a sense of humor. "Our merchandise and organizational activities tend to have an urban sophisticate feel mixed with professionalism and the right touch of 'rabbitude.'"

The organization opposes the production, sale or use of rabbit fur, rabbit skin and rabbit meat; these campaigns are run by volunteers. "We welcome compassionate, responsible people to help us advocate and care for these special little companions who deserve protection, respect and love," says Marcy.

Vancouver Rabbit Rescue and Advocacy (Canada)

Their name pretty much says it all. VRRA founder Olga Betts says her organization does quite a bit of outreach, educating the public about rabbits, and they have plenty of opportunities for activists who would like to get involved. "We will train people to help with rabbits, but there are a lot of other things we need," she says. "Education help, event help, fundraising, marketing, promotion, graphic design, Web design – the list is endless. Quite frankly, there is so much we would like to do and we talk about but it never can get done because we need people to do it."

Resources

Animal Place

www.animalplace.org

Bunderground Railroad

www.bundergroundrailroad.org

Center for Animal Rehabilitation and Education

www.primatecare.org.za

Eastern Shore Sanctuary

www.bravebirds.org

Edgar's Mission

www.edgarsmission.org.au

Farm Sanctuary

www.farmsanctuary.org

The Fox Project

www.foxproject.org.uk

Hillside Animal Sanctuary

www.hillside.org.uk

House Rabbit Society

www.rabbit.org

Kingbilli Wildlife Rescue

www.kingbilli.com.au

Performing Animal Welfare Society

www.pawsweb.org

PETA's shelter resources

www.helpinganimals.com

Rabbit Rescue

www.rabbitrescue.ca

SaveABunny

www.saveabunny.org

Vancouver Rabbit Rescue and Advocacy

www.vrra.org

WildCare

www.wildcaremarin.org

Wildlife Rescue Association

www.wildliferescue.ca

Woodstock Farm Animal Sanctuary

www.woodstockfas.org

CHAPTER 8

ANIMAL PLANET: THE GLOBAL REACH OF MULTIMEDIA

All truth passes through three stages. First, it is ridiculed. Second, it is violently opposed. Third, it is accepted as being self-evident.
Arthur Schopenhauer

Karl Losken and Lindsay Bickford enjoyed talk radio, but they found little sympathy whenever they'd phone in to their favorite radio shows to discuss animal rights. "Basically we became tired of calling in on other hosts' talk shows and then being cut off when raising the animal issues," says Karl. "So we started our own radio program." They found a home for their show, "Animal Voices," on Vancouver's community-based Co-op Radio in 2001. The weekly program explores a wide variety of animal-related concerns and is heard throughout much of British Columbia and northern Washington State over the air and around the world via the Internet. Perhaps best of all, no one interrupts when "Animal Voices" is addressing such topics as vivisection, endangered species or animal activism.

In recent years, Karl twice attempted to submit films into the Vancouver International Film Festival: *The Witness*, which explores how Eddie Lama embarked on his street-level animal activism, and *Peaceable Kingdom*, the groundbreaking film about factory farming. Karl's application was flatly rejected both times. "Instead of accepting *Peaceable Kingdom*, they played a movie on how to skin a cat," he says. Buoyed by his success on the air, he created the Animal Voices Film Festival, devoted to, as Karl describes, "celebrating the glory of the animal kingdom." The event plays to a full house every year and includes guest speakers such as Howard Lyman and entertainers like Dana Lyons, whose comic song "Cows with Guns" has become an animal-rights anthem.

Welcome to the modern age of animal activism.

While their success may seem like an anomaly – how many of us could hope to have our own radio show or launch a film festival? – Karl and Lindsay simply put their talents to use for animals in the best way they could. And their story is really not that uncommon; as we'll see, the emergence of the digital realm has created a truly universal activist community, with one person's outreach message received and shared by a global audience. Some of the tactics now being implemented include:

- Web sites – not just personal sites, but Facebook, MySpace, Zaadz and other virtual communities
- Videos – posted to YouTube, Google Video and more
- Podcasting
- Blogging
- Email and enewsletters
- Digital images – Flickr, Photobucket, Webshots, et al.

There are old-school tactics, such as using radio and newspapers, that are still successful as well. Indeed, multimedia offers the activist so many opportunities to make an impact that it's unlikely we could cover them all in a single chapter – perhaps not even in one book. But there's one medium we can probably all agree has profoundly enhanced the scope of animal activism.

The Activist's Web

"The Internet has dramatically changed how we interact as individuals and within our society," says Erica Meier, executive director of Compassion Over Killing (COK). A small animal-rights organization, COK is especially concerned with making every penny count as they target the broadest audience possible. Naturally, the Internet is an ideal tool for this. "While TV is still heavily watched – advertising on MTV is incredibly successful for us – it's clear that more people are relying on the Internet for communications. By tapping into that resource, which in most cases is free or of limited cost, we can reach a whole new audience more effectively than we have in the past." Erica says their profile on MySpace has greatly increased the number of people who contact them for more information.

"The Internet is a wonderful tool, if only because it is radically democratizing," says Bob Torres. He and his wife, Jenna, both of whom also teach full time at a university in upstate New York, started the Vegan Freak Radio podcast in 2005 and published their popular book *Vegan Freak: Being Vegan in a Non-Vegan World* a year later. "Instead of being rigorously hierarchical, the Internet is more rhizomatic, and it allows for interconnections between people that previously were impossible. This relatively non-hierarchical structure means that we no longer have to be dependent upon large, managed organizations to participate in this movement. We can begin to build something unique, authentic and truly grassroots."

> Consciousness is a gift. And even consciousness about suffering is a gift. We experience the suffering but we are also given the gift of the consciousness about it, and it's better to be awake than asleep most of the time. We're committed to living life with integrity, and integrity means not being split off from who we ourselves are.
>
> **Carol J. Adams**
> *Satya* magazine, July/August 2001

The Vegan Freak forums section allows people to post their own comments about the podcast, being vegan or just about anything else; it is an important component of the virtual community activists participate in. "We started the forums on a whim after publishing our book," Jenna explains. "We thought that it would be a simple place to discuss where to get vegan goodies and chat with other vegans. Since we started, we've seen the forums grow into a vibrant community of vegans who act as a support structure for each other. The forums give them a place where they don't feel so alone in their joys and frustrations, and I think many of them are more likely to stay vegan when they realize that there are plenty people out there that are like them." The Vegan Freak forums also serve as a focal point for those looking to participate in a variety of activism, including letter-writing campaigns, leafleting, cooking classes or just acting as a vegan mentor for those around them. "The forums have even created a real-life community as well. Since we've started, there have been meetups all around the world, and we've even had two couples who met on the forums get married."

Maximizing Sites

"Campaigning without the Internet is unthinkable," says Kate Fowler-Reeves of Animal Aid, the UK's largest animal-rights organization. "We have a Web site that is constantly changing and being updated. We use short, punchy viral films to make our point. We send out E-News to around sixteen thousand people every month. We have a MySpace page." A lot of this work is being done by just one person: Chris Anderson. Chris is as comfortable using terms like "web 2.0" and "viral video" as he is campaigning against animal cruelty. Whether he's quoting Buckminster Fuller or encouraging people to pledge veg, Chris is all over the Internet, extolling the virtues of veganism and beautiful design. When he's not publishing an enewsletter, videotaping inside factory farms, blogging on one of his Web sites or recording a podcast, he's writing articles or doing radio interviews. As the Web editor for Animal Aid, Chris orchestrates the group's vast multimedia outreach effort. In other words, Chris is making full use of technology to help change the world. "Web 2.0 technologies involve people rather than treat them as an audience," he says. "I think that if people are actively engaging with a subject, then they take it onboard in a much deeper manner than if they just read a book or watch a film. Our whole web effort, like those of other campaigning groups, is in a process of reorientation to allow our supporters to participate in them, rather than consume them. This is a radical change, and it brings a lot of new challenges, but I think it's worth the risks."

Karin Ridgers is another great example. On the face of it, her idea was both simple and revolutionary. But when Karin took her plans to create a TV program focusing on healthy, compassionate eating to England's television stations, they told her she was ahead of her time and that such programming would only appeal to a narrow audience. So the actress and former director of the Vegan Society UK began searching for a new home for her vegan TV show – and looked as far as her computer. "I realized the Web was the perfect venue for promoting compassionate and healthy animal-free eating in a fun and positive way worldwide twenty-four/seven," Karin says. And "Veggie Vision" was born. Her play-on-demand programs are viewable pretty much anywhere there's an Internet connection, and Karin says she's gotten a very positive response from all over the UK, as well as the US, Australia, India, Argentina, Italy, Holland, Germany, Spain, Sweden and Israel. Karin's show keeps things upbeat and fun, so it won't scare away meat-eaters. "Anyone can send in a clip," she adds.

The PETA Model

No discussion of how activists are using the Internet would be complete without a look at what PETA is doing. Not only do they have a vast array of ancillary Web sites, but they are enabling local activism by using the same model that powers social-networking sites like MySpace.

When most people think of People for the Ethical Treatment of Animals, they likely imagine a mammoth organization with an unlimited budget. After all, everyone has heard of PETA and their campaigns, right? In reality, PETA cannot come close to matching the many billions of marketing dollars spent every year by the industries that profit from exploiting animals; instead, they rely on creativity to promote their message. "We do this in a lot of ways," says Joel Bartlett, marketing manager for PETA. "We get people more involved with us by fostering a community. We also reach them where they already are: MySpace, YouTube and blogs. This is so we can fit better into their lives. And we make our content and our message impossible to ignore and irresistible to talk about."

In other words, PETA is taking full advantage of multimedia for its outreach efforts and is especially adept at capitalizing on the Internet. Because they've been doing this for so long and they're so successful at it, we can learn from their experience and see how grassroots activists might apply the same strategies.

The community PETA has created using the Internet is their youth network, the peta2 "Street Team," an ever-growing group of activists who earn points for participating in animal-rights campaigns – points they can redeem for PETA swag like clothing, concert DVDs and jewelry. "The hub of this campaign is peta2.com," explains Joel. "This keeps them interested and coming back to our site to do more activism in a way we'd never seen before."

Let's briefly explore just three of the inter-related technologies PETA is using to engage activists and win campaigns.

Videos

The combination of undercover video and expanded broadband accessibility has allowed PETA to take activism to a new level, reaching people in a way they never could before. "We consider videos the most powerful advocacy tool available," says Joel, who explains the videos document what goes on behind the closed doors of slaughterhouses and fur farms. "Nothing will inspire someone to take action against cruelty more than actually watching it." But most of the footage isn't likely to end up on commercial television, or even most cable channels, so Joel and his team post the videos on the PETA Web site. They launched PETATV.com in 1999, but have had videos on their main site since 1997 – almost ten years before the use of online videos became commonplace with YouTube and its imitators. "The feedback we have received is beyond anything we could have imagined. This it is why we try to include links to videos in every email we send out and on every Web page we publish."

PETA videos like *Meet Your Meat* (www.meat.org) are also used at tabling events, demonstrations and shared among friends. "Videos have played a crucial role in all of our major campaigns. For instance, since the release in 2005 of our investigation into the fur industry in China, many leading clothing retailers and designers have pledged to never use fur again."

MySpace

"Our love affair with MySpace began when one of our Street Teamers started a chain letter on MySpace about our campaign to get youth clothing retailer Wet Seal to go fur free," says Joel. "As a result of his action, more than three hundred and fifty thousand people came to peta2.com in one week, watched a graphic video of animals being skinned alive for fur in China – the largest exporter of fur to the United States – and signed a petition. Traffic-wise, this

Actress and PETA spokesperson Pamela Anderson narrates a video exposing KFC cruelty.

was PETA's biggest online success to date. Wet Seal didn't know what hit them. Just one month later they signed a moratorium pledging they would not sell fur the coming season." Joel says that MySpace and peta2 make a good match because they are both community-based sites that share the same strategy of using popular bands to drive traffic and new users. "It's really just our animal-rights agenda and lack of a multi-billion dollar budget that separate PETA from MySpace," he says.

Video-Sharing Sites

PETA has expanded its reach through online video sites such as YouTube. Joel explains PETA's approach: "Our first step was just getting all our content on the various popular video-sharing sites like YouTube, MetaCafe, iFilm.com and Google Video. Our goal is for people to find PETA videos whenever and wherever they're searching for videos online. If someone is searching for John McEnroe, for instance, they'll find his spay and neuter public service announcement. From just our efforts of uploading videos, we estimate we've received almost two million video views."

Their experience with multimedia has taught PETA some valuable lessons. Here are a few that Joel shared:

1. People like to create things. That's why ninety-nine percent of the Web is user-generated content. We encourage it. All of the buddy icons we have on peta2.com, and many of the web banners and desktop wallpapers we have available, were made by our users. We want kids to take our stuff and make it their own because we know that once they feel ownership they'll show something to everyone they can.

2. People like to show off what they care about, especially when it's made easy for them. That's why we provide our users with the HTML code they need to put streaming videos of undercover footage and web banners on their own profiles. We aim to make it easy enough that even the biggest technophobe can make their online profile a digital, interactive billboard for animal rights. We don't copyright any of our Web text, videos or leaflets, and we encourage people to use this material on their own sites.

3. People want to see the face behind the curtain. We understand that people don't want to interact with an organization – they want to talk to individuals from MySpace. Peta2 has recently created a staff profile section of the site. New Web features and blog entries are published that not only include the author's name, but also a link to that staff member's profile. Many of PETA's activist liaisons include links to their MySpace pages in their email signatures so that they can connect with activists on a level normal email doesn't really allow.

4. Sending out daily bulletins to our friends brings *a lot* of traffic to our site. We're able to actually win campaigns just through the power of MySpace bulletins. For instance, Rite Aid agreed to stop selling glue traps after we posted a MySpace bulletin asking our friends to politely contact the company. Similarly, menswear brand Jack Spade stopped selling "frog dissection kits" from Carolina Biological Supply after hearing from peta2's MySpace friends. These kids have a lot of disposal income, and they and their friends will boycott companies that are cruel to animals, so it makes sense for corporations to stop abusing animals when they hear from our MySpace friends.

5. Make the content fit people's lifestyle. YouTube, Flickr, MySpace, blogs – there's one thing all of these sites have in common: They'll suck away all of the time in your day. The way people use the Internet is to waste time and entertain themselves. People go to Wikipedia, YouTube or Google and just start searching for random things. Sites like IAmBored.com and TimeKiller.com are extremely popular. We embrace this by making sure our message-based content fits in with the sorts of things people like to talk about online, but also sticks out enough that they'll definitely get noticed. We also embrace the idea that if you make people feel strongly about something, whether it be through humor or horror, they'll feel compelled to talk about it. We make sure everything we do is emotionally charged in this way.

6. All people may have been created equal, but they don't all have the same value. We actively recruit well-connected users. By reading the most popular blogs on MySpace and scanning through the most popular people, we've been able to build relationships with a number of well-connected people on the site. We've also mailed free t-shirts to some of our more popular MySpace friends so that they can post pictures of themselves wearing them. We've used those photos in our MySpace bulletins to help drive sell those products with a level of naturalism that can't be faked.

Blogging

With the advent of Web logs, or "blogs," just about anyone can publish organized content on their own Web site. And as more people turn to the Internet as a source for information on everything from fashion and entertainment to health and nutrition, blogging has become a state-of-the-art model for animal activism.

"I think that blogs help create a community for animal activists, particularly at a time when animal

> **Widening the Circle**
>
> While digital communication may be fast and cost-effective, it's important for us to remember that not every animal advocate is comfortable with new technologies. In addition to producing videos, stepping up their online presence through social and video-sharing sites and keeping most members updated via email, Animals Australia produces a magazine, advertises in publications and courts radio, TV and print media coverage. "We do need to keep a variety of communication methods going because some of our supporters are older and do not have access to the Internet," says Glenys Oogjes, the group's executive director.

activism is experiencing a resurgence, but grassroots activists are scattered throughout the world," says law student Jennifer Dillard of AnimalBlawg.com. She started the site with her husband, Joel, after reading *The Lifelong Activist* by Hillary Rettig. "It inspired me to focus my activism on the main issue of my concern – which is animal activism, particularly animal law – using the medium that I enjoy most: writing." Jennifer says she knew nothing about creating blogs, but a few friends helped her with the technical start-up issues, and using the Web-hosting site DreamHost made it easy.

"I'd first encourage people not to be afraid of starting a blog because they think they aren't technically minded," Jennifer says. "DreamHost is a very user-friendly host, and they offer amazing blog programs like WordPress, which basically installs itself." She also cites the cardinal rule of bringing traffic to your Web site: fresh content. "It's important to post something every day, or at least five days a week. Writing posts gets easier the more you do it, and readers are more likely to return frequently if they know the blog will have new posts almost every day. It's also important to keep the posts fairly short, so that readers won't be overwhelmed. Blogging is a short-attention-span medium!"

Eric Prescott, whose blogging on An Animal-Friendly Life is but one of his multimedia efforts on behalf of animals, suggests animal-rights bloggers have a good feel for what other bloggers are doing. "If someone is interested in blogging, they should be aware that there are many blogs out there already, many of which recap the news, and this has become a relatively crowded space," he says. "In other words, make sure you are offering something different from An Animal-Friendly Life, SuperVegan and Vegan Porn. Give readers a reason to visit your blog too."

In fact, assuming the purpose of your blog is to increase compassion toward animals, consider a blog site that is *not* focused on animal rights. Take one of your other interests – travel, running, crop circles, sock puppets or whatever – and create a blog around that, occasionally weaving in discussion about veganism or animal-rights issues. In the same way that an op-ed critical of vivisection will likely affect more hearts and minds by being published in your local newspaper than in an anti-vivisection publication, a smattering of blog entries on veganism or a link to a powerful video could result in helping more animals than spending all your activist time preaching to the choir.

Eric also recommends that bloggers syndicate their writing through Really Simple Syndication (RSS), a family of web-feed formats used to publish blogs, podcasts and other frequently updated digital content. "RSS feeds that allow readers to subscribe to their blogs by email or RSS-capable applications and browsers. This way they are 'pushed' information in which they have expressed an interest. I personally use Bloglines.com to stay on top of all the feeds I read, and I can scan all my daily headlines from one browser window every morning."

Blogger Mary Martin (AnimalPerson.net) believes animal-rights bloggers should be clear and upfront about their beliefs: "Decide if your site is a showcase or a forum or a link-fest. Mine is mostly a showcase for my commentary. There are loads of animal discussion boards out there already. And many sites that have oodles of links about animal-related material."

If you're thinking of starting a blog but are intimidated by the technology, Jason Doucette of VeganPorn.com may be your role model. "When I started Vegan Porn, I didn't know what a blog was," he says. "But now there are a ton of free resources available to get people going in as little as a few minutes. Blogging about veganism is a great way to generate topics to write about, and if you keep at it with a post every day or two you'll quickly find your voice." Jason says most blogs take time to build an audience, so newcomers should expect traffic statistics to be low at first. "Above all, encourage feedback from your audience. Managing spam can be a hassle, but you'll stay a lot more motivated if you get emails and comments from your readers that mention how you've touched their lives. You might even make a few new friends."

Podcasting

Think of podcasting as akin to an audio blog. Both technologies use digital files, are updated often and they're both distributed over the Internet. Both terms are even derived from other words – "podcast" comes from "iPod," the portable media player designed and manufactured by Apple Inc., and

"Webcast," which describes Internet-based audio and video. Apple's iTunes application allows listeners to download digital media, including podcasts, though you can also enjoy podcasts directly from your computer.

The animal-rights-related podcast market that began with Erik Marcus (Vegan.com) in 2004 is growing, though as Eric Prescott points out, the audience for podcasting is smaller than the blogoshpere, at least for now. "For those who are iTunes- and iPod-friendly, podcasts can be more portable than blogs, plus you can listen to a show while you are walking, cooking or working out," he says. "It's harder to multitask while you're reading."

Eric observes, however, that creating a podcast can be time-consuming. "It can take an entire day to put together a good show, which means – if you're aiming for one show a week – that you have just made yourself that much less available for other activism. Your listeners have limited time, too, and there are already so many good podcasts being recorded. Before you go through all the trouble to launch yet another podcast into the world, would-be podcasters should again be sure to find a niche that isn't already being well-covered, keep shows relatively short and engaging and be yourself. My experience shows that people gravitate toward shows that reflect the host's personality."

He also advises that activists know why they're blogging or podcasting. "If you're doing it for fun, that's one thing. But if your goal is to help animals, be aware that most of your readers or listeners are likely to already be animal-friendly and may well already be regularly consuming other blogs and podcasts. If you are respecting their time by offering something unique, it's also helpful to solicit feedback from people right from the get-go to learn who is paying attention. Tailor your work to that audience and 'activate' them as well. If you're merely entertaining activists or giving them news they can get elsewhere, you probably won't be doing as much for the animals as you could if you were doing something else with your time."

Successful animal-rights podcasts also seem to be an adjunct to ancillary efforts. Vegan cooking instructor Colleen Patrick-Goudreau, for example, produces the popular "Vegetarian Food for Thought" podcast, while Bob and Jenna Torres have created a thriving community around their "Vegan Freak" premise. Jenna says she and Bob found in podcasting a way to engage in activism that shared their enthusiasm with others. "When we first started our podcast," she says, "we envisioned that it would be a support network for people who were already vegan. But as time went on, we realized it was not only that, but also a tool to let people know about the various reasons for going and being vegan. I can't tell you how many emails we get from listeners to our podcast who have gone vegan after something we said reached them, and for everyone it's something a little different that resonates. Both the podcast and the forums have been successful beyond what we could have ever imagined in terms of vegan outreach."

Email

You probably use it so often that its potential power may be forgotten, but email can be an effective tool in your outreach efforts. Not only can email disseminate information around the world, but we use it to submit op-eds and letters to the editor, to rally support, to organize protests and to forward petitions. Many activists create a special signature at the end of their emails, appended automatically each time they hit the send button, asking readers to take a specific action for animals or including a link to a video.

Thanks to email, digital media has the ability to go viral. Viral marketing is word of mouth for the twenty-first century, but rather than telling one person at a time, you can spread the word (or photo or video or Web link) to thousands of people, all over the world. The emails with the most viral potential are those you can't wait to share with your friends – the "you've got to see this" email that can take on a life of its own. Sometimes it's a funny piece of flash animation or a news story. Recently I received an email with the subject line "Fun with veggies." An imaginative artist had transformed fruits and vegetables into animals:

Colleen Patrick-Goudreau records her popular "Vegetarian Food for Thought" podcasts at home.

eggplant was turned into penguins, cauliflower and olives became sheep, green peppers were carved and arranged to look exactly like frogs – it was amazing. Apparently, a lot of other people felt the same way, because I received that email three times in one day. Now, imagine the worldwide impact that email could have had with a call to action, such as a link to *Meet Your Meat* at the very end. Before you pass along a collection of cute cat photos or an inspirational poem someone emailed you, add a line or two of text that will benefit animals.

Better yet, don't wait – you can create your own viral email with an animal-rights angle. Sites like CuteOverload.com feature countless images and video clips of animals. Pick any of them, like the otters "holding hands" clip or the chickens breaking up the rabbit fight (called "Chicken Police"), and blast it out

> **The Power of the Press**
>
> Be sure to tell investigative reporters in your local media outlets about animal-abuse issues. Reporters sympathetic to animal rights can have a real impact. For example, the ABC-TV affiliate in San Francisco broadcast a report on the battery-egg producer supplying Trader Joe's markets in the area with their store-brand eggs and showed shocking images, supplied by an activist who had secretly visited the farm, of the hens' living conditions. This report bolstered the hard work of activists who had been critical of Trader Joe's, and four days later the company announced they would be going cage-free with all of their store-brand eggs nationwide.

with a brief note explaining that this is just one example of the sentience of animals, and direct readers to a link with more information (see Resources at the end of this chapter for a few suggestions).

Video & Film

As Joel Bartlett said, video is an extremely effective outreach tool. In terms of activism, using video can be as simple as posting an animal-rights documentary on YouTube. Other activists, however, fully embrace this technology as an indispensable resource for furthering the interests of those who cannot speak for themselves. Actually, say these activists, video is perhaps one way defenseless animals *can* speak out, announcing to the world through the sights and sounds of their suffering that they feel pain, experience emotions and deserve to be treated with respect.

Some viewers are so moved by what they see on the screen that they not only go veggie, they devote their lives to animal rights. Christine Morrissey was watching the HBO cable channel one night when she happening to see the 1996 film *To Love or Kill: Man Vs. Animal*. This award-winning documentary graphically depicts animals around the world being killed in the most horrific ways. "I was completely shocked," she says. "I didn't know what to do with myself; I was on the verge of having a breakdown just watching the jarring footage. Two days later, I had my last meat-based meal." Soon afterward, Christine founded East Bay Animal Advocates and was going undercover in agribusiness to create short films like *Rabbits: Pets or Poultry?* and *Fostering Cruelty*, which documents the

abusive practices of Foster Farms, one of the largest poultry producers in the US.

When it comes to compelling video footage to argue against trapping animals, activist groups around the world rely on the films of Fur-Bearer Defenders. Staffed by only a handful of people, this Canadian organization began when George Clements, the group's director, stepped into a beaver trap and got a very painful lesson in what trapped animals endure.

"We have made countless presentations demonstrating the traps across Canada," says George, "as well as showing our association's unique film footage of trapped animals, taken on a

Members of Animal Liberation Victoria use multiple video cameras to document the rescue of battery hens and the conditions in which they live.

trapline by a registered trapper, showing a brief bit of the suffering to the viewer. We have enjoyed even greater coverage throughout Western Europe, and as a result, the European Parliament has tried to ban all wild fur imports from any country still using leghold traps: Canada and, to a greater degree, the US." George says thanks in large part to their video, exports of wild fur to Europe, for decades the number-one market, have plummeted from eighty-five percent to less than fifteen percent.

But speaking out against his country's fur industry has come with a price. "All the anti-trapping and all the anti-fur groups have been warned by our federal government that if they persist in criticizing the fur industry, they risk losing their registered charitable status. Thus we are basically the only vocal group consistently doing this work in Canada." Yet the number of animals trapped in Canada has declined dramatically over the last five years from five and a half million to less than one million animals per year. George laments that television stations are reluctant to show the group's footage. "They claim that too many of their audience just turn off such visuals," he says.

For Aaron Koolen, it was a film about the annual killing of whales and dolphins off the Faeroe Islands that changed his life. "There were hooks and spears being rammed into the heads and bodies of these animals who were blocked from escaping and were thrashing around, nowhere to go," he says. "On the land you saw little kids laughing and enjoying the show, feeling nothing about what they were taking part in, totally desensitized. Then it hit me: Cows, sheep, pigs, whales and dolphins are all the same. They all can suffer, and they all fear for their lives before the slaughterman kills them. I decided at the exact moment that I wasn't going to be part of that."

Aaron founded Meat Free Media in Auckland, New Zealand, to both educate the public and record animal-rights events throughout the country. They also maintain an online library of undercover video footage and photos taken of battery-egg farms, slaughterhouse and other places of animal abuse. "Animal-rights footage has generally floated around the movement, often being lost at some point, so we felt it was important to attempt to keep an archive of this," says Aaron, adding that the videos are also made available to mainstream media.

Photography & Beyond

Although he characterizes himself first as a photographer, Derek Goodwin fully embraces the "multi" in multimedia. Derek's activism includes not only photographing farmed animals (his images grace animal-rights literature and the Web sites of several animal sanctuaries), but blogging, an online showcase for vegan artists, graphic design and a radio program called "Vegan Radio."

"I think that the more formats the better," he says. "Some people are moved visually, some people are moved on an emotional level, some are more intellectual and need a well thought out argument to persuade them. When I first started creating Veganica, the online gallery for vegan artists and musicians, I was motivated by the fact that most of the graphic design that was used by major animal-rights organizations looked very amateurish. We are up against giant corporations with bottomless pockets putting out glossy messages of consumption. To effectively combat that we need to be taken seriously, and not have literature and other media that looks like it was created by crazy loners with a clip art CD. I am glad to see that the media many organizations are using now has greatly improved. I think art is essential to any movement, and the better the art the more effective the message will be at reaching certain types of people who are visually and emotionally motivated."

Derek is now planning to take his

Public Screenings

Screening a film or video at your library or on your college campus is a great way to help people see animals as more than just things to be exploited. Documentaries like *Earthlings* or *Peaceable Kingdom* – or even commercial films like *Fast Food Nation* or *Babe* – can inspire lively discussion. Check with your public library, community center or student activities office about arranging a screening. Set up a table at the screening with plenty of animal-rights information, and let people know that the purpose of the event is to promote compassion for animals. Even hosting a video screening in your home and inviting all your friends can make a difference!

activism on the road through a project called "The Vegan Bus" – an old school bus he and his confederates are converting to run on vegetable oil. The specially painted bus will even include a raw vegan kitchen with solar dehydrators and appliances that run off of extra energy the bus generates. "We will eventually have a FaunaVision video screen on the outside to show documentaries and also slide shows of my farm animal photographs," Derek says. "We are organizing performers and educators to do tours to schools and events. I am most excited about this project now, collaborating with other people to build something that will be a work of art that will travel around and influence people who we can't reach on the Internet as easily. It will be a multimedia extravaganza and in many ways a culmination of everything I have been investing my activist energy into for several years now."

Public Service Announcements

Getting a public service announcement (PSA) on radio, television or in print is a tried-and-true method for reaching a wide and varied audience. Also called a community service announcement, this is free air time or print space that is made available to advocate groups, non-profits, community associations and for-profit organizations that are promoting a non-profit event. Begin with the stations, newspapers and magazines you already watch, listen to and read. "If someone really loves their local classic rock station, reads their daily paper every day, watches a certain news station frequently or subscribes to a magazine and reads it religiously, they can and should contact them about PSAs," says Bruce Friedrich of PETA. "I have personally gotten tens of thousands of dollars' worth of free print placements in progressive and Catholic newspapers and magazines that I read, and I know others who have done the same."

Steps to Getting a PSA on the Radio

- Contact an animal-rights group in your area and ask if they are eligible for PSAs. If they are, ask if they have a recorded PSA they can send you and explain you want to get it on the air. Or...
- PETA has PSAs you can download and burn onto a CD. Label the CD

by listing the PSAs on the CD and the length of each one.

- Or if you can't burn a CD, request a peta2 radio PSA CD by sending a message to PETApsa@peta.org.
- Call or visit your local radio station or college station and ask to speak to the person who handles public service announcements. This person's title is often "community service director" or "public service director." At college radio stations, this may simply be the DJ.
- Explain the PSA you have and ask if they will play it. If they can't or won't meet with you, download the files from the site and email your pitch to them with the PSA files attached.
- Call the radio station a few days after delivering or sending the materials to see if they plan to air the PSA. If so, find out when it will play.
- If they have not yet reviewed the PSA, ask when you should follow up to determine their interest. Don't be afraid to be a little pushy.

Steps to Getting a PSA on Television

Television stations receive many PSAs from various non-profit organizations on the local and national level, and they can pick and choose what they will play. Because stations will require a high-quality production, you may want to rely on a large animal-rights organization to supply you with a professional videotape. Again, PETA makes this easy for activists anywhere in the world.

- Visit www.petapsa.com and click on "Television" at the top of the page. You can view the PETA public service announcements and determine which one you would like to place.
- Once you determine which PSA you want to pitch as well as the TV station(s) in your area, contact PETA's PSA coordinator via email at PETAPSA@peta.org. They will get you the contact information for PSA people at the appropriate stations.
- Send an email to the station(s) asking for free placement and explaining why the PSA is beneficial to animals and to the community.
- If you are emailing multiple people at once, put the contacts' email

addresses in the "bcc" field of your email and put your email address in the "To" field.

• Once you've emailed your pitch, follow up with a phone call a few hours later. Ask if the person received your email and if the station would like a copy of the PSA. If the person wants a copy, ask what format is preferable. The most common is BETA or BETA SP. PETA cannot provide DVC Pro, so if that format is requested, ask if the station can handle MiniDV or BETA SP instead.

• Contact PETA's PSA coordinator with the name of the TV station, the PSA you pitched, and the format you need. They'll make a copy of the PSA and either send you the PSA or send it to the TV station for you – as soon as possible and in the required format.

• Send a thank-you letter or card to the contact person at the station once they have aired the PSA.

Steps to Getting a PSA into Print Media

• Contact an animal-rights group in your area and ask if they are eligible for PSAs. If they are, offer to help them place a PSA into a local publication. Note that PETA can help you place a print PSA anywhere in the world.

• Compile a list of the newspapers and magazines in your area.

• Contact each publication and ask who handles donated space.

• Send an email to the appropriate person, asking them to run the PSA and explain why it is beneficial to animals and the community; make sure to include your name, affiliation and a telephone number with the best times to reach you.

• If you are with a large organization or are working with several groups, consider having other representatives sign on to the letter to show support.

• Follow-up. Call your contacts at each publication a few hours after sending the email. Ask if they are willing to consider running the public service announcement. Remember to be brief and polite.

• If the publication has space, ask for the space size, their spec sheet (which includes the publication's production information), whether the

PSA will be in color or black and white, what format it should be submitted in (PDF, jpeg, etc.), whom to send it to, the deadline and if there is anything else you need to know before submitting it.

- Make sure to thank the outlets that run the PSA with a letter or card.

Television

Viewers of commercial television generally see animals the way multinational corporations want animals to be seen: as a source of food, fiber or fun. So the major networks mostly present programs featuring animals trained to do tricks – which parallel the advertisements filled with dogs, chimpanzees and other animals exploited in the name of capitalism. If there's a farmed animal on the show, chances are he or she is the centerpiece of a holiday dinner. Rarely are animals depicted as having a full range of emotions or engaging in their natural behaviors. For that, viewers must turn to cable networks or documentaries.

If you have a cable television station in your area, you probably have access to a virtually untapped resource for advancing the interests of animals. Public access television stations around the world permit members of their community to submit documentaries for broadcast on a wide range of topics. This is a very effective tactic, and animal-rights organizations report that many people tell them they ordered a veggie starter kit or other information because of a documentary they saw on cable television.

You can request high-quality documentaries in various formats from Animal Place, Compassion Over Killing, Farm Sanctuary, GourmetCruelty.com, Mercy For Animals, PETA and many other organizations. If you're not familiar with the public access stations in your area, the Global Village has links to hundreds of stations (see Resources at the end of this chapter).

To get the most out of the broadcast, promote each program the station airs for you. If you're part of a group that the documentary might interest, ask the email manager to send a notice to all members. You can also ask local vegan, vegetarian and humane societies to post a notice of the broadcast on their Web sites. Finally, ask your local paper if they'll print a program listing in their television schedule.

More ambitious activists may follow the example of Helen Rosser. Looking to increase coverage of animal-rights and animal-welfare issues in the mainstream media, Helen created a program for Australia's public television called "Animals Matter." The show offers information on vegan and compassionate living but doesn't shy away from featuring video of animals in confinement or discussing animal rescues.

"This is definitely something others can try in their country," says Helen, formerly with Animals Australia. "I think the most important thing is to find a good production company that understands your motives for wanting to do this." In Helen's case, it was the production company that approached her with the idea. "They had already been doing a lot of work with community television and so had the contacts there. I originally thought it was an impossible dream, but they knew how passionate I was about animal-rights issues and convinced me that I could really do it – and we did!"

Activists able to invest a bit of money can now place short animal-rights videos on television and online as advertisements. Although national TV stations often shy away from some of the hard-core videos, such as PETA's *Meet Your Meat in 30 Seconds*, you'll generally have success with local affiliates and their Web sites. Compassion Over Killing, Mercy For Animals and other groups rely on support for buying ad space, and you can work directly with PETA to place a pro-vegetarian commercial on local television stations or their Web sites anywhere in the world. Both are extremely cost-effective methods for reaching thousands of people.

> I think anybody who cares about animals should be so thankful that anybody does anything to help animals, even if they don't do everything we think they should. If they are out doing trap-neuter-release work or working to bring about a no-kill shelter or protesting rodeo, how can we not be thankful? We are all imperfect creatures, in an imperfect world.
>
> **Tom Regan**
> *Satya* magazine, August 2004

Your (Free) Ad Here!

Newspapers that sell advertising space frequently run short of paid advertisers to fill the allotted display ad area. This shortfall is called "remnant space," "remainder advertising" or "last-minute advertising." Although media often sell this remnant space to businesses at steep discounts, they frequently give the space away for free to worthy causes. Because newspapers publish daily or weekly editions, they offer many opportunities to get your message seen by their readership.

What to advertise: Vegetarian starter kits, food fairs, animal shelter adoptions and fundraising events are all a great fit for remnant ad space.

Creating the ad: Your ad doesn't have to be fancy, though it will need to look professional and be submitted in the publisher's required format (this generally means a digital file). One indispensable resource is some kind of desktop publishing program, such as Quark or InDesign, but even Adobe Distiller will allow you to turn a standard text document such as Microsoft Word into a portable document format (PDF). You can also download PDF-style writing software for free online: just type "create free pdfs" into your favorite search engine for a selection.

Create a few designs that include the contact information and Web site address, if appropriate, and then ask friends what they think of the ad. Remember that the ad must fit the paper's width and height specifications.

Steps to Getting a Remnant Ad Placed

- Create a list of the print publications in your area (this is easy to do online), as well as those you read regularly.
- Don't forget local TV and radio stations – especially the ones you enjoy most.
- Determine who handles the advertising at each publication (this is generally the advertising sales manager).
- Send an email or place a phone call to introduce yourself and ask if they have any remnant space in their next issue; explain what it is you'll be advertising.
- If they do have space, a typical response may be, "Yes, I have a one-column spot that's two inches high. Can you email me your ad as a PDF

by three o'clock p.m. Thursday?"
* Ask if they have any special requirements – some publications, for example, want you to insert their logo in your ad.
* Check the page on their Web site that shows the display ad dimensions, or ask them to email the ad specs to you.
* Be sure to get your ad file to them by the deadline!
* A publication will usually not know until the last minute if they have any remnant space available, so be prepared with an ad in all the publication's ad sizes.
* After the ad has run, send a thank-you note (not an email) to the ad manager or person who helped place your ad.
* In my experience, newspapers don't mind if you keep asking, even if they have published an ad for you already – so ask again!

Tips for Maximizing Multimedia
* Use your MySpace page, Zaadz and other social Web sites to promote animal issues; invite animal-rights groups to become online friends.
* Remember that anyone can edit the online encyclopedia Wikipedia: add information about animal-rights issues to listings on entertainment, medicine, agriculture, fashion, etc.
* Post videos to YouTube, Google Video and other video-sharing sites.
* Use public access television to show documentaries.
* Get public service announcements on television and the radio. You can try any radio station, but activists seem to have more success with college stations.
* Take advantage of remnant ad space.
* Add an action item to your email signature, asking recipients to take action in support of your campaign. Be specific: Tell them what you want them to do and provide links, if any.
* Add video links to news sites, your email signature and popular blogs that allow comments (i.e., AlterNet.org, CommonDreams.org).
* Popular blogs on issues that matter to you are great places to start a conversation about animal issues: email the blog owner and ask him or her to comment on a video, news story, current issue, etc.

• Appeal to influential people. Contact the editors of your favorite magazines, informing them about animal issues. And don't forget the power of the press: Tell investigative reporters about animal abuse!

The Medium is the Message

Media can sometimes transform an advocate's efforts into something beyond her wildest activist dreams – all the more now that so much is archived online, to be downloaded and emailed in seconds. Just ask Karen Davis. Karen runs United Poultry Concerns and didn't like that National Public Radio was characterizing domestic fowl as unlovable. For several years in the 1990s, an NPR program called "This American Life" did an annual show that ridiculed turkeys, ducks and especially chickens. So Karen started a letter-writing campaign to the program and the show's host, Ira Glass, heard from animal advocates throughout the United States. Surprised by this outpouring of support for animals he considered to be "a pain in the ass," Ira ended up visiting Karen's sanctuary and interviewing her for his radio program. She introduced him to many chickens that day – birds like Ella and Henry and Dolores – and you can hear the seeds of a new attitude being planted as Ira gets to know these "refugees from the commercial poultry industry," as he calls them. His voiceover, recorded sometime later, belies his earlier criticisms as he tells listeners about the poultry industry's practice of using selective breeding and specially formulated feed to make a "meat" chicken grow to full size in just six weeks, rather than the six months nature intended. Karen explains this is just one reason all the chickens at her sanctuary suffer illness and will die prematurely. When Ira defends his NPR show as harmless, Karen is adamant that it perpetuates the myth that chickens are stupid. "You're one of the many components of the abuse," she says. "You're part of the problem!"

Fast forward six years. Ira Glass is a guest on a different NPR program and he recounts his tale of visiting Karen and the chickens, admitting it had an impact on him. Then, in April of 2007, Ira appears on television's "Late Show with David Letterman" and shares his story with Dave, the studio audience and four and a half million viewers at home, explaining that chickens have real personalities (the clip has also been viewed thousands of times on YouTube and continues to attract comments). Many in the audience laugh as Ira speaks of Karen's activism, and even Dave chuckles at the term "chicken advocates." But no one laughs when Ira says he became a vegetarian because of what he had learned from Henry and Elise and Lois and Lambrusco and Karen Davis. "She got the last laugh on me," he says.

The scope of multimedia is so broad that it may seem daunting to some activists. Yet fueled by new technologies, animal advocates are using different media to create everything from simple Web sites and blogs to elaborate video productions and radio shows. Being entertaining has value too, a point clear to many podcasters and the creators of animated shorts like "The Meatrix" and "Cows with Guns." The chosen media needn't even be high-tech: members of the Animal Rights Collective of Halifax (ARCH) recently put the *act* into *act*ivism by writing and performing a play about animal testing. The short production, which features a rabbit, a mouse, a dog, a cat and a scientist from Proctor & Gamble, neatly sums up P&G's history of abuse and explains the humane alternatives to testing on animals. "It was set up like a debate between the non-human animals and the human," says Jennifer Surrette of ARCH. "We performed it in front of the Halifax Public Library since it's a high pedestrian traffic area."

Perhaps the best way to sum up the use of multimedia to advance the interests of animals is to give a few of its proponents the final word.

"With respect to multimedia, I think the best advice I have is not to venture into something you won't have the time to maintain on a regular basis," says Eric Prescott. "The ventures that succeed are rigorous about updating with fresh content." He also emphasizes originality. "I would ask that activists interested in using the Web as a base for any kind of activism thoroughly research what is already online and use that information to fill in the gaps, or to tie it all together in a novel way. On one hand, the more the Web is overrun with animal activists, the harder it will be for anyone to avoid it. At the same time, we don't want to end up like the modern cable TV universe: Hundreds of channels, but nothing interesting to watch."

"To optimize success on the Web, it's important to be passionate about the Web, as well as passionate about the interests of animals," says Jason Das, who blogs for SuperVegan.com. "The methods and techniques for reaching people on the Web are constantly changing. It helps to be something of a Web nerd, and enjoy shaping and following these trends." Jason also advises activists to think outside the cause. "Too many activists live in a bubble of their scene. To change the real world, you need to live up to real-world standards. A writer has to write on a level that would get them hired outside the movement; a podcaster has to have radio skills and presence that would impress in any context."

"Internet advocacy is the wave of the future," says Christine Morrissey. "The work of East Bay Animal Advocates would be nowhere without the Internet – just ask Foster Farms or Cloverdale Rabbit Company. In addition to our group Web site, we operate six campaign sites and five MySpace accounts. Internet advocacy is cheap and it works!"

"Be self-motivated," says Aaron Koolen. "Realize that people won't always be there, and sometimes you'll have to carry on yourself. If you can't do that, you're in trouble."

Lauren Corman, who produces and hosts the "Animal Voices" radio program out of Toronto, suggests activists with an interest in starting their own show first volunteer at their community or campus radio station. "Not only will this demonstrate that you're dedicated and reliable, but it will also give you a chance to familiarize yourself with the technology, political climate and culture of the place," she says. Lauren adds that in her experience, you'll need to show how your program will involve some level of balance. "As an animal-rights show, you will likely be seen as having a clear agenda, which may or may not be acceptable for the station. Depending on their political perspective, you might be asked how you intend to represent 'the other side.' Talk about the diversity of programming you'd like to offer, including the diversity of perspectives you'll feature, and demonstrate how you're interested in initiating dialogue rather than pushing propaganda."

"If you have a great idea, then bring it to life, no matter how intimidating it is to do so," says Derek Goodwin. "Don't be afraid to ask for help in doing it – or at least for advice. If you don't have a big original idea, then maybe you can find someone else who is doing something you find interesting and help them to make it even better. We need to be here for the animals and for each other. We need to think less about 'MySpace' and more about 'OurSpace.'"

"My advice for individuals who want to help spread information about animal rights is to incorporate promoting animal rights into your daily routine," says Joel Bartlett. "This means talking about animal rights with people in real life or making sure that there are vegan and vegetarian options in your school or office, but it also means that you should make animal rights a part of your online presence. If you have an account on YouTube, upload a couple of PETA's videos to your account. If you have an account on Flickr, include a few images of you doing activism for animals. If you have an account on MySpace, stream a video on your page – you'll be amazed at how many people will email you telling you that you've opened their eyes to animal abuse. With this in mind you can play to your strengths and your interests. Don't create a blog just because it's the new thing to do. Write a blog if you like to write and you want to make a daily commitment to keeping the blog updated."

Finally, Karl Losken offers this simple advice: "Follow your intuition. Enjoy what you do and fill a need that you feel exists."

Resources:

An Animal-Friendly Life
http://ananimalfriendlylife.com
AnimalBlawg
www.animalblawg.com/wordpress
Animal Person
www.animalperson.net
Animal Protection Institute (documentary)
www.bancrueltraps.com
Animal Rights Collective of Halifax
www.archalifax.com
Animal sentience links
www.ciwf.org.uk/education/animal.html
www.fishinghurts.com/feat/fishlives
www.goveg.com/f-hiddenliveschickens.asp

www.stopanimaltests.com/feat/hiddenrats

Animal Voices (Toronto)

www.animalvoices.ca

Animal Voices (Vancouver)

www.animalvoices.org

Animals Matter

www.animalsmatter.com.au

Blogging

www.blogger.com

http://wordpress.org

Compassionate Cooks

www.compassionatecooks.com

East Bay Animal Advocates

www.eastbayanimaladvocates.org

Fostering Cruelty

www.fosterfacts.net

Fur-Bearer Defenders

www.banlegholdtraps.com

Global Village

www.communitymedia.se/cat/linksus.htm

Meat Free Media

www.meatfreemedia.com

Peaceable Kingdom

www.tribeofheart.org/pk.htm

PETA

www.petapsa.com

www.petatv.com

Podcasting

www.how-to-podcast-tutorial.com

www.podcastingnews.com

Rabbits: Pets or Poultry?

www.rabbitproduction.com

Vegan Freak Radio

http://veganfreakradio.com

Vegan Radio
http://veganradio.com
VeggieVision
www.VeggieVision.co.uk

184

CHAPTER 9

ANIMAL LIBERATION: DIRECT ACTION

Unless someone like you cares a whole lot, nothing is going to get better, it's not.
Dr. Seuss

Beneath the warm glow of a half moon, across a muddy field, Christine Morrissey is running for her life. Actually, she's running for three lives: cradled in Christine's arms are two chickens she rescued moments ago from the confines of a factory farm. Although she was able to partially document on film the conditions in which these "broiler" (meat) chickens were living, no camera could capture the acrid smell that permeated the huge, jam-packed shed these birds had called home. Nothing except firsthand experience could convey the utter despair a compassionate person feels at the sight of lame, feces-encrusted birds limping about and dead chickens, their ammonia-scalded breasts denuded of feathers, lying where they collapsed from inhumane breeding practices. Knowing that these systematic abuses are common in animal factories throughout the world only makes tonight's mission more dire – and heartbreaking.

Christine, president of East Bay Animal Advocates (EBAA), darts nimbly over the yielding terrain, ducks under a barbed-wire fence, and the two birds she's holding become the latest animals saved using the activist model known as "open rescue."

Like most open rescuers, Christine is passionate about her work, citing the need for transparency in agribusiness as the motivating factor behind her liberations. "The authorities have largely ignored our pleas for further investigation and law enforcement," she says, adding that her activism helps bring to light some of worst abuses endured by animals. Christine photographs or videotapes every rescue, usually making the images available to the media and to the public through one of the many Web sites EBAA operates.

Ever the ag agitator, Christine is also single-minded in her resolve. "I love the E-40 rap lyric 'Go hard or go home,'" she says firmly. "I live and will die by this motto." While different people will have different definitions of direct action, this chapter will address actions that bring the activist into closer contact with businesses responsible for animal abuse: factory farms, vivisection labs, slaughterhouses, et al.

It is important you understand that many direct actions against animal exploiters are considered illegal and should be undertaken with the knowledge that you could be arrested and go to jail, even if you are acting on ethical grounds, such as offering your home to a hen rescued from a battery shed. Other direct actions, including investigative

Christine Morrissey of East Bay Animal Advocates liberates a sick "broiler" chicken from a factory farm.

work to document abusive practices, though legal, are likely to prove both upsetting and nerve-wracking. Primatologist Sarah Baeckler, for example, spent more than a year working undercover at a Hollywood "training" compound for exotic animals where she witnessed staff members brutally beating chimpanzees used in movies and television. The good news is the owner of this concentration camp for animals is no longer allowed to own or work with primates, and the rescued chimps are now safe in sanctuaries. "My small part in saving them is absolutely my finest accomplishment," says Sarah.

Rattling Cages

Pioneered in the 1980s by Patty Mark of Animal Liberation Victoria, open rescue is one of many tactics that fall under the general heading of direct action. It's a popular model that has been used for many decades: Mohandas Gandhi's direct-action campaigns in India are among the most famous examples, and his passive resistance inspired activists such as Martin Luther King, Jr., Cesar Chavez, the Dalai Lama, Nelson Mandela and Aung San Suu Kyi to use non-violent activism as a means to achieving social change.

Framed in the tradition of these advocates, open rescuers are activists who have grown frustrated by what they see as a lack of interest on the part of government officials to make improvements in the lives of animals used for food, entertainment, clothing and research. Armed with cameras and a passionate determination, they record the conditions inside an animal enterprise and the treatment of animals, often removing some to provide them with veterinary care and place them in loving homes. This can be grueling work, since activists witness and document immense abuse and suffering. And unlike the other models of activism presented in this book, open rescues generally involve unlawful activity, which means there is also the threat of being caught and prosecuted for a variety of crimes, including trespassing. But every activist who engages in this tactic of direct action agrees that it's worth the risk and that the danger they face in exposing inhumane treatment is nothing compared to the cruelties animals must endure. It is vital, they say, to report their findings to authorities and the public.

As the world's hunger for cheap animal protein continues to grow, factory farmers in the poultry industry have succeeded in making the chicken the most exploited animal in meat production: according to United Poultry Concerns, worldwide more than fifty billion chickens are raised and slaughtered every year. And the egg industry only compounds the abuse these intelligent creatures suffer, with hens forced to produce an unnatural number of eggs before they too, their bodies exhausted, are slaughtered. Their male counterparts, who are of no economic value to egg producers, are killed immediately after hatching: suffocated, buried or macerated (ground up) while still alive.

With such egregious abuse considered business as usual, it is little wonder animal activists have focused on the "broiler" chicken and egg industries. In 2004, Auckland Animal Action (AAA) launched an investigation of a Tegel Foods Limited broiler farm, documenting the conditions that more than forty-four million chickens are subjected to every year in New Zealand. "Our investigation took place over a six-week period in one shed," says Suzanne Carey, "from the first week when the chickens are placed in the shed to the week when they are removed for slaughter." AAA's objective was to document how fast the birds grew and their quality of life. "What we discovered was appalling," she says. "More than forty thousand birds kept in a dimly lit, ammonia-filled, windowless shed totally void of anything even remotely natural. Many of the chickens were suffering from crippling deformities and were in obvious distress, the consequence of being bred to grow to such a huge size in a minimal amount of time." Rochelle Rees of AAA adds that investigators found many birds die of starvation, heart disease and other conditions before they reach the ideal size and weight for the consumers' dinner plate. "We removed many of the sick and injured birds and got them much-needed medical attention," she says.

AAA posted their findings on a Web site devoted to their investigation – www.tegelchicken.co.nz – and Suzanne says the site receives a lot of visitors. "We regularly hear from people who are horrified after viewing the conditions that millions of chickens are raised in," she says. "Many of these people have gone vegetarian or have said they will never buy Tegel products again." AAA reports this was the first investigation of its kind in New Zealand.

Deirdre Sims holds a piglet being rescued from a farrowing crate. Because piglets require very special care, rescues of pigs are not common. This little guy is in a happy home now. (Note that the activists document the rescue.)

"Open rescue is a great model of activism because others can see that ordinary people like themselves are so outraged by what is happening to animals on factory farms that they are driven to take the law into their own hands," says Deirdre Sims of New Zealand Open Rescue, a collective of animal-rights activists from cities all over the country. Deirdre became involved in open rescues because she wanted to do more to directly help animals in factory farms. "I wanted to see for myself the conditions and the suffering. I wanted to get animals out of these places and to give them a chance at a decent life," she says. "And I realized that I could do exactly that, simply by getting over my fear of the possible consequences and taking action."

Deirdre says that police raided the house of one of their team members shortly after their first battery-hen rescue. "However, despite an investigation called 'Operation Chicken,' no charges have been laid," she adds. "Since then, we've openly rescued many more animals from factory farms and have had no apparent interest from the authorities." Why don't authorities press criminal charges? "We believe that the factory farm industries are unwilling to prosecute as they know this will simply lead to more media coverage. This means more images of suffering animals on TV that they don't want their customers to see. If we ever do end up in court, our argument will be that we were not 'stealing property' – we were saving lives."

Breaking In Down Under

The modest woman credited with launching the open rescue model in the 1990s would much rather be out helping animals than discussing her exploits; nonetheless, Patty Mark paused long enough to recall the first rescue she organized. "It wasn't a matter of me saying or thinking, 'Well now, let's start doing open rescues and see how we go with them' at all," she says. "Nor did I think at the time, or even wonder, if open rescues had happened anywhere else; I really don't know if they had. I was very aware of the ALF with their balaclavas, bravely breaking into the animal prisons to save as many suffering animals as they could, and I understood their anger at destroying the equipment used to torture animals, but for whatever reasons I didn't have this ability in my nature. Perhaps it was my strict religious upbringing and the implicit allegiance to authority that religion instills. All I know is when I saw the look on the faces of the animals the ALF rescued, I was happy."

Whatever latent reluctance held Patty back would be overcome by a force familiar to many activists: vivid images of animals suffering. "In 1992 I received a call from an employee inside a huge battery hen farm [north of Melbourne]. She told me horror stories of how the hens were packed so tightly in the back cages of the shed they couldn't move at all. Some of the hens pushed their way out of the old cages or escaped when dead birds were removed and fell down into the manure pit below." The caller described farm workers shooting these hens for fun. "It all sounded too weird to believe," recalls Patty.

So she sent a volunteer from her organization to work undercover at the battery farm for three days. "We talked every day on the phone, and he was teary at what he saw and what the birds suffered," Patty says. "He verified everything and more of what the worker told me. The birds were brutally ripped out of the cages, carried four or five in each hand by one leg and slammed into plastic crates. Some fell to the ground and were run over by the transport trucks below. The hens

Jamie Yew (left) and Patty Mark of Animal Liberation Victoria rescue a hen from a battery shed; the hen is now safe and healthy in a sanctuary.

were placed in row after row of cages up on the first floor and the ground floor was an enclosed area under their cages where all their droppings piled up, sometimes six feet [1.8 meters] high. There was no care taken whatsoever during the removal of the hens from their cages, and he could hear their bones pop from the rough handling. Some of the workers kicked the birds who had fallen to the floor."

A video, taken undercover by another volunteer on a follow-up visit to the same farm, pushed Patty to take direct action. "Everything in my mind, body and heart screamed out at me, 'Just go up there and get them out of that manure pit ASAP!'" By this time, Patty had spent fifteen years campaigning against battery cages, using every legal means at her disposal. She'd had enough. "I knew too well about the cover-ups, the clean-ups, the 'Don't

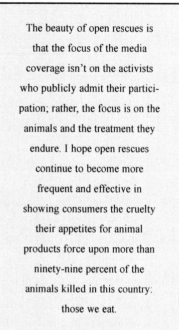

The beauty of open rescues is that the focus of the media coverage isn't on the activists who publicly admit their participation; rather, the focus is on the animals and the treatment they endure. I hope open rescues continue to become more frequent and effective in showing consumers the cruelty their appetites for animal products force upon more than ninety-nine percent of the animals killed in this country: those we eat.

Miyun Park
Satya magazine, October 2002

worry, she'll be right, mate' attitude. But what I saw totally disgusted and haunted me. It was vital and overwhelming, in my mind, to get to those birds as quickly as possible and get them out of there. I contacted a few brave people around me who did undercover work at the time and told them I wanted to contact a leading current affairs program and take them onto the property to film this obscene cruelty and suffering and rescue these animals openly; that is, we will go in undercover to gain entry to film and rescue, but then not hide our identity, as it was the owners of this property who should hide their faces!"

"Hinch at Seven," at the time one of Australia's top-rated current affairs programs, accompanied Patty and her confederates on their uninvited visit to the battery farm. The segment the production team put together, titled "The Dungeons of Alpine Poultry," aired nationally on November 9, 1993. "The suffering of battery hens was on TV screens around Australia," says Patty, "and open rescue was born."

In 1999, Karen Davis brought Patty to the United States to speak at United Poultry Concerns' Forum on Direct Action, the first conference of its kind to discuss direct action for animals. Participants in the forum also included Bruce Friedrich of PETA, Miyun Park and Paul Shapiro of Compassion Over Killing (COK) and Freeman Wicklund of Compassionate Action for Animals (CAA). US activists were familiar with the covert rescue method used by the ALF, but Patty's open rescue approach was a revelation. "The response to Patty's presentation was absolutely awesome," says Bruce. "People were *blown away* by the simplicity and beauty of the personal, political, powerful witness that also had real results."

Freeman and members of CAA carried out the first open rescue in the US, removing eleven hens from a battery egg farm in Minnesota in 2001. A few months later, activists from COK openly rescued eight hens from a factory farm in Maryland, sent out a press release and held a press conference at which they showed the media compelling, high-quality video footage taken inside a battery shed. Soon activists across the country were learning about – and engaging in – the open rescue model.

Gaining Traction

As we've seen, authorities may not press charges against activists engaging in open rescue, but that's not always the case. The US animal-rights organization Compassionate Consumers made headlines in 2006 when three members of their group were arrested after they made public the results of an investigation and rescue of chickens from a factory farm in New York State. The group's president, Adam Durand, was eventually sentenced to six months in jail. We will explore Adam's experience a bit in Chapter 10, but his encounter with authorities is symptomatic of the general post-9/11 climate, coupled with an increase in animal activism, that has resulted in US courts growing less tolerant of anything they believe smacks of "domestic terrorism." Activists in other countries, notably Australia and New Zealand, have not experienced such legal woes, however, and have if anything increased their open rescues. There's even an activist in the Czech Republic who is doing this full time. Michal Kolesar told the daily Czech newspaper *Právo* that he's been liberating hens since 2006, and he posts videos documenting his chicken-saving missions online at www.realita.tv. "It is just like top sport," Michal said. "I have no time for anything else. If I worked eight hours a day, I would have time to do about one-third of the work." He explained that he lives off his small savings and the generosity of close friends who support what he's doing.[1]

For Deirdre Sims, rescuing animals is the ultimate activism. "To me, open rescue is about three crucial things: saving lives, documenting abuse and raising awareness by exposing what is hidden behind closed doors to as wide an audience as possible," she says. "Activists wanting to participate in open rescues need to accept the possible consequences of their actions. You need to know that your house might get raided and you might end up in court. If you can handle that, then get started!"

Following is Deirdre's advice on becoming involved in open rescues:

• Organize a group of like-minded people and start planning.

• First, you'll need to locate a safe place to bring the animals you rescue. You can't take them back to your house because that places the animals at risk if the authorities should happen to turn up. The animals will need to be placed with people who know how to care for ex-factory farmed animals, as they have special needs.

• Use the Internet or phone book to locate factory farms, or go out for some drives in the country. You'll also need video and photographic equipment to document the conditions. Safe and comfortable transport boxes or cages for the animals are another essential.

• Get familiar with your animal welfare laws so you can point out breaches of them on camera. Know your facts about the animals you are rescuing so that you can talk about this to the camera. For example: you've found a "broiler" chick with splayed legs, but why are they splayed? Because they are bred for maximum growth rate in a minimum timeframe to increase poultry industry profits.

• Your job isn't done after saving some lives: Now you've got to get that footage on TV and those photos in the papers and on the Internet. Get your message on the radio. Hold workshops, film screenings and stalls (tables) and talk to people about what you've seen and why you did it. Raising public awareness and keeping the debate alive is one of the crucial aims of open rescue and probably one of the most important elements that will create change for these animals.

Freeman Wicklund advises activists not to use violence during rescues. "Our non-violent code included not causing any property damage, or minimizing damage if it was necessary to gain access or to offer immediate help to an animal," he says. "Thankfully, the factory farms were never locked and we never needed to cause any property damage. Still, if we had to cut a lock to gain entry, we were willing to replace it with a new one or reimburse them for the damage."

"Open rescue work is an extremely effective way of directly protecting animals and educating the public about the systematic abuse of animals," says Christine Morrissey. "It allows the public to examine the plight of abused animals through the lens of compelling experience."

"I believe that open rescue is a very public-friendly form of direct action," adds Deirdre. "When we get media coverage of a rescue or show footage at a film screening, people can

Tom Wright, Deirdre Sims and Mark Eden (L to R) of New Zealand Open Rescue brought ten hens out of this South Auckland battery egg farm in April 2007. The activists left vegan Easter eggs for farm workers and a Happy Easter card explaining the reasons for the rescue.

see that we are just like them in a lot of ways. We are just ordinary people who feel so strongly that our legislation is failing animals that we can no longer sit by and do nothing."

Animal Liberation Victoria has developed a guide to open rescue. Though the guide is not published online, you can learn more about it at www.openrescue.org/guide.

Other Rescue Models

Another, some say more pragmatic, form of direct action is the covert rescue model exemplified by an international confederation of underground activists called the Animal Liberation Front. ALF members work in small, autonomous groups. They don masks to remain anonymous as they carry out the liberation of animals from factory farms, research labs and fur farms, often inflicting financial losses by damaging or destroying property. Sites of economic sabotage may include actual places of animal exploitation (i.e., laboratories and fast-food restaurants) as well as vehicles, boats or other property owned by animal abusers.

An additional difference between open rescue and the model embodied by the ALF is that the open rescuer generally takes animals like chickens and pigs who can easily be placed into a safe home, while the covert teams also liberate animals, such as mink and deer, into the wild. ALF members do document their activities on video, but they keep their identities hidden. Whatever their reputation (the FBI calls them "domestic terrorists"), the ALF has never physically attacked a human being.[2]

Some animal activists who engage in rescue work do so without taking direct responsibility for their actions, thus avoiding both the ski masks and their fifteen minutes of fame. These liberators have gone into factory farms, documented conditions on videotape, removed animals and then leaked the video anonymously to authorities. No one but the exploited chickens, pigs or ducks (from foie gras farms) need appear on camera.

Homer's Odyssey
He sat in a tank of sea water in a grocery store as people passed by, marveling at his size. At nearly ten pounds (4.5 kilograms), this lobster was coveted by meat-eaters from all over Halifax, Nova Scotia, each one hoping to guess the crustacean's exact weight and therefore win the right to boil him alive in their kitchen.

But activists from the Animal Rights Collective of Halifax (ARCH) had a kinder idea. They mobilized members to submit their own guesses to the Atlantic Superstore contest, and in the end, compassion won.

ARCH transformed the victory into an animal-rights event. On the Saturday afternoon they picked up the lobster, whom they called Homer, activists distributed *Being Boiled Hurts* leaflets outside the store and spoke to customers about animal cruelty. They emphasized that lobsters have nerve endings and pain receptors and experience physical suffering just like any other animal.

Later that evening, a few ARCH activists, accompanied by a marine biologist, set Homer free at an undisclosed location somewhere along Nova Scotia's South Shore. The only concern was that Homer, whom local biologists estimated to be between twenty and thirty years old, may have been weak from living for days in the grocery tank with no food and rubber bands on his claws. But the last time activists saw Homer, he was moving on his own and undoubtedly happier to be back in the ocean.

And the media covered the entire event.

Lesson: Direct action, including animal liberation, can take many forms.

Investigations

Kate Turlington had just graduated from college when she landed a job as a laboratory animal technician at the University of North Carolina. Kate worked in a research lab with rats and mice, providing the animals with food, water and clean cages. She also notified the vet staff of any signs of illness she noticed in the animals. A keen observer, Kate kept complete notes on the animals' care – or lack thereof: At one point, she witnessed an experimenter using household scissors to cut the heads off of fully conscious baby rats. He admitted that the approved research protocol called for him to numb the babies with ice first, but he told Kate he chose his method because it saved time. She found live mice shivering and distressed in the dead-animal cooler, forced to eat the remains of other animals to survive; she discovered cages so severely overcrowded that animals died from being trampled and from suffocation; and she routinely encountered animals who were undergoing painful, lingering deaths, yet were denied veterinary care and euthanasia.

Sven Reider and Amanda Brown of ARCH with Homer the lobster, just after his rescue. They returned him to the sea.

Perhaps to the surprise of her colleagues, after six months of working at the UNC lab, Kate quit her job. The next day, it was revealed that she had been even more thorough in her observations than anyone had expected: Kate was an undercover investigator with PETA, and in addition to making notes about the treatment of the rodents in the lab, she had documented the abuses with hidden cameras. The front page of the local paper carried the story, and PETA submitted a formal complaint to the National Institutes of Health, which supports UNC with hundreds of millions of dollars in federal grant money every year.

"We learned that as a result of our investigation, several experimenters were placed on probation and my building supervisor resigned and was replaced," says Kate, now PETA's manager of undercover investigations. "In response to the numerous cruel killing methods I documented at UNC, the NIH issued a directive to every research facility in the nation regarding approved rodent killing methods."

Although regulations do exist to enforce certain areas of animal welfare, it often takes a covert investigation like this one to discover how enterprises are actually treating the animals used for medical research, food, breeding and the like. This form of direct action is extremely useful in collecting evidence against animal abusers, because most of the businesses exploiting animals are generally off limits to the public. But what does it take to make a good investigator?

"Contrary to what most people might think," says Kate, "investigators must be – and remain – sensitive, compassionate and empathetic. I assumed that the only way that a caring person could function in such a job would be to emotionally numb themselves out in an attempt to not internalize the animals' suffering." But she learned that the worst thing she could do as an investigator would be to harden herself to the suffering she witnessed every day. "After all, if we do not maintain our keen sensitivity to what the animals are going through when we infiltrate the industries that use and abuse animals, then we are no better than the ordinary employees who cause the animals to suffer." Kate also points out that investigators who become desensitized lose the ability to be critical observers, and therefore run the risk of accepting a cruel practice as the norm.

Because investigative work is so emotionally loaded, it's critical that activists engaged in this model have realistic expectations and deal with their feelings as they arise. "Don't expect a lab or slaughterhouse to be shut down as a result of your efforts," Kate warns. "Every investigator handles stress differently but, in general, I believe it is incredibly important for investigators to be emotionally mature and honest with themselves about their feelings. As tempting as it is, we cannot push down or otherwise avoid or deny our feelings; otherwise, we will go insane and will not be able to help the animals!"

One of the feelings Kate and many others experience being undercover is fear. "For me, working undercover was *very* scary," she says. "In addition to the difficulty of being a witness to animal suffering, investigators live with the fear of being caught. They must always be on their toes, not only to follow up on animal concerns and document them to the fullest, but also to make sure they don't accidentally slip up and say something to give themselves away, get caught with a camera or be seen associating with known animal activists."

My attitude is not "If I didn't think we'd win, I'd quit," to which I would say, "Then quit." Working for animal rights isn't a football game or a beauty contest. It's working to modify our species' attitudes and behavior at a deep level, to develop a different set of genes – fundamental elements of human nature that have largely been ignored, overridden by other elements thus far.

Karen Davis

Satya magazine, July/August 2001

Is It for You?

While not for every activist, undercover investigations generate the most compelling evidence of animal suffering and have resulted in many victories for animals; moreover, because these cases generate lots of media attention, they help educate the public and encourage discourse on animal rights. To help activists decide whether they have what it takes, Kate and her team have put together this list of the qualities shared by PETA's effective undercover investigators helping animals around the world:

- **Unshakable work ethic.** Investigators essentially work two full-time jobs, as their days are spent laboring at a job where animals are used and often abused, and their nights are spent reviewing documentation that was gathered on the job (i.e., logging photos and watching video) and generating log notes detailing every aspect of the day's events.

- **Ability to travel.** Investigators must have a fly-by-the-seat-of-your-pants attitude with regard to undercover assignments and travel.

Investigators spend months on end on the road and on location for under-cover jobs, which is a clear area of conflict for those who have families, significant others or animal companions.

• **Confidentiality.** An investigator's ability to remain undercover is the most critical aspect of any investigation, which means that investigators can tell no one that they work for PETA. This factor, coupled with the geographic distance from friends and family, makes the job of an under-cover investigator very isolating.

• **Strong writing skills.** Investigators must draft log notes detailing everything that they experience on the job with coherence and accuracy and without editorializing.

• **Team-player mentality.** Investigators must develop and maintain positive working relationships with co-workers at their undercover jobs. Additionally, investigators work closely with their colleagues at PETA and must follow instructions and communicate openly and honestly.

• **Emotional management skills.** Investigators witness immense animal suffering and must find a healthy balance between masking emotions at their undercover jobs and acknowledging and working through those emotions after hours. Investigators cannot share their on-the-job difficulties with friends and family but do have access to former investigators who can relate to the emotional hardships of the job and offer advice or simply an understanding ear.

• **Ability to focus on the big picture.** Investigations are intended to document the conditions that the animals would be forced to endure even if PETA were not there. The forceful objections or aggressive actions of a single investigator would probably not do much to help animals – the investigator would merely be fired and thereby unable to continue documenting the lives and deaths of the animals behind the scenes. As a result of investigators' documentation, however, the shocking reality of animal suffering is exposed to the world, campaigns are born and change is effected for the greatest number of animals possible.

• **Investigative mind**. Investigators must pay close attention to – and retain – details and be proactive in their efforts to document conditions for animals.

• **Common sense**. Investigators must work autonomously, make sound decisions under pressure and push through inevitable fear and paranoia while constantly operating under a shield of caution.

"Additionally, of course, investigators must be able to think well on their feet, act quickly and fit in with employees at their undercover jobs in addition to working well with their PETA colleagues," says Kate. "I recommend that anyone who thinks they have what it takes to work undercover contact PETA to apply for a position as an undercover investigator." Interested applicants should submit their resume and a cover letter describing their experience with animal rights and interest in the position, as well the skills they possess that would benefit them in this job.

Activists have a long history of using direct action to expose the atrocities committed against animals. It's an effective method that relies on video and photographic evidence to bring into public discourse the indefensible abuses animal enterprises work hard to keep concealed. These businesses profit from perpetuating the disappearance of animals into a system of full-scale, institutionalized exploitation – a state that in turn enables corporations to create an alternate reality featuring "happy cows," depict only human faces when promoting medical research and avoid mentioning what becomes of male chicks in the egg industry. Rescues and investigations directly threaten the status quo, revealing the hidden truth in undeniable detail. While direct action may not be right for everyone, at least one activist encourages you to give it a try.

"Challenge yourself by getting active," says Christine Morrissey. "It will be the best decision of your life."

[1] "Vegetarian steals hens reared at large-scale farms," *Právo*, May 16, 2007.

[2] For an insightful examination of the ALF's tactics, read *Terrorists or Freedom Fighters?: Reflections on the Liberation of Animals* (Lantern Books), an anthology of essays by supporters and critics of the ALF from within the animal-rights movement edited by Steven Best and Anthony J. Nocella, II.

Resources

Animal Liberation Victoria
www.alv.org.au
Animal Rights Collective of Halifax
www.archalifax.com
Auckland Animal Action
www.aucklandanimalaction.org.nz
Compassionate Action for Animals
www.exploreveg.org
Compassionate Consumers
www.compassionateconsumers.org
East Bay Animal Advocates
www.eastbayanimaladvocates.org
PETA
www.peta.org
Note: New Zealand Open Rescue does not currently maintain a Web site, though they may be reached via www.openrescue.org.

CHAPTER 10

ANIMAL LAW: THE LEGAL SYSTEM

The person who understands what I have to say about justice
understands everything I have to say.

Meister Eckhart

Ordinarily the disclaimer "What I'm about to say now does not constitute legal advice" does not elicit laughter. But attorney Len Egert is addressing a Harvard Law School lecture hall full of law students, lawyers, academics and activists from around the globe, and when he uses those familiar words to preface his response to an activist asking how to engage in activism while avoiding the wrath of the Animal Enterprise Terrorism Act (AETA), knowing laughter echoes off the vaulted ceiling of the imposing hall. It also breaks the ice that tops a chilling topic: how even legal activism can be construed as terrorism.

Len is among a score of speakers who have convened at one of the most prestigious law schools in the world to discuss the ways in which advocates can use the law to benefit animals. Animal advocates throughout the US are currently faced with a law that could impose stiff penalties for engaging in certain types of activism, but as Len observes, the AETA is so vaguely worded that even lawyers who specialize in the United States Constitution have difficulty determining exactly how this legislation can be applied. "How is an activist supposed to know?" he asks.[1]

Activists in other countries have cause for concern as well: the UK, for instance, has enacted the Serious Organized Crime and Police Act of 2005 – a set of laws to specifically address the "illegal activities" of animal activists.

The main focus of the conference, organized by the Animal Legal Defense Fund (ALDF), is animal law, which can be defined as the body of statutory and case law related to non-human animals. It's a field ALDF knows well: since 1979 they have been working for stronger enforcement of anti-cruelty laws and more humane treatment of animals. "I think that law students and potential law students should recognize animal law as an up-and-coming field that will need many more academics and practitioners in the coming years," says Jennifer Dillard, who attended the ALDF conference with her husband, Joel. "In its early years, environmental law was seen as a marginalized area, and now it's becoming a common concentration for law students. I believe that animal law will have a similar path, and, as students, we're currently in the position to gain an expertise that will be much sought after in the future."

Though the field of animal law is growing rapidly in the United States and other countries (there are currently almost ninety colleges offering animal law courses in the US, up from nine in 2000), most animal activists will never see the inside of a law school. Nevertheless, legal means to advance the interests of animals are available to everyone, and indeed some of our biggest victories on behalf of animals are the result of ordinary citizens who care enough to get involved. For example, grassroots activists in Arizona recently proposed a citizens initiative, Proposition 204, to prohibit the confinement of calves in veal crates and breeding sows in gestation crates. Voters agreed such indefensible cruelty should be banned, and the measure passed by an overwhelming majority. "This is direct democracy," says Stephanie Nichols-Young, chair of the Arizona State Bar Animal Law Section and an attorney who helped shepherd Prop 204 onto the ballot, with much support from Farm Sanctuary and the Humane Society of the United States.

Gene Baur of Farm Sanctuary believes that activists who participate in legislation such as Prop 204 and the initiative to ban gestation crates that Florida voters passed in 2002 (the first law enacted to prohibit a standard factory farming practice in the US) make an invaluable contribution to the process. "As people become aware and take a position against certain cruelties, you have a tipping point where you can pass laws," he says. "And that's what these initiatives do. By passing laws through the initiative process or other processes that garner media attention, you're also continuing to educate. Ultimately, most people agree these practices are cruel and should not be allowed."

Agribusiness is taking notice, too. Just months after the Arizona ban, Smithfield Foods – the largest pig producer in the US – announced that it is phasing out its use of gestation crates. One week later, Maple Leaf Foods, Canada's largest pig producer, joined the shift toward change and said it is doing the same.

"Activist pressure is where it starts," says Gene. "Smithfield has said McDonald's was a big part of their decision, but the reason McDonald's was pressing Smithfield in the first place was because customers were pressing McDonald's, and that's because of activist pressure. So it all starts with activists raising awareness."

Legislation

Laws intended to advance the interests of animals are an important tool in generating reform, and countless grassroots activists have campaigned for legislative changes or assisted animal-rights organizations in their efforts. In fact, assisting animal organizations is probably the easiest way for activists to engage in this form of activism, so check with one of the large animal-rights groups in your country (Animal Aid, Animal Rights Africa, Animals Australia, Compassion in World Farming, HSUS, PETA, Uncaged, etc.) to ask how you can get involved in current legislative efforts. Such legislation can be used to:

• Ban egregious business practices, such as using confinement crates and battery cages
• Protect wildlife by creating refuges, prohibiting hunting or trapping, etc.
• Advance welfare by setting minimum standards, such as veterinary requirements for rodeos
• Ban specific forms of animal abuse, such as circuses, blood sports or tethering animals
• Protect farmed animals and public safety by banning the slaughter of "downed" animals or regulating the use of antibiotics in factory farms
• Overturn existing laws that permit cruelty, such as the sale and slaughter of wild horses and burros

- Regulate the sale of exotic animals
- Make animal abusers accountable for their cruelty
- Provide funding for spay and neuter programs
- Strengthen existing laws, such as those regulating the sale of fur from domestic animals.

Before embarking upon a legislative campaign, activists must examine what they wish to accomplish and then decide if legislation is the most effective model for achieving that objective. It may turn out that another strategy would be a better approach. If the goal is a law mandating at least one vegan entrée selection in every school, for example, the activist or group should consider if a law is really necessary. Could the same result be obtained through outreach? Chances are that speaking directly with dining hall decision-makers and school administrators will yield better results for a fraction of the cost.

If legislation is indeed the best course of action, either by trying to create a new law or improve an existing one, activists will want to consider what kind of public support they can expect. This can be achieved through a survey or by collecting voter signatures (which you may have to do anyway). Any changes in the law will come down to a vote of either the citizens or their elected officials, so knowing beforehand what kind of backing your issue will have is likely to be a deciding factor in whether or not you pursue legislation.

Pursuing Legislation

Although they may be protected under certain laws, animals are considered property, which means humans can do pretty much whatever they want with them. Naturally, we'd be living in a very different world if animals were granted rights, the most basic of which may be the right to simply exist for themselves and not as a service to humanity. "Animal rights" do not yet exist, and hence there is no real "animal rights law." Advocates can, however, use laws and regulations to aid animals, since many forms of mistreatment are considered illegal.

Unfortunately, not only do animals not have rights under the law, but not all animals are considered equal; consequently, laws that apply to one species may not apply to another. In the United States, for example, the Humane Methods of Slaughter Act specifies that animals must be rendered insensible to pain before being slaughtered, yet this law does not include poultry, so there is no federal protection for chickens, who represent more than ninety percent of farmed animals killed in the US. These birds – as well as turkeys, ducks, geese and rabbits (considered "poultry" by the USDA, for some reason) – suffer some of the most horrific deaths imaginable.

Through legislation, activists have the opportunity to enhance the protection of animals. Such legislation can cover a spectrum of legal improvements, from the European Convention's efforts to protect pets and stray animals to laws targeting the most egregious industrialized abuses of farmed animals. Legislation may be urged on local or national levels and may even use international agreements, such as those from the International Whaling Commission or the International Air Transport Association, which sets standards for the international transport of animals.

Think Globally, Act Locally

Legislation begins at the local level, says Farm Sanctuary's Gene Baur, who recommends that activists become acquainted with the elected officials in their city or county. "Legislators need to come to know and understand animal people as reasonable, as sensible and as having a good argument about things," he says. "Activists may be able to get their city to enact a ban on foie gras, which is what happened in Chicago." (In 2006, Chicago became the first US city to ban the sale of this cruel delicacy.) "But the way to make this happen is to get to know your elected officials." Community support helps too. "Whenever we've done foie gras campaigns, we've always reached out to restaurants, getting them to sign pledges not to serve it," Gene says. "That support can be used to demonstrate to legislators that citizens agree that foie gras is cruel."

Gene Baur believes that in addition to improving the lives of animals, legislative campaigns help make overall activism more effective. "A large

Issues like the environment or human rights are further advanced down the stages than animal rights are. The stages as I understand them are: 1) public education, 2) public policy development, 3) legislation, 4) litigation and enforcement, and 5) public acceptance. Although we do some litigation, legislation and some public policy development, I think the animal rights issue is still very much in stage one – public education. I think that's why media coverage is still the goal. We need to understand that the more we can propel the issue of animal rights into the public policy development and legislation stages, the more that we will expedite the cause.

Kim Stallwood

Satya magazine, December 2001

part of what we as animal advocates need to do is determine how to reach out to people who are not animal advocates and communicate in a way that they will listen to us and recognize these issues as important and deserving of their time and attention," he says. "These campaigns are like a living laboratory of social science, helping us understand how to reach out in the most effective way."

Lobbying

Democratic governments throughout the world – including Australia, Canada, New Zealand, South Africa, the United Kingdom and the United States – recognize the value of lobbying to attain legislative goals. Citizens and organizations have the right to communicate with elected officials, urging them to support issues that are important to them. By directly targeting lawmakers, activists can help create new legislation or improve existing legislation. You may even find yourself defending recent legislation, as activists in the UK have experienced with the 2004 Hunting Act, which bans hunting with hounds. The pro-hunting lobby has funneled considerable resources toward unseating anti-hunt Members of Parliament (MPs), and Conservatives have vowed to repeal the law, enacted by the Labor party, should Tories return to power.

UK activists work hard to ensure the hunting ban stays in effect, mostly through lobbying. This method of trying to influence MPs is called "a Lobby of Parliament," explains Joyce D'Silva of Compassion in World Farming (CIWF). "We hire a big hall near Parliament, have a rally, and then people can queue up to see their MPs," she says. "If you're lucky, they'll come and talk to you; if you're very lucky they'll take you for a cup of tea and talk to you. It's a way of getting issues to a lot of MPs on a quite personal level."

Joyce says that MPs are sympathetic about animal issues, perhaps because they hear about them so often from constituents. "Many MPs in England have said they get more letters on animal-welfare issues than anything else," she says. "One MP's secretary even said the MP wasn't interested in animal welfare, but he gets so many letters on it that he thought he should show up and vote, because he's representing his people. So, letters really can have an effect." Joyce cites as an example a massive letter-writing campaign they organized with the aid of the Royal Society for the Protection of Animals to encourage MPs to vote for a bill banning gestation crates for sows. The bill passed, and the crates were banned in the UK as of January 1999.

The anti-vivisection group Uncaged, meanwhile, has taken the UK lobbying effort into the twenty-first century with their Protecting Animals in Democracy (PAD) campaign, which employs a dedicated Web site (vote4animals.org.uk), to make it easier for citizens to use the political system and elections to combat animal abuse and exploitation.

Angela Roberts, founder of Uncaged, explains how PAD works: "The main aim of the campaign is to make candidates aware of the issues and rank their responses to various questions, and then to let their constituents know where the candidates of all parties stand on animal issues, thus allowing people to make an informed decision about who to vote for. A high number of MPs responded to our questionnaire saying that they had more mail generated from this campaign than from any other issue. And we have carried out a series of interviews with the most supportive MPs in our magazine."

Registered members of the PAD network receive regular email updates about new animal protection issues that are on the political agenda. The user-friendly PAD system enables activists to lobby their MPs on key issues that affect the lives of animals and raise public awareness in their constituencies and nationally about the need to protect animals.

MPs in New Zealand, on the other hand, can generally be lobbied in person. "New Zealand has the advantage of being small enough that in most cases you can simply call up your local MP and arrange a visit," says Anthony Terry director of Save Animals From Exploitation (SAFE). He also suggests a hand-written letter has more impact than an email, while consumer postcards sent to MPs often show the lawmakers a level of support.

While grassroots activists may think the business of lobbying is just that – a business better left to "professionals" – individuals can actually hold more sway with their elected officials.

"Legislators tell us that citizen lobbyists carry a stronger message than a hired gun," says Jake Oster, director of grassroots advocacy in the Government Affairs department of the Humane Society of the United States (HSUS). "The absolute best advocate for animals is a citizen who lives in the legislator's district." To ensure your message is heard, Jake recommends meeting with your elected official, which legislators say is the best method of communication. "Citizens who get up and take the time to make appointments to meet with their legislator, attend a town hall meeting or make some sort of face-to-face contact tend to carry the strongest message. Phone calls, emails, letters – those are all great, but there's no substitute for a personal meeting."

If you cannot meet with your legislator, a phone call is the next best thing. "Letters to Capitol Hill take a very long time to get there in the post-Anthrax scare world because letters have to be irradiated," says Jake. "Offices get so many emails, they don't always answer them all. There's no accountability; we have no way of knowing if they open an email, if they read a fax or open a letter. But we know when we call they pick up the phone." Be sure to keep calls brief and to the point. "Your call is not a time to debate or tell them about your cat. Just say you're a constituent and that you're urging them to support or oppose this legislation." (On the other hand, email is usually the best way to reach state legislatures. "In fact, a lot of them don't have offices or staff to answer phones," says Jake.)

US activists unfamiliar with Capitol Hill may feel put off by the federal government's hierarchy and staff process. Every legislator has a staff, which could comprise as many as one hundred people, and meeting with your Senator or member of Congress will likely involve one or more staff members. But don't be offended, says Jake. "On animal issues, staff make most of the recommendations to their bosses on how to vote, so lobbying and developing relationships with staff is as important – sometimes more important – than the legislator. You should never feel slighted if you make an appointment and you get a staffer rather than your elected official."

Here's some more advice from the HSUS:

How to Effectively Lobby Your Lawmaker

- Don't be intimidated by the thought of approaching elected officials. State legislators especially are receptive to constituent comments.

- Be concise. Your message should be short and direct. It is fine to express your opinion.

- Use all available resources. Request position papers, fact sheets, or other documentation from animal protection groups such as the HSUS. You don't need to be an expert, but the more facts and arguments you have on your side, the better.

- Personalize your appeal. Tell how you are concerned about an issue and how it affects you, your family and your community.

- Cultivate legislative staff. Establish a positive relationship with staff persons. They are usually more accessible and can have tremendous influence over an issue.

- Be honest. If you don't know the answer to something, admit it and try to get the information later. Also, when working with legislators who sponsor your bill, be sure to be upfront about any potential problem areas.

- Research your legislators. Ask around, talk to others who have worked for legislative change – on any issue – and ask their advice on which legislators are most effective or which committees are most likely to approve of your bill.

- Identify your bill or issue clearly. Whenever you get a chance to lobby elected officials, don't just refer to your effort by the bill number. And always make it clear whether you are asking for their support or opposition to the matter.

- During the legislative session, constantly check your bill's status. Most legislative entities have a bill status information office. At certain times, action occurs quickly and with little notice.

- Keep things friendly. Maintain a positive relationship with all legislators – they may be in this office or a higher one for decades. Threats and hostile or sarcastic remarks are not productive. Do not create any enemies.

- Avoid party politics. Animals have friends on both sides of the aisle.

- Be flexible. Sometimes compromise is a must. Support legislative strategies that may save an otherwise doomed bill: adoption of sunset provisions, grandfathering clauses, and placing provisions into regulations instead of statute.

- Express gratitude. Thank everyone and let your members know how helpful key legislators were in your success.

Do's and Don'ts of Lobbying

Do's:

- Do know who represents you at all levels of government. You can obtain this information from your local library or board of elections and usually through the Internet. Keep phone numbers and addresses handy. Help others do the same.

- Do identify yourself by name and organization (if any) when talking with an elected official. (Politicians always act like they remember who you are to avoid offending anyone.)

- Do state a clear and concise objective. For example, say specifically that you want to ban canned hunts – not just that you want to stop outrageous hunting practices (which is too broad). Explain the meaning of terms that may be unfamiliar, such as "canned," "pound seizure," "Class B dealers." Broad statements such as "hunting bears with hounds is inexcusable" may reflect how you feel, but don't convey a message as to what action needs to be taken by the official.

- Do explain why the issue is important to you personally. If possible, link the issue to a personal experience or a situation in the elected official's district.

• Do be aware of previous actions the official has taken on behalf of animals. You can be sure the opposition is aware of the assistance he or she gave on our behalf.

• Do get to know your elected officials. Make an effort to appear at town meetings and other events, and be sure they hear you ask at least one question on animal issues at each event.

• Do mention how important it is for your elected officials to adequately fund animal programs ranging from local animal control to state enforcement of wildlife protection laws to enforcement of the Animal Welfare Act and others. Let them know that this is how you want your tax dollars spent.

• Do join, create, or revitalize state federations or other state-wide groups to give your cause additional clout. Whenever possible, mention how many individuals your group represents.

• Do get to know and develop a working relationship with key people who have influence over animals. For example, animal control officers, veterinarians, state wildlife board members, prosecuting attorneys, and health department officials have a major impact on animal protection bills. Legislators listen to their views, so work with them whenever possible.

• Do join forces with other types of groups that may have the same position as you even if for different reasons – groups such as churches, teachers unions, chambers of commerce, local universities, or specific industries. Whenever appropriate, get school children to support your efforts.

• Do wear many hats – not just your animal advocate hat. When lobbying legislators, identify yourself as a parent, businessperson, campaign contributor, or fellow church/club/team member.

• Do work with legislative staff. They often have more knowledge of the issues, can give you vital background on the legislation's outlook, and have extraordinary clout.

• Do get involved in legislative campaigns – as an individual, not as a non-profit group. Volunteer to work, place a campaign sign in your yard, hand out leaflets, or otherwise help get someone elected.

• Do learn how to work with your local press by developing a relationship with friendly reporters and editors.

• Do respond to action alerts sent by the HSUS and other groups. Alerts are usually sent when legislation is close to passage or in a precarious position, so your action can make a tremendous difference.

Don'ts:

• Don't threaten or antagonize a legislator even if he or she deserves it. If an elected official opposes your viewpoint, but respects you and bears you no animosity, you may find common ground in the future on another issue. But if you make an enemy, that person may take extra steps to defeat the bill you support. A legislator who doesn't agree with you on wildlife issues may be great on companion animal issues and vice versa. Don't make enemies. Today's city council member can be tomorrow's governor.

• Don't refer to bills by their numbers alone.

• Don't fail to listen to elected official's comments and questions on an issue. If she asks how a bill will impact jobs, or medical care, or the budget, you'll know where her concern is focused. Find ways to address those issues.

• Don't ever lie to or mislead a legislator – especially someone who is on your side and needs to know the truth about an issue. Trust is essential for a working relationship.

• Don't overwhelm a legislator with too much information or paperwork. They don't have time for it. Provide them with whatever is key to their efforts and be ready to supply any other needed information.

• Don't be inflexible. Sometimes we have to compromise. As long as such a change won't harm any animals, consider the situation carefully. Learn legislative strategies that might save a bill otherwise destined to die, such as sunset provisions, grandfathering clauses, and placing provisions into a regulation instead of a statute.

• Don't forget to thank someone who was helpful. Whenever possible, let your membership know how helpful the person has been.

- Don't use terms or abbreviations that may be unfamiliar to an official without explaining their meaning, such as WLFA, PIJAC or even the HSUS.

What Influences a Legislator?

Elected officials are, first and foremost, politicians. When lawmakers are up for re-election, they are often more willing to listen to interests outside their normal concerns. The issues of special interest groups are important to them because they may need that support to win re-election.

One of the easiest and most direct ways to get to know and influence legislators is to help them. You can do so by volunteering to work on a campaign. Although assisting politicians does not ensure that they will always vote your way, it does allow you to spend time with them and their staff. Building and maintaining working relationships is always important.

The following are important questions to keep in mind when lobbying elected officials. The answers to these will influence how a legislator responds to the issue.

The Issue:

- What are the merits of the issue?
- What impact does it have on his/her district?
- Does it involve possible job losses?
- What is the cost?
- What is the issue's impact on the economy or business?
- Would the issue create too much government interference?
- Do issue opponents have more clout than proponents?
- Is there a general lack of knowledge about the issue?
- What is the executive branch position?

Political Considerations:

- Is there an upcoming election in which the legislator faces tough competition?
- Is the legislator a lame duck?
- Have issue proponents or opponents made campaign contributions?

- Does the issue have the commitment of an interest group? In other words, are there many voters tied to this single issue?
- Does the issue have support from the president, governor or mayor?
- Does the legislator know that Scorecards are closely monitored on this issue?

Media:

- Have there been many news articles written on the issue?
- Have there been many editorials written on the issue?
- Have readers submitted letters to the editor on the issue?
- Are there more opportunities to gain press attention?

Legislative Considerations:

- Is the legislator the chairman of the committee that would handle the issue?
- What are the legislator's committee assignments?
- What trade offs has the politician made with fellow legislators?
- What are the positions of others in state or district delegation?
- Are other legislators lobbying for or against the issue?
- What is the staff advice on the issue?
- What is the position of the legislator's political party?

Personal:

- Does the legislator have personal experiences and feelings on the issue?
- What are the positions of the legislator's family members, friends, and (especially) children?
- Does the issue impact the legislator personally or others important to the legislator?
- Does the issue have any connection to the politician's alma mater?

Outside Influences:

- Does the legislator have frequent grassroots contact with constituents who could influence him?

- What's the general public sentiment about the issue?
- Do celebrities or sports figures endorse the issue?
- How often does the legislator have chance encounters with the public?

(Source: The HSUS)

Citizens Initiatives & Referendums

Twenty-four states in the US allow citizens to submit proposed changes in the law to voters for approval. The initiative process (also called the "ballot initiative" process) allows citizens to gather petition signatures to place a proposed statutory or constitutional amendment before the voters and is most often used as a last resort effort when other means of effecting reform have been exhausted. Citizens initiatives like Arizona's Prop 204, mentioned earlier in this chapter, come with a hefty price tag, making them a last resort. They are worth mentioning, however, since they are another avenue to legislative improvements for animals.

Activist Camilla Fox helped coordinate Proposition 4, which ultimately banned several wildlife traps and poisons in California in 1998. "I think the public ballot initiative process has provided an opportunity for animal advocates to put forth measures to the public where they have not had success in the legislature or through the regulatory process," she says.

Nevertheless, Camilla urges grassroots activists to do their homework and get support from animal-protection organizations. "Ballot initiatives are very expensive, and I do not encourage activists to attempt to pursue a ballot initiative without the backing of major animal-protection groups because of the resources that are necessary to win such a campaign. If you don't have the polling data that shows you have a winnable campaign early on, it can be a tremendous waste of resources, both financially and in terms of activists' efforts."

Before even thinking of embarking on a ballot initiative campaign, Camilla suggests activists use the other tools at their disposal, such as voicing your concerns at legislative and other public policy hearings or working for change through state and federal wildlife management agency rulemaking processes. "If such efforts fail, you have a better case for taking your measure to the public through the initiative process because you've demonstrated that you've exhausted all other means and now you have no other recourse but to allow the public to weigh in on the matter."

Another tip she offers from the activist trenches: Read the opposition's literature. "These publications often provide an update on the legislation and regulatory agency reform efforts they plan to put pursue," she says. Knowing this information beforehand can be of extremely helpful when creating your campaign.

New Zealand's first citizen-initiated referendum for animals was on behalf of battery hens, according to SAFE's Anthony Terry, who doesn't put much faith in this tactic. "The petition gained over three hundred and thirty thousand signatures," he says, "but the signatures were severely refuted and they rejected a sufficient amount to not reach the six percent of registered voters needed. The government effectively axed it as it seemed they did not want the issue to reach a referendum."

Activists in a number of European countries, including the UK, are now campaigning for the European Union to grant citizens the right to create initiatives; if implemented, this would be the first trans-national tool of citizens' participation. In the meantime, activists in the UK lobby lawmakers and sign petitions.

"Petitions to the PM are widely used – and forgotten as no official system exists for dealing with them," says Joyce D'Silva. "Petitions to the European Parliament actually end up with the Petitions Committee and may get endorsed by the Parliament, so they are much more useful. Our petition to have animals recognized as sentient beings in EU law was endorsed by this European Parliament in 1994."

Joyce says that a proper body such as CIWF can take the government to "Judicial Review" where they challenge their actions as being illegal under a certain law. "CIWF has judicially reviewed the government on at least three occasions and never yet won. The cases were on the export of animals to continental Europe and the welfare of broiler chickens. One case was referred to the European Court of Justice in Strasbourg, but we lost there too."

Voting Blocs

Used by all other issue advocacy movements that pursue laws and public policies, the voting bloc is generally a missed opportunity for animal advocates. The voting bloc system comprises a coalition of citizens who are so motivated by a specific concern that it helps them determine how they vote in elections. Julie E. Lewin, political trainer and president of the Connecticut-based National Institute for Animal Advocacy, says the voting bloc system has four components:

- It organizes supportive citizens by legislative district.

- Before voting on a piece of proposed legislation of concern to the issue group, lawmakers know that constituents who care will find out how they vote.

- Before voting, the lawmaker knows his/her voting record on the general issue will determine whether the political organization endorses him/her for re-election, or endorses his/her opponent.

- The lawmaker knows that the voting bloc organization will deliver votes on Election Day to its endorsed candidates.

Thus, a voting bloc is an information-delivery system. It coordinates the voting behavior of its members; these citizens hold their lawmakers accountable, and the lawmaker knows his or her voting bloc organization has the clout to sway other constituents. "That's where the power comes from: the power to use endorsements and political mobilization to swing elections," says Julie. "Voting blocs turn advocates into true power players. Think of the National Rifle Association and Christian Right. In my state, licensed hunters are only one and a half percent of the population, but because they understand all this and use it to their advantage, they control wildlife policy in the state. Animal advocates are huge in comparison but aren't political, so therefore they have no power in the lawmaking arena."

Across the United States, lobbying for animals – when it is done at all – is performed by charitable organizations and concerned individuals, who are largely powerless when it comes to achieving strong legislation; that is, legislation that has organized opposition. Julie defines a strong law as one that bans outright a certain practice, substantially raises the legal minimum standards of care for a group of animals or makes it easier for humans to gain standing in court to represent animals. For example, Julie does not consider felony cruelty laws strong legislation, because they fail to give animals any additional legal protection. They have no organized opposition, and thus have been won without voting blocs.

Animal advocates, Julie says, are missing a vital opportunity to leverage the legal system by creating voting blocs. "We are a sleeping giant. The tragedy of the animal-rights and animal-rescue movements to date has been the failure to view *formal* political organizations – voting blocs – as a mandatory component. We must get political, or the animals will continue to pay the price."

You'll find step-by-step instructions for creating a voting bloc for animals in Julie's how-to manual for rights and rescue advocates, *Get Political for Animals and Win the Laws They Need: Why and How to Launch a Voting Bloc for Animals in Your Town, City, County or State.*

No matter how organized we are as activists, using legislation on behalf of animals can be a protracted process. "Be patient," advises Erika Ceballos, director of Canada's Campaigns Against The Cruelty To Animals. "Things don't change overnight, despite your big efforts to change the world or at least stop a specific kind of cruelty. Things in this very ugly animal-rights world take months and years to change. Look at the seal slaughter here in Canada. It

> Jail and prison are life experiences and like any experience it can be pleasant or unpleasant, hard or easy, interesting or boring, depending on the psychology of the person imprisoned. People can adjust to any environment if required. The best thing to do is find a niche and survive and, if possible, find the means to flourish. Prison also provides insight into the state of conditions for all the animals imprisoned on farms, ranches, zoos, laboratories, game parks and aquariums. Most of the world's citizens spend their entire life in captivity; and the death penalty is the most common sentence given to non-humans after serving their time.
>
> **Paul Watson**
>
> *Satya* magazine, March 2004

takes *decades*. Many people feel so frustrated when things go wrong and their efforts don't make much of a change for the animals, but, hey, perseverance pays eventually."

The Other Side of the Law

Bryan Pease was sixteen years old when he became an animal activist – and when he started getting arrested for his activism. There was the time, for example, when he was holding a protest sign on a public sidewalk in front of a fur store in Syracuse, New York. "The tactic was first the police would arrest people, and then they'd get a restraining order while the case was pending," Bryan says. "That can take months to be resolved. In effect they were preventing you from going back there, even if the charges aren't valid. So I was arrested on a charge of unlawful assembly and I received a temporary restraining order. The arresting officer seemed to think 'unlawful assembly' meant a protest he didn't authorize."

He ignored the judge's order and returned to the same spot on the sidewalk, where he leafleted. "So then they arrested me for contempt of court." At his trial, Bryan was found not guilty of unlawful assembly, but the judge found him guilty of violating his order. "He sentenced me to thirteen weekends in jail, but I appealed it and I won," says Bryan, who is now an attorney practicing animal law and co-founder of the Animal Protection & Rescue League.

Being arrested at a protest or for some other animal-rights campaign is always a possibility. While an activist who chains herself to the door of a slaughterhouse may have a pretty good idea she'll be taking a ride in a police car that day, other activists are quite surprised to find themselves in handcuffs.

In 2006, activist Adam Durand was convicted of trespassing and sentenced to six months in jail for his part in an investigation and open rescue of hens from a battery farm. A first-time offender, Adam thought he would be getting probation. "But the judge saw otherwise. He decided to give me the maximum sentence times two, because I was convicted on three trespassing counts." After thirty-five days in jail, Adam was released on appeal and is awaiting the judge's decision.

"I didn't expect to go to jail up until the day I was sentenced because I had been assured by the prosecutor that I wasn't going to jail," he says. "But then his recommendation *was* jail."

Adam and another prisoner shared a ride in a patrol car to begin their sentences. "He said, 'Man, you're a political prisoner. I'm really proud of everything you're doing.' I thought that was a good sign. And that's the way the other inmates treated me. They were very friendly and respectful. The corrections officers were not always as nice. Some of them wanted to see who this vegan guy was and make fun of him."

But being vegan in jail wasn't easy for Adam. "I was not offered any kind of dietary exemption," he says. "I did file papers with the jail. They never responded to them. I think the internal forms in the jail are designed to be ignored. My attorneys tried to get the jail to change their policy, but they didn't offer any kind of exemption for ethical dietary choice – they called it a preference." Luckily, Adam got a job in the kitchen, so he had a little control over what he ate.

"This was a wake-up call to the conditions in which two million Americans are living. I learned a lot. It's definitely a fight I want to include in my future activism: better treatment for prisoners. For example, the Thirteenth Amendment to the Constitution abolishes slavery, but it exempts prisoners who have been convicted of a crime, and I just think that's ridiculous. I didn't realize that until I was in there and I was being forced to work."

In the end, Adam remains proud of exposing the cruelty hens endure in battery cages. "This case is really a classic example of civil disobedience. I don't think anyone really wants to go to jail, but the amount of publicity that this case got because I went to jail was well worth it."

Patty Mark, meanwhile, estimates she's been arrested thirty times as a result of her animal activism, though so far she's only served two brief stints behind bars: three days and ten days. "There are currently eight warrants out for my imprisonment for unpaid fines for open rescues," she says. "I refuse to pay these fines on ethical grounds. I was ordered to serve seventeen days in prison in July 2005 for these unpaid fines and to date I'm still 'on the run.' I'm still doing open rescues and the police don't take me in – they turn a

blind eye. I believe they know we have the public opinion on our side."
As the activism of Adam and Patty demonstrates, open rescues and other tactics that involve sneaking onto private property, removing animals and even planning such activities may be considered crimes (trespassing, burglary and conspiracy, respectively). While the chances of getting caught might seem slim, it can happen, so be aware that governments around the world are more likely now than ever to prosecute you.

You will not be arrested for any activities that are guaranteed by your government, however. For example, the freedom of speech (defined as any act of seeking, receiving or imparting information or ideas, regardless of the medium used) is guaranteed under the First Amendment of the United States Constitution as well as through many human-rights instruments, including Article 10 of the European Convention on Human Rights and Article 19 of the Universal Declaration of Human Rights. Thus, leafleting, protesting or other acts of speaking out for animals are protected under the law.

Surviving Jail

For Bruce Friedrich, who has spent years in various jails and prisons for his peace activism before he joined People for the Ethical Treatment of Animals (PETA), being arrested is another outreach opportunity. "An activist shouldn't feel like jail guards and inmates are the enemy," he says. "Feel free to talk with them about vegetarianism and animal rights and you'll find many sympathizers, just like in any other line of work." Bruce warns, though, that you should not talk with anyone about whatever it is they're claiming you did until after your trial is over, since law enforcement may try to get you to incriminate yourself. "Part of their job is to get you to say things that could come back to haunt you. Often if you're arrested, even for something completely absurd like standing on the sidewalk with a sign, in order to get you to talk and say something possibly incriminating, many will tell you that they're going to hold you for a week or a weekend or something; they'll try to scare you about the jail conditions and how 'You don't want to spend a weekend there – those guys will eat you alive.' It's all nonsense. Other prisoners are always nice and respectful if you're nice and respectful to them, and a night in jail is something that you'll be able to tell your friends about later – don't worry about it. So whatever you do if you're arrested, don't talk with anyone about what you've been arrested for, even though you are certainly completely innocent. It will not help you be released more quickly to speak with the police or other inmates, one of which could be an undercover police officer; nothing you say will help you in any way, but many things can hurt you. Don't do it. Of course, *most* police will not try to manipulate you or be mean to you; they're just doing their jobs and they find the 'good cop, bad cop' duplicity stuff to be beneath them. But some will, so be wary."

If you end up being processed into the system for more than a night or a weekend, you are likely to be strip searched and booked. "The process is *boring*, but painless," says Bruce.

Bruce also makes these salient points:

• Most of us involved in animal rights are not likely to find ourselves in a situation of powerlessness that is similar to that of other animals; jail is going to be the closest we get. This is an opportunity to experience powerlessness, which may help us to empathize with other animals to some degree.

• No matter how bad it is, it's better than being in a zoo, vivisection lab or factory farm. No jail I've ever been to or heard of was physically horrible. Some were bad, but none of them were anything approaching as bad as every moment of an animal's life on a factory farm or in a slaughterhouse.

• For activists who are working very hard, jail can be a forced retreat. You can sleep, play cards, read, write and so on. It's a forced vacation of sorts, and if you look at it with a positive attitude, it can be quite relaxing.

• Vegan food: Work to get your judge to order it. If your judge orders it, you're set. PETA is always ready to work to get vegan food for anyone who is having trouble.

The thought of actually spending time behind bars may intimidate the toughest activist, but Bruce believes the reality is not so bad. "Incarceration is not a big deal," he says. "Again, it's mostly boring, and it's hard on loved ones a lot more than it's hard on the inmate. If you're in federal prison, you'll have very liberal visiting hours, though you may find that you'd prefer to keep with your routine, rather than to have a lot of visitors. Jails tend to offer a fair amount to amuse you, since a bored inmate population is likely to be unruly. Also, the concept of jail is supposed to be that you're in jail as your punishment, not for your punishment – that is, being in jail shouldn't be miserable, beyond your being away from your life. That said, there are a lot of really shitty county jails – really shitty. And they're getting worse as jails privatize. But even there, you should have things to read and other inmates to talk with, and my most interesting jail stories are from the ones that were least pleasant."

Please see *Appendix C – Know Your Rights* for more information.

[1] Although many US animal activists are nervous about how the "chilling effects" of AETA may impact their advocacy, others are not concerned. Erik Marcus of Vegan.com states: "Based on the final wording of the Animal Enterprise Terrorist Act, there's nothing that would dissuade me from any of the tactics I use or advocate to others." And PETA's Bruce Friedrich observes that any action that was legal before AETA is still legal, regardless of whether a company's profits are affected. "It is important that all of us who believe in kindness toward animals redouble our efforts; such a response will be the strongest action in opposition to the Act," he says.

Resources
Animal Law
www.animal-law.biz/talk.php
Animal Legal Defense Fund
www.aldf.org
Animal Protection & Rescue League
www.aprl.org
Animal Rights Africa
www.animalrightsafrica.org
Animal Rights New Zealand

www.arlan.org.nz

Australian Parliament

www.aph.gov.au

Canadian Office of the Registrar of Lobbyists

www.orl-bdl.gc.ca

The Humane Society of the United States

www.hsus.org

National Institute for Animal Advocacy

www.nifaa.org

National Lawyers Guild, National Office

www.nlg.org

New Zealand MPs

www.parliament.nz/en-NZ/MPP/MPs/MPs

South African protest rights

www.fxi.org.za

UK legal advice

http://freebeagles.org

www.release.org.uk

Uncaged

www.uncaged.co.uk

US right to protest

www.nlg-la.org/righttoprotest.htm

CHAPTER 11

ANIMAL CARE:

ACTIVISTS ARE ANIMALS TOO

*When I despair, I remember that all through history the way of truth
and love has always won. There have been tyrants and murderers,
and for a time they seem invincible, but in the end, they always fall.*
Mahatma Gandhi

Although it was shocking and sad to see hens being yanked by their fragile
legs, necks and wings from battery cages, it was the vision of thousands of
them packed onto a flatbed truck that eventually made me lose it. The tears
would come later ... after I had helped rescue hundreds of "spent" hens from
an avian nightmare known as a battery-egg farm. The owner of this egg farm
had decided to convert his battery-cage operation into something less
inhumane, and he had invited animal-protection groups to take away as
many "spent" hens as they could before the birds went to slaughter. (A hen
is considered "spent" after laying eggs for one to two years – a fraction of
her natural lifespan.) Kim Sturla of Animal Place was taking part in the
rescue, and she had asked if I could help. *Of course I can do this to help
animals.*

A gloomy shed filled with one hundred and sixty thousand hens greeted
us. The stench of ammonia burned our eyes and assaulted our lungs.
Carefully removing as many as eight frail hens from each small cage, we
worked against the clock, amid dead chickens and curtains of cob webs,
knowing that at some point in the afternoon the "catchers" would arrive and
begin their work. The catchers would also be in a hurry. *I don't want any
animals to get hurt.*

As we raced in and out of the shed, filling boxes with hens who had never
before seen daylight, I grew wearier with each step, having to choose from

among tens of thousands of birds. Our actions decided who would end up in a safe home and who would end up in dog food. I cradled nearly lifeless hens in my arms, giving them fresh water, determined they not perish without knowing a tiny bit of kindness. By three-thirty the catchers were removing hens for slaughter, yanking them out of battery cages, stuffing them into even smaller wire crates and loading them onto a large truck. *Stop doing that! Can't you see you're hurting them?*

Packed into their mobile prison, the traumatized hens awaited a grueling ride. *I'm so sorry I could not save you.* I made it home, got through the front door, and the image of all those hens on the truck caught up with me. My face felt hot and my eyesight blurred, though I could see so many tired faces looking out through the wire, as though imploring me to help them, their used and broken bodies crammed into more cages, waiting hours without food or water to be transported for yet more abuse. *I'm so sorry.* Before long I was sobbing like a freight train, my body and soul consumed by an inconsolable anguish. I felt ashamed to be part of the human species. *What kind of an activist am I, anyway? How can I cope? How can I live?*

With few exceptions, anyone who is active in animal advocacy long enough experiences some form of emotional pushback. Whether we're coping with grief, depression, anger, stress or that psychic demon known as burnout, we activists often bear the burden our compassionate work engenders, facing an assortment of mental and sometimes physical challenges. Trying to change consumer behavior can feel like we're drowning as we struggle against the tide of corporate hegemony that keeps animals oppressed. The result is that we often question our ability to speak out for animals. Even doing nothing can hurt: As Carol J. Adams will explain in this chapter, just *knowing* about animal abuse can cause us to suffer.

So, how do we move past the pain? How do we not just keep our heads above water, but continue to make positive strides amid a potential sea of despair and flourish in our activism? The answer is to be found somewhere in a delicate balance: We have to set boundaries as activists even as we are striving to realize our full potential as human beings. But recognizing your limits – and respecting them – takes practice.

Coping with Guilt

"You can bear anything if it isn't your own fault," wrote the novelist Katharine Fullerton Gerould. She obviously was not on a first-name basis with many animal activists. Countless activists suffer feelings of guilt, most often because they believe they aren't doing enough for animals. Perhaps they are comparing themselves to other activists (try reading *Ethics Into Action: Henry Spira and the Animal Rights Movement* by Peter Singer without telling yourself you're not doing enough). Or maybe the constant exposure to animal abuse makes them feel no amount of time and effort could possibly have an impact on so colossal a task.

But unless you're working for an animal-advocacy organization, you are likely to be a student or busy with a full- or part-time job outside the movement – or both. The activism you engage in is conducted in your so-called "free time," and every bit you do, whether it's leafleting for thirty minutes a week or devoting several hours a day to corporate outreach, is important. If you're using your time wisely, active in efforts that can make a real difference for animals, then be proud of that! Celebrate your compassion knowing you are contributing more to making the world a kinder place than most people ever will.

Even if you *are* employed by a group fighting animal exploitation, there is no guarantee you won't experience the pangs of a guilty conscious – however unwarranted that guilt is.

"I have a lot of guilt," says Dawn Moncrief, who works ten hours a day as executive director of the Farm Animal Reform Movement. "Not just from the tangible experiences of seeing animals and not being able to save them, but experiencing that sensation on a regular basis – knowing they are suffering and dying and not being able to save them. I also have guilt associated with taking part in recreational activities or other non-advocacy activities. I have guilt from being comfortable in the midst of their discomfort. I have guilt from being upset about my personal, relatively trivial matters."

Lisa Franzetta also works full time on behalf of animals and is no less vulnerable to activist guilt. "Honestly, I feel like I live under the constant shadow of guilt of not doing enough, or not being effective enough in what

I do," Lisa says. "And the way I deal with it is the time-honored approach of just trying not to think about it. I feel guilty every time I see a woman in a coat with fur trim walking down the street and, for whatever reason, I look the other way instead of engaging her in a conversation – or at least expressing my disgust. And while I rationally believe in the importance of incremental reforms, I do often feel a kind of guilt for not being 'hard-line' enough, both as a professional working for an animal-rights organization and just in my day-to-day personal life."

For some activists, guilt is simply not an issue. "There is always guilt that you can't do more, but just because you can't do everything doesn't mean you are not being effective," says Kate Fowler-Reeves of Animal Aid. "It is just a measure of how corrupt and amoral this human-run world is. And, even though you may not be able to save every chicken in every battery unit in the world, you can save a handful, and to them, that is everything."

Christine Morrissey agrees. "I refuse to feel guilt," she says. Christine focuses instead on the lives she is able to save doing outreach and conducting rescues. "In my mind, guilt is reserved for those who harm animals and humans, not the individuals helping animals. Rescue work allows individuals to empower the voiceless and build a better future."

Zoe Weil, president of the Institute for Humane Education, shares a story about driving next to a truck full of pigs, presumably headed for the slaughterhouse: "It was so cold, and going sixty miles [96 kilometers] an hour, the pigs must have been freezing. One caught my eye – literally – and we stared at each other for as long as was safe with me driving my car. When the truck pulled off the highway at an exit, I felt like I should follow it, but what could I have done? I made a promise to that pig that I would continue to educate others and speak out. And that's what I've been doing as a humane educator my entire adult life."

Zoe quotes the singer and social activist Joan Baez, who said "Action is the antidote to despair." "I think that action is also the antidote to guilt," Zoe says. "But when we can't take an action to save specific animals – like all the ones in a factory farm we happen to be visiting – then it's important to take some other action. We can take photographs of those animals and educate others and work for change for all the animals in factory farms. As long as our guilt does not become debilitating, it can be a powerful motivation to action. I'd recommend that people feel their guilt and let it inspire their work. Doing the work, the guilt abates."

That's exactly what Josh Balk of the Humane Society of the United States does, embracing guilt as an aid to his activism. "I find that, for myself, a healthy amount of guilt can be a motivating factor when working to help animals," he says. "I know that the worst I'd ever feel would be if I didn't work as hard as I could at my job, which in effect, would cause more animals to suffer. This healthy guilt would be too much for me to bear, so I try to avoid it the best I can."

And do not allow yourself to get too disillusioned or disheartened. We have lost too many people to a feeling of hopelessness. To that end, it's important that people pace themselves and try to achieve some balance in life. It's vital to take time for yourself in order to maintain your long-term participation in the cause.

Wayne Pacelle

Satya magazine, June/July 2005

Relieving Stress

We all know that just living can be stressful. Dealing with the frustrations and pressures of life takes a toll on our bodies, minds and emotions. But the angst of animal activism can easily turn everyday stress into a major hazard – not just for your health, but for your ability to speak out for animals. Moreover, the constant stress experienced by those who investigate abuse, rescue animals, spend time in a shelter or perform other potentially disturbing work makes these people vulnerable to the crippling effects of Post-Traumatic Stress Disorder. Stress can sneak up on you; therefore, watch for the signs so you can take steps to reduce them.

Physical symptoms of stress include:
- Headache
- Digestive problems
- Muscle tension

- Sore jaw, grinding teeth
- Change in sleep habits
- Chronic fatigue
- Chest pain, irregular heartbeat
- High blood pressure
- Change in body weight
- Nervous ticks (sniffling, nose twitching, foot bouncing, etc.)
- Vision problems (if your stress is this serious, go to the doctor!)
- Excessive alcohol or drug consumption (again, seek help)

Mental symptoms of stress include:
- Memory loss
- Difficulty making decisions
- Inability to concentrate
- Confusion
- Negative viewpoint
- Poor judgment
- Loss of objectivity
- Desire to escape or run away

Emotional symptoms of stress include:
- Depression
- Anger
- Hypersensitivity
- Apathy
- Restlessness, anxiety
- Feeling overwhelmed
- Lack of confidence

"I think it's good to try to pinpoint the cause of the stress," says Mia MacDonald, whose activism includes work in human rights and the environmental movement as well as animal rights. "Of course, thinking about the state of the world for animals and the breadth and scale of the cruelty is overwhelming in and of itself. Trying to see your way through your role in stopping the suffering can make you feel very tiny and very ineffectual. So it's probably best to try to understand those thoughts but not dwell on them." In addition to practicing yoga and meditation, Mia unwinds by spending time outside. "I try to realize I can't work all the time," she says. "I try to get enough sleep and eat well and plan ahead." She also emphasizes the importance of friendship. "Circles of support for activists can be good. I think stress is certainly more intense when you're alone and dwelling in and on it. Talking about it with others, seeing others trying to find ways of dealing with stress can demystify it and let you find more solutions than feeling stuck in it. That said, life is stressful and there will be times when you feel really stressed and the tools to help you with it don't work that well. I have these periods from time to time and kind of have to accept it and believe that it won't last forever, that I'll get some sense of equanimity back."

An Activist's Advice for Relieving Stress
pattrice jones has spent a lot of time contemplating the stress and other issues activists endure. She is an activist and author (*Aftershock: Confronting Trauma in a Violent World: A Guide for Activists and Their Allies*), has practiced clinical psychology focusing on trauma, and she runs the Eastern Shore Sanctuary in Maryland, where she confesses to suffering her fair share of grief each time a rescued chicken dies. Here is pattrice's advice on how animal activists can best cope with stress:

• Be reasonable in your expectations of yourself and others.
• Eat well and get enough sleep.
• Deliberately relax before and decompress after stressful actions or encounters.
• Respect your own animal rights and don't expect your body to do more than it can do.
• In your off time, seek out a variety of pleasurable activities and sensations.
• Have empathy for yourself and others.
• Maintain healthy relationships with your comrades, and be sure to have one or two friends with whom you do not work.

The Curse of Traumatic Knowledge

The sudden awareness we experience when we first learn of the enormous suffering of animals can prompt feelings of loneliness and despair – a deep well of sadness that leaves us unable to communicate our pain to others. Activist and author Carol J. Adams calls this awareness "traumatic knowledge."

"Traumatic knowledge makes us feel the suffering of animals acutely," she says. "We are shocked – horrified – as we learn about the treatment of animals: 'I have been a part of that system!' We may feel revulsion at our own complicity. We have a need to forgive ourselves for our enmeshment within a system that daily destroys animals by the millions. We are unable to relate to others, and we are unable to explain what is happening to us. Our desolation cuts us off and amplifies the loneliness the knowledge brings."

Compounding the problem, Carol says, is that our culture shields consumers from the truth about the cruelties animals suffer. We don't witness the horrors of the slaughterhouse; instead, we see only neatly packaged animal flesh in the meat section of the supermarket, so we need not consider where the meat came from. She calls this phenomenon "the structure of the absent referent," and this theory is a central theme of many of her books, including *The Sexual Politics of Meat* and *Living Among Meat Eaters*.

"People are much happier eating some*thing* than some*one*," she says. But that "happiness" is merely the result of being ignorant about the realities of agribusiness – an ignorance not shared by the animal activist, who experiences traumatic knowledge when the referent is restored. "It is very difficult to live with this information. It is painful to know what animals endure. But, the response to this is to say, 'I would rather know than not know, and I will find the inner strength to know and not collapse under the weight of knowing.'"

Living with traumatic knowledge requires that we share it. "Sometimes," says Carol, "our friends and co-workers think we are going to drive them crazy saying, 'Do you know about how chickens are treated? Do you know about this? Do you know about that?' We want to be heard, but sometimes indirectly rather than directly is more effective. Give your friends and co-workers pamphlets and books rather than voicing everything yourself. Allow them to hear in their own voice, rather than yours, what is happening to non-humans."

Carol also emphasizes the need for activists to remember their own needs. "No matter the activism we do for animals, we have to take care of ourselves. We cannot do it all, so as we do what we can do, we must do it with love for our own animal body. We can't exhaust ourselves or we don't end up helping the animals. We have to develop interests outside of the animal-rights movement – music, poetry, going to movies – something that meets our needs for nurture and growth. This way we don't ask the animal-rights movement to be everything and all things to us. We can come to it with energy rather than feeling overwhelmed. Having healthy boundaries allows for healthy activism."

Traumatic knowledge affects the animal-rights movement by fueling activists with an urgent desire to vindicate the suffering and trauma animal experience, Carol explains. "One of the attractions of the more militant activities of the animal-rights movement, including targeting someone's home for a demonstration, is that it provides several antidotes to traumatic knowledge: it offers a way to be heard, to have a sense that you are working for change and a way to express anger. But this urgency is dangerous. We sometimes make decisions based on this urgency, losing sight of the need to evaluate. Traumatic knowledge may cause us to see everything in black and white. The problem is we live in a grey world." The key, she says, is to keep theory and activism linked, because theory helps us see this grey world.

"Living with traumatic knowledge, as we all do, means there will always be a crisis. That is because this knowledge causes an inner crisis. We must take care of our bodies because each of our bodies is processing incredibly difficult, demanding, depressing information, and we must be careful and take care as we relate to others. Traumatic knowledge requires that we take care of ourselves, spiritually and physically and emotionally."

Carol suggests that activists acknowledge the pain but not give in to it. "We have to develop an inner capacity, an inner discipline so that traumatic knowledge doesn't destroy us. We must find ways to say, 'Yes, here you are again, this feeling of pain and hurt and desperation. But I know I can live with it. I can take the time to acknowledge it, take a deep breath, regain my

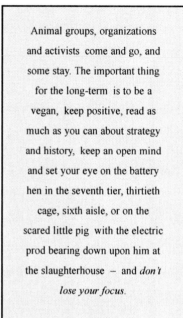

Animal groups, organizations and activists come and go, and some stay. The important thing for the long-term is to be a vegan, keep positive, read as much as you can about strategy and history, keep an open mind and set your eye on the battery hen in the seventh tier, thirtieth cage, sixth aisle, or on the scared little pig with the electric prod bearing down upon him at the slaughterhouse – and *don't lose your focus.*

Patty Mark

Satya magazine, September 2006

grounding, and then move forward.'"

Finally, she observes that traumatic knowledge causes us to feel needy, and that's okay, as long as we have a good support network. "We need so much," she says. "To win – that would be great – to be acknowledged for trying, to have more time and energy. But sometimes we bring that neediness *to* the animal-rights movement. In this sense, the animal-rights movement cannot meet our needs. We must be nourished elsewhere. Make sure you have loving, supportive friends who love you simply for who you are. Take time to exercise or develop a spiritual practice. Take time to rest.

"An example of my own traumatic knowledge was the realization thirty years ago that there was a connection between a patriarchal world and animal oppression. This knowledge needed to be expressed. This knowledge forced me to become a writer. Georgia O'Keefe said that as an artist she lived on the edge of a knife. I live on top of it as well. Traumatic knowledge is sharp, but it is powerful and it can empower us, if we can stay balanced upon it."

Avoiding Burnout

Take the effects of stress – such as fatigue, depression, diarrhea, confusion and anxiety – combine these with a failure to set limits, add a dash of guilt, and you've got a recipe for burnout. Burnout occurs when we ignore the warning signs of an impending emotional meltdown and continue to push ourselves too hard. We may want to be superheroes and never stop working for animals, but activists are animals too, at the mercy of bodies, minds and spirits that need constant nourishing. The threat of burning out follows us like a late-afternoon shadow, casting a dark presence over our efforts to shed light on a world of suffering. Fortunately, many hard-core activists have plenty to say about burnout.

"Burning out is not an option," declares Kate Fowler-Reeves. To ward off collapse, Kate recommends a tried-and-true tonic: friends. "Surround yourself with good, committed and compassionate people and they will buoy you up. Take a little time to be with animals – at a sanctuary, for example – and they will give you the strength to carry on. Don't wallow in the negatives. There is no point spending hours watching films of abuse if it does nothing more than depress you. You'd be better of spending the time writing campaign letters or organizing demos in your local town."

Take Your Time

"One thing I've been seeing in the movement is this attitude that the more you sacrifice, the cooler you are," says Dallas Rising, a personal coach who helps animal activists increase the effectiveness of their advocacy. "People may feel, 'The animals are suffering so much, how can I take time for myself?' They may also have some issues with actually enjoying themselves, because it is so guilt-inducing."

Dallas cautions activists against attempting to turn every hobby or interest outside the movement into an opportunity to help animals, and she uses as an example a time some years ago when she needed a break. "I thought, 'Maybe I should try running.' Then I thought, 'As long as I'm running, I may as well wear a t-shirt that says something about animals because I'm going to be out in public.'" Dallas ended up organizing a group of vegan and vegetarian runners called Team Veg, and it became another form of activism. "So there's a tendency for some to not be able to turn off that part of your brain that says 'How can I turn this into outreach?'"

Because working for animal rights has been Lisa Franzetta's full-time profession for most of her adult life, she's rationalized taking "time off" from activism in her free time – evenings and weekends. This attitude has helped her avoid burnout and fueled her activism. "I have total admiration for people who work all day, either for animals specifically or whatever their chosen career is, and then go to demonstrations and participate in other kinds of activism outside of work," she says. "For me, the way I've been able not to lose steam and to maintain a pretty consistent level of motivation through the years is to allow myself the time I'm not at work as free time to balance out my life a little."

Taking time for yourself is an aspect of setting healthy boundaries: "I'll do X and then I will enjoy Y." Without these limits, there is no life beyond activism; you are simply consumed by the struggle. "It's hard," says Mia MacDonald, "but I think people need to set limits: do as much as you can, but don't do so much, think so much, agonize or agitate so much that you get really exhausted, stressed, angry or despairing." Mia suggests having some regular activities outside of activism: "A hobby, an interest, a spiritual or physical practice that gives you a break, but that might also give you some more energy, some more equanimity when you are doing activism. Talk about being stressed or burned out with others – I think there's still a lot of shame about this – but try not to wallow. Take some active steps to get yourself back from the edge. Even take a nap sometimes if that's what it takes."

Michelle Johnson knows well the value of personal time. Before she took on the role of sanctuary supervisor at Animal Place, overseeing the care of more than three hundred farmed animals, Michelle worked at an animal shelter – a stressful job with one of the highest burnout rates of any profession. "I went through extreme burnout working there, and I learned that I have to take time for myself. This is something that is very hard for activists to do, because we want to put our whole heart and mind into what we are doing – to always put the animals first. But if we don't take care of ourselves, then we're no good to them." Well aware of her limits, Michelle now relaxes whenever she can. "I try to meditate on my lunch breaks, and I take hikes on the weekends – actually leaving the sanctuary. That way, when I come back I can really be present; I can be one hundred percent there."

Though it may be counter to your intuition on how best to help animals, giving yourself some time away from activism may be just the thing to enhance your long-term efforts. Julianna Baker was engaged in a number of campaigns and poring over animal-rights books while doing her graduate work. After years as an activist, she found herself growing progressively angrier at the egregious abuses perpetrated on the defenseless. She stepped back from activism for a year, avoiding the movement's literature but still advocating compassion and answering the questions of those inevitably drawn to her calm resolve. "I was actually better at promoting vegetarianism when I wasn't pissed off about what I was reading," says Julianna. "People don't like or respond to the 'angry vegan' or the 'angry activist.'"

Find a Good Fit

One of the best ways to avoid burning out is to match your style of campaigning with your interests and strengths, creating activism that nourishes you. Although Dawn Moncrief recommends pushing past comfort zones to increase your range – especially if you want a leadership role – knowing your comfort zone provides a safe space when needed. "Plus, not everyone wants to be a leader," she says. "Some people are better behind the scenes and some like the spotlight. Some people like to protest, while others like feed-ins or mainstream networking. Regardless, people can use their skills and interests for the cause. If they are working in their comfort zone, they're less likely to burn out."

Indeed, Zoe regards this as the *most important* approach to preventing burnout. She believes too many people sign up for a campaign without first assessing their skills and interests, as she found out the hard way. "When I first learned about animal exploitation, I wanted to do something," she says. "I called an animal-protection organization in the city I was living in and asked to be on their activist list." Zoe quickly received a call from the organization asking if she would leaflet. Although she had never leafleted before and didn't think she'd enjoy it, she convinced herself such thoughts were selfish and she should do it anyway – for the animals.

"So I leafleted ... and I hated it. People ignored me, or took my flier and threw it on the ground, or sneered at me. I was headed for burnout after my first effort at activism!" Rather than give up on activism altogether, Zoe relaxed long enough to evaluate her talents and passions, imagining what type of activism she would enjoy most. "I realized that I wanted to teach," she says, "and so I offered some week-long summer courses to secondary school students on animal and environmental issues. I *loved* teaching those courses; I discovered that I'd found my life's work – humane education – and that I could do this work forever. Not only have I not burnt out after twenty-plus years, but I am energized, heartened and enthused by my chosen form of change-making. It feeds me."

Zoe explains that each activist must discover this alchemy for themselves. "Some are energized by lobbying legislators, others by creating and executing campaigns, others by writing books, others by protesting and others by, yes, leafleting. It's not selfish to consider what your talents and interests are. The animals are served far better by someone doing work they love than by those doing work they think they *have* to do, but which they can't stand doing." It's these latter activists who are most likely to burn out, according to Zoe.

"A lot of times people feel frustrated because they have a preconceived notion of what the most effective form of activism is," says Dallas. "Take leafleting, for example. I'm a huge fan of Vegan Outreach, and I love leafleting – I think it's very effective, and I will recommend it for many activists who want to make a difference and don't have a lot of time; however, it's not for everybody, and sometimes the emphasis on what is effective for the movement can really be counterproductive for an individual. Some people are not comfortable with it or are not ready to do that kind of frontline work. So I work with individuals and ask, 'Okay, what are you really interested in?' I look for ways for them to use their natural talents and abilities and character traits to make a difference for animals in a way that really works and will be sustainable for them, because if you're out there trying to force yourself to leaflet and you're uncomfortable, you're going to shy away from it and there's a danger of losing that activist. For example, there's a guy in our community who is very interested in helping animals, but he's super shy. So he will drive activists to a crowded area, drop them off for leafleting and then come back and pick them up."

Make a Change
And what if you pursue your life's work for animals, yet still experience the stress and overwork that can lead to burnout? "It may be that you're ready for a change," advises Zoe. "You don't have to give up on making a

difference for animals, but you may need to find a different avenue. We all change and grow, and it's important to allow ourselves to grow in our activism too."

pattrice agrees with this attitude and acknowledges the many opportunities activists have to alter their efforts if burnout creeps up on them. "There's so much work to do on so many problems that you can give yourself a break from one set of problems by turning your attention to another," she says. "If you start to feel like you cannot possibly answer the same old arguments for vivisection yet again, maybe it's time to switch focus and work on factory farming instead. If you need to take a break from direct contact with animal suffering, work on global warming. If you're burned out on working with the public, work on behind-the-scenes research and let somebody else do the leafleting."

One reason activists engaging in a group effort may be reluctant to make a change is the fear of disappointing their peers, Dallas observes. "There's a feeling of scarcity in our movement: there's not enough people working on behalf of animals, there aren't enough vegans – or animal-rights groups may feel there aren't enough volunteers or not enough money – so there can be this experience of pressure that says 'I'm going to be letting everybody down if I give up this role.'" Dallas advises her clients who want to make a change within a group to write a detailed guide for someone else to be able to do that job well. "Also, you can make it known that you are available as a resource for anyone else who wants to step up."

Achievable Goals

A longtime activist, pattrice recommends remaining wary of spending too much time on problems without seeming to make a difference – another path to burnout. "To guard against that, individuals and organizations should make sure that their strategic plans include not only long-term aims that might not be achieved for decades, but also achievable short-term goals that can be acknowledged and celebrated when they are met."

Dallas suggests that activists break every campaign down to small pieces. "I mean *really* small pieces," she says. "For example, in Minneapolis there's a campaign that's been going on for seven years to ban circuses in the city limits. This is a *huge* undertaking. If the group had simply said, 'Well, we just want to get this banned, period,' that's such a far-off goal it would be really easy to lose sight, and they have a couple of times." So the group separated each of their objectives. "They took on simpler goals, like 'We really want to make sure that every single council member gets this information. We will have meetings with them, and we want to find out where they stand on the issue either way so that we can work on that.' That is a much more realistic and practical goal to set, and it helps to keep people motivated in the long run."

Even when your goals are achievable – such as handing out five hundred leaflets at a busy location in a couple of hours – remember to keep things in perspective and concentrate on the positive changes being made. "It's human nature to focus on the conflict," says activist Freeman Wicklund. "If we leaflet for several hours at a university, what stands out is the one person who flew off the handle and shouted and swore at us, not the hundreds of people who gladly accepted our brochures. As activists we need to see the positive changes that are going on around us every day for animals. Focus on the good conversation on vegetarianism that we had with the person at the bus stop who saw the button on our bag, not the one where our uncle waved away our valid concerns with a flippant 'They're here to be eaten!'"

Tips for Avoiding Burnout

In addition to the tips listed for relieving stress, consider this "ACTIVE" approach for beating burnout:

- **A**llow yourself to be human. Give yourself permission to fail; hard as we try, we don't win every battle. Take a real vacation.
- **C**reate a file or scrapbook of your activist achievements to remind yourself of the positive changes you've helped to bring about.
- **T**alk to other animal advocates whom you respect and trust; share your concerns and don't be afraid to open up about your fears. If necessary, talk to a therapist.
- **I**gnore graphic sights and sounds, including animal-rights magazines, newsletters and videos that feature upsetting text and visuals – at least

until you feel stronger.

• Visit an animal sanctuary. Many activists have never met a cow, chicken, pig, rabbit, turkey, goat or sheep. Treat yourself. These sanctuaries are home to animals rescued not only from slaughterhouses and factory farms, but from research labs, vet schools and the entertainment industry. Pet a lamb. Watch a former battery hen spread her wings and enjoy a dust bath. Rub a pig's belly. Get some face time with the faces you're working so hard to help.

• Exercise regularly. Consult your doctor if you're not sure how to begin; otherwise, get out there and sweat. Also consider walking, yoga or meditation. These will all do wonders for your mental well-being.

Humor

If Woody Allen's theorem that "Comedy equals tragedy plus time" were true, then animal abuse would have to be the richest source of humor for the last ten thousand years. But of course it's not. This doesn't prevent animal activists from laughing, though. Whether they're watching "The Simpsons," reading absurd stories in *The Onion* or simply unwinding with friends at the pub, activists recognize the importance of laughter and share it whenever they can.

Humor is one of the most effective coping mechanisms humans have. It has been shown to relieve tension, reduce anger and enhance our ability to carry on with tasks. Laughter even aids our physical well-being by increasing oxygen exchange, boosting our immune system and producing a high level of cognitive functioning.

The Power of Solidarity

Letting other activists know that you appreciate them and their efforts has enormous power, says activist coach Dallas Rising. "It reminds one another that we're making a difference." Dallas says such encouragement gives both parties more energy and helps sustain their activism. "Write a letter, send an email, make some cupcakes for the next meeting – whatever. People are often surprised others have taken notice, and it can strengthen the bond between people and counteract the peer pressure among activists."

Moreover, as you laugh, your brain releases endorphins – the body's natural painkillers. For activists working in campaigns with others, humor helps to break down hierarchies and build rapport: "Laughter is the shortest distance between two people," quipped the humorist Victor Borge. It's also one of the best tools activists have for managing stress.

Although Christine Morrissey has witnessed some of the worst animal abuse imaginable, she continues to move forward, enjoying the fellowship of animals and humans alike. I have yet to see her anything but upbeat about her activism (she also has a full-time job outside the movement). "Above all," she says, "laughter is the key to reducing or avoiding burnout. Also, spending time with family and friends is a perfect cure for stress."

"I need the humor to keep sane," says Jason Doucette, creator of the Vegan Porn blog site. "I doubt very much that I'd still be maintaining Vegan Porn if I didn't throw some jokes in the mix. The news is often depressing and infuriating, and while writing about it can be a means of venting and possibly calling others to action, I'm also spreading that depression and anger to my readers, which could lead to multiplying the burnout. I use humor to blunt the force of the blow when things get bad, while hopefully still respecting the seriousness of the issues. Also, a significant portion of visitors to the site aren't vegan, and the humor can catch people off guard if they've made the 'vegans equals angry' association in their mind and could lead some to re-think their position on vegans and veganism."

Her job managing the care of hundreds of animals sometimes takes a toll on Michelle Johnson. Chickens, pigs and turkeys bred in today's industrialized farms are not meant to live long, and their bodies suffer a variety of ailments and premature death at the sanctuary. While caring for an ill animal, Michelle says, humor helps keeps everyone's energy up. "Your focus so much of the day is on that sick animal. What I and the staff have found is that we don't need to stay in that place of sadness when the animal is sick; in fact, it's not even best for them. By laughing and joking about other things and being able to focus when you're other places in a more joyful state, when you come back with that animal, you're more present and able to do what needs to be done. I've found laughter really helps to keep moving through difficult times."

Death at the sanctuary hits everyone hard, but Michelle focuses on the positive. "When we lose an animal, we cry – it is a loss – but later we can talk about him and what we loved about him and we can keep going. We always remember that we were able to give them a wonderful life. Knowing we've given an animal the best life we could is a real comfort."

Other Emotions

Because activists are generally motivated by emotion – the love of animals, for example, or rage against companies practicing abuse – it is axiomatic that they are more likely to be especially sensitive to the pains that accompany the fight against indefensible cruelty. Grief, depression, anger and despair are all common feelings activists must learn to cope with.

"I think that one of the most important issues that any activist faces is dealing with dark emotions, specifically hatred, sorrow and rage," says Zoe. "We all know activists who are embittered, nasty and so enraged that they push everyone around them away. It's important to realize that this harms animals. We must model a message of kindness, compassion, integrity, honesty and love." As Zoe observes, no one wants to join a group of angry, hateful people unless they are angry and hateful themselves. "And, unfortunately, the image in many people's minds of animal activists is that they're misanthropes," she says. "We need to find a practice – whether it's meditating, praying, singing, dancing, being in nature or whatever – that enables us to be whole, joyful and emotionally healthy. The animals need this from us as much as they need our time and energy directed toward their liberation."

pattrice believes that much of the "burnout" activists feel is actually depression. She advises people to minimize their risk of depression by taking care of their body, maintaining healthy relationships with supportive people and finding ways to express and work with – rather than ignore or suppress – the natural feelings of anger and sadness that will arise in the course of activism. "If you do start to feel depressed, don't ignore it," she says. "Often something as simple as a vitamin supplement or talking to somebody about your feelings can bring relief."

Our Call to Action

Shortly after the battery hen rescue that begins this chapter, as I struggled with a variety of emotions, an art therapist offered me some advice. She recommended I take a box, a receptacle for all the pain I experienced on behalf of animals, and decorate it. So I painted a small wooden box with a chicken, goat, pig, cow and rabbit. When I am hurting, the therapist said, I should create something to represent the emotional thrashing my spirit is taking – a drawing, a poem or anything else that might speak to me in that moment of anguish – and place it in the box. The grief, sorrow or anger then resides in the box and is (in theory) no longer within me. What helped my healing most after the rescue, though, was the national media coverage we were able to garner after saving the lives of eighteen hundred hens. Many members of the public expressed their shock upon learning how battery hens are treated, and I suspect more than a few people were inspired to go veggie.

> We should rage against the dying of the light in every animal's eyes that results from human cruelty and abuse. The thing is to transform that pity and rage into one's case for animal rights. It's hard to burn out once we see ourselves as advocates with a case to put before the public. What matters is making the most of the opportunity of being on the right side, win or lose, while we are living.
>
> **Karen Davis**
> *Satya* magazine, July/August 2001

Although the work of the activist can be painful, the potential for emotional pain exists in nearly all rewarding work: firefighters, healthcare professionals, therapists, social workers and many others experience both the exhilaration and the stress that accompanies helping someone. Engaging in animal activism brings you a profound sense of satisfaction knowing your effort to relieve suffering is the right thing to do. The key to being an effective activist over the long haul is learning and embracing self care. If you remember only one thing from this chapter, let it be this: *Take care of yourself.* As Zoe says, "If we don't take care of ourselves, we're of no use to the animals, and we're terrible role models. Self care is part and parcel of activism."

Respect your limits – know how much you can take on and be prepared to take a holiday or shift the focus of your activism, if necessary. Megan Hartman, PETA's assistant director of international grassroots campaigns, believes that activists consistently guided by the misery of animals stand the best chance of succeeding. "Keep your eyes on the prize," she says. "Having a sense of humor, taking time for yourself and not letting your anger overwhelm you are all important, but the activists who have been most successful in not burning out are the people who have kept their focus on the suffering of animals."

The world of animal suffering is hidden from most of the world. As activists, we offer a gift not only to non-human animals, but to the people who live beneath a shroud of ignorance. Most people do not want to contribute to animal abuse – that's your weapon. Give a person some knowledge – throw some light into the dark recesses of animal factories, testing labs, puppy mills, circuses, fur farms, rodeos and all the other sources of misery – and be prepared to answer some questions about what you've shown them. You are the enlightened one, offering information that is both shocking and hopeful.

Unfortunately, those who profit from exploiting animals have weapons too, and they see each successful animal-rights campaign as a threat to their livelihood. As you read this, businesses with a financial interest in animal suffering are organizing their resources and creating strategies to combat activism. They have the deep pockets and political clout to try to maintain the status quo of consumer ignorance. What they do not have is integrity.

Being not just an activist but an effective activist over the long haul takes an abiding commitment – a conviction shared by each of the more than one hundred activists from around the world who contributed their time and thoughts to this book. If you're just beginning your activism, try out what seems comfortable to you. I hope one or more of the models presented here sounds appealing and that you now feel you have the information and resources to begin.

If you're already engaged at the vanguard of activism, I hope this book has inspired some new thinking in your struggle to reduce suffering – and some new approaches to sustaining yourself through the difficult times.

Wherever you are on your path, remember to celebrate each victory you help achieve for animals. As Hillary Rettig, author of *The Lifelong Activist*, observes, "It's recognizing and acknowledging the positive, not harping on the negative, that creates growth." So enjoy the successes more than you mourn the losses. If you need to, step back from the movement once in a while. And mind the words of pattrice jones: "Every successful social-change movement has involved a multiplicity of people using a multiplicity of tactics to approach a problem from a multiplicity of angles. Some people push against the bad things that need to be changed while others pull for the good alternatives. Some people work to undermine destructive systems from within while others are knocking down the walls from without. We all need to recognize that and find our place within a multifaceted struggle, being sure to be generous and appreciative of those who are working toward the same goals using different tactics."

Though the abuses of animals are myriad and the battles we must engage in on their behalf appear daunting, our goals *are* achievable. Moreover, if we are to nurse this ailing planet back to health, if we are to ensure no one goes to bed hungry, if we are to bequeath to future generations the promise of a lasting peace, then our vow should be to actively challenge the long-held view that animals exist for us to breed, eat, wear, experiment on, use for entertainment, sacrifice in the name of religion or exploit for any other human purpose. Their suffering is our call to action, and we must act for them. We must act for ourselves.

Resources

Aftershock
http://aftershock.pattricejones.info
Carol J. Adams
www.triroc.com/caroladams
Dallas Rising
www.dallasrising.com
Institute for Humane Education
http://humaneeducation.org

The Lifelong Activist
http://lifelongactivist.com
Mia MacDonald
www.miamacdonald.com
Zoe Weil
http://zoeweil.blogspot.com

APPENDIX A

RECENT MILESTONES FOR ANIMALS

• Vegetarianism is gaining in popularity: vegetarian restaurants, veg entrees in other restaurants and people switching to a plant-based diet are all increasing.

• Bans on veal crates and gestation crates have taken effect in the EU, the UK and in parts of the US.

• Beverage makers Coca-Cola, Pepsi and POM Wonderful have agreed to stop using animals to test their products.

• Clothing makers Tommy Hilfiger, J. Crew and Ralph Lauren have gone fur free.

• Mary Kay, Revlon and other cosmetics firms no longer test products on animals.

• Many school systems offer alternatives to dissection in science classes.

• The US has stopped breeding chimpanzees for research.

• Top fashion designer Marc Bouwer has launched a cruelty-free collection, eliminating fur, leather and wool.

• Chimp experimentation has been banned (legally) or abandoned (stopped in practice, but without laws) throughout the EU, New Zealand and Liberia.

• MasterCard, Visa and Sears have stopped sponsoring the Ringling Bros. and Barnum & Bailey Circus because of concerns about animal treatment.

• Chicago became the first US city to ban the sale of foie gras, while Denmark, Germany, Israel, the UK and other countries ban its production. California's ban on the sale and production of foie gras goes into effect in 2012.

• Zoos in Detroit, Chicago, New York, Philadelphia, San Francisco and other cities have stopped housing captive elephants.

• Live hare/rabbit coursing has been banned in many parts of the world, including England, Scotland, Wales and in some US states.

- McDonald's and Telstra Corporation stopped sponsoring rodeos in Australia.
- Campbell Soup Company and Pace Foods no longer sponsor rodeos in the US.
- Many universities, from Harvard to the University of Science and Technology of China, now offer programs in animal law.
- Many cities throughout Australia, Canada, Ireland, the UK, the US and other countries now ban animal acts, such as circuses.
- Major retail chains have stopped selling glue traps, devices that rip patches of skin off animals' bodies as they struggle to escape and cause them to suffer for days until they die of starvation or dehydration.
- Panasonic stopped sponsoring the annual Iditarod sled dog race.
- Fox hunting with hounds is banned in England and Wales.
- Cities throughout the world ban rodeos.
- College and corporate dining halls continue to eliminate the use of eggs from hens confined in battery cages.
- Fur farming is banned in the UK.
- Abercrombie & Fitch, J. Crew, Limited Brands and many other retailers have stopped buying wool from mulesed or live exported Australian sheep.
- More than one hundred jurisdictions nationwide, including the entire state of California, have passed legislation restricting or banning the tethering of dogs.
- PETCO agreed to stop selling large birds in their stores and make provisions for the millions of rats and mice in their care – a precedent-setting victory for all animals suffering in the pet trade.
- The Balearic Islands have supported a legal statement (the equivalent of a resolution) that favors granting great apes basic rights, and a similar proposal is going before Spanish parliament soon.

APPENDIX B

ELEVEN THINGS YOU CAN DO TODAY

TO HELP ANIMALS

1. Go vegan. If you can't, try giving up meat, eggs and dairy products one day a week, then add another day every week.

2. Set up an account with a site like iGive.com or goodsearch.com, which allow you to support animal groups with a percentage of your online shopping.

3. Contact a local animal shelter or sanctuary and ask about volunteering.

4. Order leaflets from PETA or Vegan Outreach; begin leafleting when they arrive (see Chapter 1).

5. Ask your school cafeteria or one of your favorite restaurants to carry (more) vegan or vegetarian entrees (see Chapter 6).

6. Write a letter to the editor of your local paper (see Chapter 2).

7. Visit your local bookstore and pick up a book on animal rights.

8. Visit cok.net, humaneeating.com, mercyforanimals.org or peta.org and order a veggie starter kit; give it to a meat-eating friend.

9. If you have companion animals who are not spayed or neutered, make an appointment with their veterinarian to have this done, or ask your parents to.

10. Order buttons and shirts with anti-cruelty messages from PETA, Compassionate Cooks, Pangea, etc.

11. Include a signature line in your email with links to one or two of your favorite animal-rights videos or current campaigns.

APPENDIX C

KNOW YOUR RIGHTS

Police powers and a citizen's legal rights obviously differ from country to country. This section offers some basic guidelines and advice from legal groups in Australia, Canada, New Zealand, South Africa, the United Kingdom and the United States, but this is not meant as legal advice from a qualified professional. This is for information purposes only.

Australia
Source: Legal Aid – Western Australia

Police Powers
The information below sets out the powers of police to arrest, hold, search and question you.

It is important to understand what your legal rights and obligations are in these circumstances.

If you have been arrested, it is important that you speak with a lawyer as soon as you can.

Arrest
When can the police make an arrest?
The police can arrest you without a warrant if they reasonably believe or suspect that you have broken the law. Most arrests are made without a warrant.

An arrest may be lawful even if you have not committed an offense.

What do the police have to do to make an arrest?
When the police make an arrest they should:
- Tell you that you are under arrest
- Tell you why you are being arrested
- Touch you and ask you to accompany them or to stay at a certain place.

If you resist or struggle, you can be charged with obstructing police. A police officer can use as much force as is reasonably necessary to restrain a person, affect an arrest or execute a warrant.

Reasonable Force

If you think that unreasonable force has been used, or if you have been injured by the police, you should:

- Report the matter to the officer in charge of the police station straight away. A written complaint that is dated and signed is best but at least a verbal report should be made.
- Have a doctor examine and document your injuries as soon as possible. If possible have photographs taken of your injuries.
- Get legal advice about your situation.

What should you do if you are arrested?

If you are arrested, you should:

- Confirm that you are under arrest and ask the police what charges are being laid against you.
- Keep calm and be polite. If you resist arrest and are abusive, other charges may be laid against you.
- Ask to make a telephone call and phone your lawyer, a relative or a friend. It is *not* your right to be allowed a telephone call. However, if you ask you may be allowed to make a telephone call.

Do you have to answer questions?

Generally you do not have to answer questions, sign a statement or take part in a video interview.

You *must*, however, provide your name and address, date of birth and, if the police request, your current address as well as the address at which you normally reside if they are different.

You should generally get legal advice before answering any questions, whether or not you have been arrested. In some circumstances you are required to provide the police with information.

Anything you do say or sign will probably be used as evidence in court.

What rights do the police have to search?

The police can stop, search and detain (hold) any person or vehicle, if they reasonably believe that:

- An offence has been committed
- An offence is about to be committed or
- You are carrying something relating to an offence.

Generally the police may search your premises if you agree or if they have a search warrant. In certain circumstances the police may enter premises *without* a warrant.

You should obtain legal advice after the police have conducted a search of your premises.

The police are allowed to search a person and any property in their possession once they have been arrested.

The police can have your body searched and this usually must be done by a medical practitioner or a nurse.

Search Warrants

The laws relating to search warrants and searching a person can be complex. Often different laws will apply, depending on the situation. If the police have searched your body, belongings or premises, and you want to know if it was lawful for them to do this, you should get legal advice.

If the police have a reasonable suspicion that a person has committed a crime, they can enter a property without a warrant to make an arrest.

Once you have been arrested, the police can search you and any property you have in your possession.

If the police have reasonable grounds to suspect that someone has committed certain offences under the Misuse of Drugs Act, they have very wide powers, which include entering onto a premises without a search warrant and searching your person and your property.

Canada

Source: The Canadian Charter of Rights and Freedoms

Section 10 - Rights when arrested

If you are arrested or detained, you must be given reasons for this right away. The police must tell you of your right to a lawyer. If you say you want a lawyer, police must stop questioning you until you have a chance to speak with a lawyer privately. If your detention is not legal, you must be released.

Section 11 - Rights when charged with an offense

Section 11 rights are basic principles of criminal law – like being presumed innocent, the right to a speedy trial and the independence of the Courts.

If you are charged with a criminal offense you have the right:
- To be informed of the offence without unreasonable delay
- To a trial in a reasonable time
- To be silent (the right not to testify at your own trial)
- To be presumed innocent until proven guilty
- To a fair and public hearing by an impartial and independent court
- To reasonable bail (unless there is good reason to be refused bail)
- To trial by jury for serious crimes (except for military offences decided by a military tribunal)
- Not to be convicted of a crime unless the act was a crime at the time it happened
- Not to be tried or punished twice for the same crime (the rule against double jeopardy)

If the law has changed between the time an offence happened and time of sentencing, a person has a right to be sentenced under the law where the punishment is less.

Section 12 - Protection from cruel and unusual punishment

People are protected from cruel and unusual punishment such as punishment that degrades human dignity, is out of all proportion to the offence, or shocks the public conscience.

Section 13 - Protection from self-incrimination

If you are a witness, what you say in court cannot be used against you in another court case. But if you are charged with perjury, what you said in court can be used to prove perjury.

Section 14 - Right to an interpreter

You have the right to an interpreter in a courtroom if you are a party or a witness in a case and do not understand or speak the language used in the court. You also have this right if you are hearing impaired.

New Zealand

Source: The Auckland Council for Civil Liberties

Questioning, Detention and Arrest

If the police stop you or question you but you are not sure what to say or do: Tell them that you want to contact a lawyer, or your parents, or someone you trust. Stay calm and do not argue with the police.

What personal details should you give to the police?

Although you don't have to give any details to the police in many situations, these days it is advisable, if questioned, to give your name, address, age, i.e., basic identifying information only. If you're driving, you must stop and give your name, address and date of birth. You must also state if you are the owner of the car and, if not, who is. If you are a young person in a place serving alcohol, you can be asked for identification, or proof of age. If you refuse, you may commit an offense.

Should you give other information?

You are not obliged to give any other information to the police. You have a right to remain silent. It is usually better to say nothing in reply to police questions until you have consulted a lawyer, or your family, or a friend. You are not obliged to provide a written statement. If you say anything to the police, they may later use what you say against you. Be careful that any statement you do make is exactly what you mean to say. Don't lie. Make sure you read and correct the statement before signing it.

When do you have to accompany the police?

You do not have to go anywhere with a police officer if you do not want to, unless you are under arrest or are held by the police under a law that gives them the power to detain you. Examples of detention powers are where they suspect you have been drinking and driving, or the police suspect you may have drugs on you.

If the police are questioning your friend, and your friend asks for your advice, make sure your advice is as accurate as possible. If you offer advice without being asked by your friend, you might be arrested for obstructing the police (i.e., if they think your "advice" has made their work more difficult). Always get the officer's ID number.

What are your rights if the police want to arrest or detain you?

You have the basic right not to be arbitrarily arrested or detained. If you are arrested or held by the police, you have the right to be informed at the time of the reason why, and of your right to talk with and instruct a lawyer without delay. The police are required to inform you of that right. If you are arrested or detained, you have the right not to make a statement. The police must inform you of that right. When you are arrested, the police must charge you promptly or release you. If the police do not release you then you have the right to be brought as soon as possible before a court.

You also have the right to challenge whether your arrest or detention is lawful. If your release or detention is found not to be lawful, you must be released immediately.

When you are held against your will in any form of custody (be it by the police or any other enforcement agency), you have the right to be treated decently and with respect to your dignity.

(NZ Bill of Rights Act 1990, sections 22 and 23.)

ARREST

Always ask the police "Am I under arrest?" If the answer is "No," ask if you are free to go. If they say "No," ask what power they are detaining you under. They have to tell you whether you are under arrest. If you are under arrest or detained under a specific law, you will enjoy the full protection of the Bill of Rights.

If the police arrest you, how much force can they use?

They can use whatever force is reasonable to get you to go with them. If you think the police are arresting you unlawfully, tell them at every opportunity, but go quietly. If you resist arrest, you may be arrested either on a charge of resisting arrest, or for obstructing the police in the execution of their duty.

If you have been arrested unlawfully, you may be able to complain later to the police, or to the Police Complaints Authority, or even bring court proceedings against the police if, for example, they have breached your rights under the Bill of Rights. Alternatively, if the police have breached your rights under the Bill of Rights, they may not be able to use the evidence they have obtained later in court.

AT THE POLICE STATION

If you haven't already been arrested

It's your decision whether you answer any questions or make any written or spoken statement. You don't have to do so. It's always best to contact a lawyer before saying anything or making any form of written statement. You may leave the police station when you wish. (But if you're there for a breath or blood alcohol test and leave before the test has been completed, you will commit an offence and probably be arrested.)

Remember that if you are not under arrest, e.g., you are "helping the police with their inquiries," you may not be protected by the rights contained in the Bill of Rights.

If you have been arrested

You can be searched, fingerprinted and photographed. Palmprints and footprints can also be taken. You must give your name, address, date and place of birth, and occupation. Other than supplying identifying particulars, you have the right to remain silent and the right to consult and instruct a lawyer without delay. Ask to be allowed to contact your lawyer or family as soon as you arrive at the station; keep asking until the police let you.

What are your rights after you have been formally charged with an offence?

Under section 24 of the Bill of Rights, you have the right to:

- Be informed promptly and in detail of the nature of the charge.
- Be released on reasonable terms and conditions unless the police give good reasons for wanting to continue to hold you in custody.
- Consult and instruct a lawyer (under the Bill of Rights, people have a right to consult and instruct a lawyer at the time of arrest. Most people may have exercised this right before they are formerly charged). The police should contact the lawyer you wish to see. There should be a list of legal aid lawyers at the police station. Contact one of them if you don't have a lawyer.
- Free assistance of an interpreter.

Police Rules state that normally a friend or a relative named by you is to be told by the police that you've been arrested. Usually a friend or relative is allowed to visit you.

Can you waive any of the rights given you by the Bill of Rights?

YES, but you should never "give away" your rights without first getting independent legal advice. Make it very clear to the police that you are not waiving any of your rights.

Bail

Ask for police bail, which will allow you to leave the police station. You should always ask for bail. You don't have an automatic right to be bailed by the police, but in many cases bail can be given. You'll then have to appear in court the next day. If denied bail by the police, you should demand to be taken in front of a court as soon as possible.

Privacy of discussions with your lawyer

Any discussion you have with your lawyer should be in private unless the police put forward a very strong reason as to why they need to watch over you (e.g., for security reasons). You do not need to ask for privacy in talking with your lawyer. However, it is better to ask for privacy, because if you don't a court might say that any breach of your privacy was inconsequential. If you are not allowed a private talk with your lawyer, this may be a breach of the Bill of Rights.

Do young persons have any special rights when questioned by the police regarding an offence?

YES. For example, if they are arrested and under 17, they are entitled to have a lawyer and their parent/guardian, or some other adult nominated by them, present during any interview with the police. The young person is entitled to speak to these persons prior to answering questions (Children, Young Persons and Their Families Act 1989, sections 215-232). Ask the police what additional rights you have as a young person.

COMPLAINTS

Try to get a name and badge number of any police officer you wish to complain about. Ask the officer to provide identification. They have to give you this information. If you have been injured, ask to see a doctor of your choice, and obtain photos of your injuries as soon as possible. Write out a full description of what you want to complain about. This statement will be important and valuable. If your complaint is serious you'll want a lawyer to help you. See the lawyer as soon as you possibly can. When dealing with the police over your complaint, take a lawyer or support person with you. You can:

- Discuss your complaint with the senior police officer attached to the main police station in the area.
- Make a formal complaint to the Police Complaints Authority, 7th Floor, Local Government Buildings, 114-118 Lambton Quay (PO Box 5025, Wellington), phone 0800 503 728.

Search

You have a basic legal right to be secure against any unreasonable search or seizure of yourself, your property, or your correspondence (Bill of Rights, section 21).

When can the police search you or your property?
The police can search you, or your car, or your property, if you agree. You should always ask the police what they are searching for and whether you can refuse. A police officer has no general right of search or entry onto private property, without a search warrant. If the police have a warrant, they must show it to you. The search warrant must specify what is to be searched and what offence, or offences, the warrant relates to. The police can only search for and seize items specified in the warrant. The police can use reasonable force to carry out the warrant. If you refuse to let them in, you will most likely be arrested for obstructing them. If they have a warrant, they can even search your home when you are not there.

When can the police search you without a warrant?
The police have the right to search you or your property without a warrant where they have arrested you, or have, e.g., reasonable grounds to believe that you are in possession of drugs or offensive weapons, or they have reasonable grounds to suspect that you have firearms or explosives.

Many provisions give the police and other law enforcement officers, wide powers of search without a warrant. If the police claim they have a power to search without a warrant, always ask them to specify what that power is.

After you have been arrested, the police can search you, your property (e.g., your handbag, your motor vehicle and even your house), if they think, e.g., there is evidence which could be destroyed, or if they think you could get access to a weapon. (The law is unclear in this area.)

At the police station they will usually ask you to empty your pockets. They can even do a body search in certain circumstances. Where they suspect you may have drugs secreted within your body, they may be able to do an internal search of you (by police doctor). However, you don't need to agree to these searches, although certain penalties may apply if you refuse.

Note: Even if the police act illegally in searching you or your property, this does not necessarily mean that the search will amount to a breach of section 21 of the Bill of Rights. The evidence obtained as a result of the illegal search may still be admissible against you.

South Africa

Source: Bill of Rights, South Africa

(Section 35: ARRESTED, DETAINED AND ACCUSED PERSONS)

1) Everyone who is arrested for allegedly committing an offence has the right
    a. to remain silent;
    b. to be informed promptly
        i. of the right to remain silent; and
        ii. of the consequences of not remaining silent;
    c. not to be compelled to make any confession or admission that could be used in evidence against that person;
    d. to be brought before a court as soon as reasonably possible, but not later than
        i. 48 hours after the arrest; or
        ii. the end of the first court day after the expiry of the 48 hours, if the 48 hours expire outside ordinary court hours or on a day which is not an ordinary court day;
    e. at the first court appearance after being arrested, to be charged or to be informed of the reason for the detention to continue, or to be released; and
    f. to be released from detention if the interests of justice permit, subject to reasonable conditions.
2) Everyone who is detained, including every sentenced prisoner, has the right
    a. to be informed promptly of the reason for being detained;
    b. to choose, and to consult with, a legal practitioner, and to be informed of this right promptly;
    c. to have a legal practitioner assigned to the detained person by the state and at state expense, if substantial injustice would otherwise result, and to be informed of this right promptly;
    d. to challenge the lawfulness of the detention in person before a court and, if the detention is unlawful, to be released;
    e. to conditions of detention that are consistent with human

dignity, including at least exercise and the provision, at state expense, of adequate accommodation, nutrition, reading material and medical treatment; and

   f.   to communicate with, and be visited by, that person's

      i.   spouse or partner;

      ii. next of kin;

      iii. chosen religious counselor; and

      iv. chosen medical practitioner.

3) Every accused person has a right to a fair trial, which includes the right

   a.   to be informed of the charge with sufficient detail to answer it;

   b.   to have adequate time and facilities to prepare a defense;

   c.   to a public trial before an ordinary court;

   d.   to have their trial begin and conclude without unreasonable delay;

   e.   to be present when being tried;

   f.   to choose, and be represented by, a legal practitioner, and to be informed of this right promptly;

   g.   to have a legal practitioner assigned to the accused person by the state and at state expense, if substantial injustice would otherwise result, and to be informed of this right promptly;

   h.   to be presumed innocent, to remain silent, and not to testify during the proceedings;

   i.   to adduce and challenge evidence;

   j.   not to be compelled to give self-incriminating evidence;

   k.   to be tried in a language that the accused person understands or, if that is not practicable, to have the proceedings interpreted in that language;

   l.   not to be convicted for an act or omission that was not an offence under either national or international law at the time it was committed or omitted;

   m. not to be tried for an offence in respect of an act or omission for which that person has previously been either acquitted or convicted;

n. to the benefit of the least severe of the prescribed punishments if the prescribed punishment for the offence has been changed between the time that the offence was committed and the time of sentencing; and

o. of appeal to, or review by, a higher court.

4) Whenever this section requires information to be given to a person, that information must be given in a language that the person understands.

5) Evidence obtained in a manner that violates any right in the Bill of Rights must be excluded if the admission of that evidence would render the trial unfair or otherwise be detrimental to the administration of justice.

United Kingdom

Source: "No Comment: The Defendant's Guide to Arrest"

WHEN YOU HAVE BEEN ARRESTED

You have to give the police your name and address. You will also be asked for your date of birth – you don't have to give it, but it may delay your release as it is used to run a check on the police national computer. They also have the right to take your fingerprints, photo and non-intimate body samples (a saliva swab, to record your DNA). These will be kept on file, even if you are not charged.

The Criminal Justice and Public Order Act 1994 removed the traditional Right to Silence; however, all this means is that the police/prosecution can point to your refusal to speak to them, when the case comes to court, and the court *may* take this as evidence of your guilt. The police cannot force you to speak or make a statement, whatever they may say to you in the station. Refusing to speak cannot be used to convict you by itself.

If you are arrested under the Terrorism Act 2000, the police can keep you in custody for longer. They have already used this against protestors and others to intimidate them. Remember being arrested is not the same as being charged. Keeping silent is still the best thing to do in police custody.

Q: What happens when I get arrested?

When you are arrested, you will usually be handcuffed, put in a van and taken to a police station. You will be asked your name, address and date of birth. You should be told the reason for your arrest – remember what is said, it may be useful later. Your personal belongings will be taken from you. These are listed on the custody record and usually you will be asked to sign to say that the list is correct. You do not have to sign, but if you do, you should sign immediately below the last line, so that the cops can't add something incriminating to the list. You should also refuse to sign for something which isn't yours, or which could be incriminating.

You will also be asked if you want a copy of PACE (the Police and Criminal Evidence Act codes of practice). Your fingerprints, photo and saliva swab will be taken, then you will be placed in a cell until the police are ready to deal with you. DO NOT PANIC!

Q. What if I am under 18?

There has to be an "appropriate adult" present for the interview. The cops will always want this to be your mum or dad, but you might want to give the name of an older brother or sister or other relative or adult friend (though the cops may not accept a friend). If you don't have anyone, they will get a social worker – this might cause you more problems afterwards.

Q: When can I contact a solicitor?

You should be able to ring a solicitor as soon as you're arrested. Once at the police station it is one of the first things you should do, for two reasons:

1. To have someone know where you are.

2. To show the cops you are not going to be a soft target – they may back off a bit.

It is advisable to avoid using the duty solicitor; instead, find the number of a good solicitor in your area and memorize it. The police are wary of decent solicitors. Any good solicitor will provide free advice at the police station. Also, avoid telling your solicitor much about what happened. This can be sorted out later. For the time being, tell them you are refusing to speak. Your solicitor can come into the police station while the police interview you: you should refuse to be interviewed unless your solicitor is present.

Q: What is an interview?
An interview is the police questioning you about the offenses they want to charge you with. The interview will take place in an interview room in the police station and should be taped.

AN INTERVIEW IS ONLY OF BENEFIT TO THE POLICE.

Remember they want to prosecute you for whatever charge they can stick on you.

AN INTERVIEW IS A NO WIN SITUATION. For your benefit, the only thing to be said in an interview is "NO COMMENT."

REMEMBER: They can't legally force you to speak. Beware of attempts to interview you in the cop van or cell as all interviews are now recorded. The cops may try to pretend you confessed before the taped interview. Again say "NO COMMENT."

Q: Why do the police want me to answer questions?
If the police think they have enough evidence against you they will not need to interview you.

Q: But what if the evidence looks like they have got something on me? Wouldn't it be best to explain away the circumstances I was arrested in, so they'll let me go?
The only evidence that matters is the evidence presented in court to the magistrate or jury. The only place to explain everything is in court; if they've decided to keep you in, no amount of explaining will get you out. If the police have enough evidence, anything you say can only add to this evidence against you. When the cops interview someone, they do all they can to confuse and intimidate you. The questions may not be related to the crime. Their aim is to soften you up, get you chatting. Don't answer a few small talk questions and then clam up when they ask you a question about the crime. It looks worse in court.

To prosecute you, the police must present their evidence to the Crown

Prosecution Service. A copy of the evidence is sent to your solicitor. The evidence usually rests on very small points: this is why it's important not to give anything away in custody. They may say your refusal to speak will be used against you in court, but the best place to work out what you want to say is later with your solicitor. If they don't have enough evidence, the case will be thrown out or never even get to court. This is why they want you to speak. They need all the evidence they can get. One word could cause you a lot of trouble.

Q: So I've got to keep my mouth shut. What tricks can I expect the police to pull in order to make me talk?
The police try to get people to talk in many devious ways. The following shows some pretty common examples, but remember they may try some other line on you.

- *"Come on now, we know it's you; your mate's in the next cell and he's told us the whole story."*

If they've got the story, why do they need your confession? Playing co-accused off against each other is a common trick, as you've no way of checking what other people are saying. If you are up to something dodgy with other people, work out a story and stick to it. Don't believe it if they say your co-accused has confessed.

- *"We know it's not you, but we know you know who's done it. Come on, Jane, don't be silly; tell us who did it"*

The cops will use your first name to try to seem as though they're your friends. If you are young they will act in a fatherly/motherly way, etc.

- *"We'll keep you in 'til you tell us."*

They have to put you before the magistrate or release you within 36 hours (or seven days if arrested under the Terrorism Act). Only a magistrate can order you to be held without charge for any longer.

- *"There is no right to silence anymore. If you don't answer questions the judge will know you're guilty."*

Refusing to speak cannot be used to convict you by itself. If they had enough evidence they wouldn't be interviewing you.

- *"You've been nicked under the Terrorism Act, so you've got no rights."*

More mental intimidation and all the more reason to say "NO COMMENT."

• *Mr. Nice (good cop): "Hiya, what's it all about, then? Sergeant Smith says you're in a bit of trouble. He's a bit wound up with you. You tell me what happened and Smith won't bother you. He's not the best of our officers; he loses his rag every now and again. So what happened?"*

Mr. Nice (good cop) is as devious as Mr. Nasty (bad cop) is. He or she will offer you a cuppa, cigarettes, a blanket. It's the softly-softly approach. It's bollocks. "NO COMMENT."

• *"Look, we've tried to contact your solicitor, but we can't get hold of them. It's going to drag on for ages this way. Why don't we get this over with so you can go home?"*

Never accept an interview without your solicitor present, a bit more time now may save years later! Don't make a statement even if your solicitor advises you to – a good one won't.

• *"You're obviously no dummy. I'll tell you what – we'll do a deal. You admit to one of the charges, and we'll drop the other two. We'll recommend to the judge that you get a non-custodial sentence, because you've co-operated. How does that sound?"*

There are no deals to be made with the police. Much as they'd like to, the police don't control the sentence you get.

• *"Wasting police time is a serious offense."*

You can't be charged for wasting police time for not answering questions. The cops may rough you up, or use violence to get a confession (true or false) out of you. There are many examples of people being fitted up and physically assaulted until they admitted to things they hadn't done. It's your decision to speak rather than face serious injury. Just remember, what you say could get you and others sent down for a very long time. However, don't rely on retracting a confession in court – it's hard to back down once you've said something.

In the police station, the cops rely on a person's naïveté. If you are aware of the tricks they play, the chances are they'll give up on you. Having said nothing in the police station, you can then look at the evidence and work out your side of the story.

Additional Information

Source: FreeBEAGLES Legal Resource Centre, UK

UK laws that could affect animal activists include:

Home Demos

Section 42 of the Criminal Justice and Police Act 2001 enables the police to impose conditions on demonstrations taking place outside someone's home. Much was made of this new law at the time, as it was supposed to be one of the government's "package of measures" designed to stop animal rights extremism. But it has quickly become apparent that this law has had very little impact on home demos, and after intensive lobbying by the pharmaceutical industry and the police, the government have announced plans to make these kinds of demos illegal.

Section 42 confers power on a police officer to impose directions verbally on persons demonstrating in the "vicinity" of someone's dwelling, if he reasonably believes that they are there to protest against the actions of the resident of the dwelling or anyone else, and that their presence amounts to or is likely to cause harassment, alarm or distress to the resident. This includes the power to direct you to leave the vicinity immediately. An officer can ask you to leave even if your behavior is entirely peaceful, so long as you're in the vicinity of a dwelling. He can also impose conditions on the demonstration stating where it may take place and how many people may take part.

Aggravated Trespass

Section 68 of the Criminal Justice and Public Order Act 1994 (CJA) defines the offense as follows: *A person commits aggravated trespass if he trespasses on land with the intention of disrupting, or intimidating those taking part in, lawful activity taking place on that or adjacent land.*

Notes on Aggravated Trespass

Aggravated trespass can now take place inside as well as outside buildings. The offence was introduced in 1994 to deal with the problem caused to blood sports enthusiasts by hunt saboteurs. However, it has been widely used against other animal rights activists and road protestors as well. Section 59 of the Anti-Social Behavior Bill has amended Section 68 of the CJA, so that now aggravated trespass can occur inside as well as outside buildings. This amendment was introduced after intensive lobbying of the government by the police and the pharmaceutical industry to give them new powers to deal with office occupations by animal-rights activists and others. Previously the police only had the power to remove such protestors from the building or to arrest them for breach of the peace. They now have a specific power of arrest to deal with the trespass itself.

The law states that you cannot commit the offence from a public highway, but you may commit the offense from a public footpath or bridleway. This is because the right to use such footpaths and bridleways generally extends only to the right of passage along them. Any other act can amount to trespass.

Intending something to happen is not the same as wanting it to happen. If the prosecution can show, for example, that you knew that an office occupation would disrupt activity, then this will be enough to show that you intended it, regardless of whether you in fact wanted or desired the disruption.

You cannot be prosecuted for aggravated trespass where no actual activity is taking place to disrupt. The High Court has ruled that Section 68 CJA created a public order offence designed to deal with people disrupting persons actually engaged in lawful activity. It cannot, therefore, be used against activists, for example, who set off unattended badger traps, thus preventing the badger from entering the trap.

Arrest and Punishment

Aggravated trespass carries a maximum sentence of three months imprisonment or a fine. It is not an "arrestable offense," but the act confers a statutory power of arrest on an officer in uniform who suspects you of committing the offence.

The CPS is not been keen on the offence, as they have to show that the accused intended the offence, which is often difficult to prove in court. The police used it extensively during one animal rights campaign and failed to secure a single conviction! However, now that the power can be used to deal with office occupations, protestors can expect it to be used more widely.

Civil Trespass

If the premises are open to the public – e.g., a shop or a bank – then you have an implied license, i.e., permission to enter, and you are not trespassing. Similarly in the case of somebody's home, you have an implied permission to walk up their driveway and to knock on the front door.

However, if you are asked to leave by the occupier of the house or shop and you refuse, then you become a trespasser. And if you enter a building or part of a building which is clearly marked "Staff Only" or you jump over a security gate in order to gain entry to premises, then there is no implied license to enter and you are trespassing immediately.

The police have been known to demand peoples' details while they are trespassing, so that they can hand them over to the occupier. They have no right to demand them for this purpose and you do not have to comply with such a request. A landowner may use reasonable force to move you from his premises, and anyone – the police included – may assist him with this.

Burglary

Section 9(1)(a) of the Theft Act 1968 states:
A person is guilty of burglary if he enters a building as a trespasser with intent to either:

i) steal
ii) inflict GBH on someone
iii) rape someone or
iv) inflict criminal damage

This is therefore a much wider offense than many people realize. To justify an arrest, all the police need to say is that they reasonably suspected that you entered as trespasser with intent to inflict criminal damage. They do not have to suspect "breaking and entry" which would be a separate offence of criminal damage.

The police now have far greater powers to deal with aggravated trespass than they did before as this can now be used to deal with activity disrupted inside as well as outside buildings. However, there will be occasions where no one is actually present when the trespass occurs, and in these cases the police might use burglary when they have little or nothing else to justify an arrest.

Burglary is an "arrestable offense" under Section 24 PACE, and therefore carries all the additional powers conferred by that. Of course you are unlikely to get charged with burglary unless you actually do steal, or cause criminal damage, etc. You may well be able to sue the police for wrongful arrest and unlawful imprisonment afterward, if the police cannot give adequate reasons for believing that you intended to inflict criminal damage, etc.

Obstruction of the Highway

Section 137 of the Highways Act 1980 makes it an offense to cause a willful obstruction of the highway without lawful authority or excuse.

Many animal rights stalls and assemblies may cause an obstruction, but the key legal point is whether or not there is a "lawful excuse" for the obstruction.

Once it was the case that there could only be a lawful excuse for obstructing the highway where you were using it for passage or re-passage and for ancillary matters, for example stopping to read a map. But more recent case decisions have interpreted the right to use the highway much more liberally, so as to include, for example, the handing out of leaflets, assembling and collecting for charity. Nowadays the courts are much more mindful of the exercise of European convention rights when deciding whether or not an obstruction has been caused.

It follows that it is not necessarily the case that an animal rights stall or a picket outside a shop on the highway is causing an unlawful obstruction, even though the police and council officials often maintain that it is. Leading cases state that all the circumstances must be considered in determining whether the obstruction was unlawful, including the duration, the purpose of the obstruction and its extent on to the highway.

One of the key purposes which the courts must consider in deciding whether or not there is a reasonable excuse for causing an obstruction is whether or not it involves the exercise of one or more ECHR convention rights, for example the right to freedom of expression under Article 10.

Now that the police are legally bound to respect your rights under the European Convention on Human Rights, they have to interpret their powers so as to be consistent with those rights. And the courts must, wherever possible, interpret all legislation so as to be consistent.

In a case that went to the High Court in 2003, an anti-war protestor had erected a number of placards in Parliament Square in London. These placards protruded by one and a half feet onto a highway eleven feet wide. The council sought an injunction against him in the High Court prohibiting him from obstructing the highway. The court ruled that he had willfully obstructed the highway, but that the obstruction was reasonable in all the circumstances. The injunction was refused.

You cannot be arrested for obstruction where you are simply walking along the highway, unless you are blocking a main road. The courts have ruled that unlawful activity could never be regarded as "reasonable" for the purpose of the act.

Although breach of Section 137 is not strictly speaking an "arrestable offense," the police can arrest you to prevent an obstruction of the highway using their general power of arrest under Section 25 of PACE.

For more information, visit www.freebeagles.org.

United States

Dealing with the Police: General Guidelines for Activists
Source: The National Lawyers Guild, New York, NY

I. In General
When dealing with the police, park rangers, health officers or other law enforcement officers (collectively referred to as "police"), keep your hands in view and don't make sudden movements. Avoid walking behind the police. Never touch the police or their equipment (vehicles, flashlights, animals, etc.).

II. Police Encounters

There are three basic types of encounters with the police: Conversation, Detention and Arrest.

Conversation: When the police are trying to get information, but don't have enough evidence to detain or arrest you, they'll try to get the information from you. They may call this a "casual encounter" or a "friendly conversation." If you talk to them, you may give them the information they need to arrest you or your friends. In most situations, it's better and safer to refuse to talk to police.

Detention: Police can detain you only if they have *reasonable suspicion* that you are involved in a crime. (A "reasonable suspicion" occurs when an officer can point to specific facts that provide some objective manifestation that the person detained may be involved in criminal activity.) Detention means that, though you aren't arrested, you can't leave. Detention is supposed to last a short time and they aren't supposed to move you. During detention, the police can pat you down and may be able to look into your bag to make sure you don't have any weapons. They aren't supposed to go into your pockets unless they first feel a weapon through your clothing.

If the police are asking questions, ask if you are being detained. If not, leave and say nothing else to them. If you are being detained, you may want to ask why. Then you should say: *"I am going to remain silent. I want a lawyer,"* and nothing else.

A detention can easily turn into arrest. If the police are detaining you and they get information that you are involved in a crime, they will arrest you, even if it has nothing to do with your detention. The purpose of many detentions is to try to obtain enough information to arrest you.

Arrest: Police can arrest you only if they have *probable cause* that you are involved in a crime. ("Probable cause" exists when the police are aware of facts that would lead an ordinary person to suspect that the person arrested has committed a crime.) When you are arrested, the cops can search you and go through any belongings.

III. The *Miranda* Warnings

The police do not necessarily have to read you your rights (also known as the

Miranda warnings). Miranda applies when there is (a) an interrogation (b) by a police officer (c) while the suspect is in police custody. (Please note that you do not have to be formally arrested to be "in custody.") Even when all these conditions are met, the police intentionally violate Miranda. And though your rights have been violated, what you say can be used against you. For this reason, it is better not to wait for the cops – you know what your rights are, so you can invoke them by saying "I am going to remain silent. I want to see a lawyer."

If you've been arrested and realize that you have started answering questions, don't panic. Just re-invoke your rights by saying "I am going to remain silent. I want to see a lawyer." Don't let them trick you into thinking that because you answered some of their questions, you have to answer all of them.

IV. Questioning

Do not communicate with the police anything other than your right to remain silent. If you are arrested, you may want to give identifying information, such as name, address and driver's license, which will help secure your release by citation or be necessary to be released on bail.

It is a serious crime to make a false statement to a police officer. By talking, you could get in trouble because of two inconsistent statements spoken out of fear or forgetfulness. It is also very dangerous to try to outsmart the police. They are trained in how to extract information and trip people up who are lying to them or even telling the truth. They have learned how to get people to talk by making them feel scared, guilty or impolite. Stay strong and stay silent!

Interrogation isn't always bright lights and rubber hoses – usually it's just a conversation. Whenever the police ask you questions, it's legally safest to say these words: "I am going to remain silent. I want to see a lawyer."

This invokes the rights which protect you from interrogation. When you say this, the police are legally required to stop asking you questions if you have been detained or placed under arrest. They probably won't stop, so just repeat "I am going to remain silent. I want to see a lawyer," or remain silent until they catch on.

Remember, anything you say to the authorities can and will be used against you and your friends in court. There's no way to predict how or what information the police might try to use. Plus, the police often misquote or misrepresent altogether what was said.

One of the jobs of police is to secure information from people, and they often don't have any scruples about how they go about doing so. Police are legally allowed to lie when they're investigating, and they are trained to be manipulative. The only thing you should say to police is:

"I am going to remain silent. I want to see a lawyer."

Here are some of the statements the police might make:

- "You're not a suspect – just help us understand what happened here and then you can go." If you're not a suspect, ask to leave immediately without answering any questions.
- "If you don't answer my questions, I'll have no choice but to arrest you. Do you *want* to go to jail?" No one wants to be arrested, but regardless of their promises, talking will usually not avoid arrest.
- "If you don't answer my questions, I'm going to charge you with interfering with my investigation." You cannot be charged with interfering or obstructing a police officer by invoking your right not to talk to the police.
- "All of your friends have cooperated and we let them go home. You're the only one left." This is generally a lie – besides, even if that did happen, how does it benefit you to be a witness against yourself?
- "If you don't talk now, we'll come back with a subpoena." Most of the time this is an empty threat. The police do not have to power to obtain a subpoena. In connection with the investigation of a crime, the only subpoena that can issue is from a grand jury.
- "If you talk, we will go easy on you." Police will promise you the world to get you to talk. However, when they have people sign statements, notice they never sign anything saying the police will keep their promises.
- "You seem to be an intelligent kid with a promising future. You don't want to destroy your life over this, do you?" The truth is, the police don't

care about you. This is just another way to manipulate you into making a statement.

- "If you're not guilty, then why don't you talk?" This is one of their favorite tactics. We all have the desire to defend ourselves, especially when we know we are innocent. However, the police will attack and dissect everything you say, continually prying to get more and more information. Even if you are innocent, don't talk! A person's innocence has never stopped the authorities from convicting or jailing them. Furthermore, the more you talk, the more likely you are to mention other people's names, leading the police to them.

Police will often try to trick you into talking. Here are some of the techniques they use:

- Good Cop/Bad Cop: Bad cop is aggressive and menacing, while good cop is nice, friendly and familiar (usually good cop is the same race and sex as you). The idea is bad cop scares you so badly you are desperately looking for a friend. Good cop is that friend.
- The police will tell you that your friends ratted on you so that you will snitch on them. Meanwhile, they tell your friends the same thing.
- The police will tell you that they have all the evidence they need to convict you and that if you "take responsibility" and confess the judge will be impressed by your honesty and go easy on you. What they really mean is: "We don't have enough evidence yet, please confess."

Jail is a very isolating and intimidating place. It is really easy to believe what the cops tell you. Insist upon speaking with a lawyer before you answer any questions or sign anything.

The police do not decide your charges; they can only make recommendations. The prosecutor is the only person who can actually charge you.

V. Searches
Never consent to a search! If the police try to search your house, car, backpack, pockets or other private property, say "*I do not consent to this*

search." This may not stop them from forcing their way in and searching anyway, but if they search you illegally, they probably won't be able to use the evidence against you in court. You have nothing to lose from refusing to consent to a search and lots to gain. Do not physically resist police when they are trying to search because you could get hurt and charged with resisting arrest or other serious crimes.

If the police have a search warrant, nothing changes – you should not consent to the search. Again, you have nothing to lose from refusing to consent to a search, and lots to gain if the search warrant is incorrect or invalid in some way. But remember not to physically resist police when they are trying to search.

VI. Taking Notes

Whenever you interact with or observe the police, always write down what is said and who said it. Write down the names and badge numbers of the police and the names and contact information of any witnesses. Record everything that happens. If you are expecting a lot of police contact, get in the habit of carrying a small tape recorder and a camera with you. Be careful – police don't like people taking notes, especially if they are planning on doing something illegal. Observing them and documenting their actions may have very different results; for example, it may cause them to respond aggressively, or it may prevent them from abusing you or your friends.

APPENDIX D

RESOURCES

ANIMAL RIGHTS GROUPS

Australia

Against Animal Cruelty Tasmania
www.aact.org.au
Animal Liberation Victoria
www.alv.org.au
Animals Australia
www.animalsaustralia.org
Anti Vivisection Western Australia
www.avwa.com.au
Edgar's Mission
http://edgarsmission.org.au

Canada

Animal Rights Collective of Halifax
www.archalifax.com
Campaigns Against the Cruelty to
Animals
http://catcahelpanimals.bravehost.com
Canadian Voice for Animals
www.canadianvoiceforanimals.org
EarthSave Canada
www.earthsave.ca
Fur-Bearer Defenders
www.banlegholdtraps.com
The Responsible Animal Care Society
www.tracs-bc.ca
Toronto Vegetarian Association

www.veg.ca
Vancouver Humane Society
www.vancouverhumanesociety.bc.ca

New Zealand
Animal Rights New Zealand
www.arlan.org.nz
Auckland Animal Action
www.aucklandanimalaction.org.nz
Meat Free Media
www.meatfreemedia.com
Save Animals From Exploitation
www.safe.org.nz

South Africa
Animal Rights Africa
www.animalrightsafrica.org
Seal Alert
www.sealalert.org

UK/Europe
Animal Aid
www.animalaid.org.uk
Animal Rights Action Network
www.aran.ie
British Union for the Abolition of
Vivisection
www.buav.org
Coalition to Abolish Animal Testing

www.ohsukillsprimates.com
Coalition to Abolish the Fur Trade
www.caft.org.uk
Compassion in World Farming
www.ciwf.org
European Anti-Rodeo Coalition
www.anti-rodeo.org
European Coalition to End Animal
Experiments
www.eceae.org
Hillside Animal Sanctuary
www.hillside.org.uk
League Against Cruel Sports
www.league.org.uk
The Vegan Society
www.vegansociety.com
Viva!
www.viva.org.uk

US
Animal Legal Defense Fund
www.aldf.org
Animal Place
www.animalplace.org
Animal Protection & Rescue League
www.aprl.org
Animal Protection Institute
www.api4animals.org
Compassion Over Killing
www.cok.net
Compassionate Action for Animals
www.exploreveg.org
Compassionate Consumers
www.compassionateconsumers.org

Compassionate Cooks
www.compassionatecooks.com
East Bay Animal Advocates
www.eastbayanimaladvocates.org
Eastern Shore Sanctuary
www.bravebirds.org
FARM
www.farmusa.org
Farm Sanctuary
www.farmsanctuary.org
GourmetCruelty.com (foie gras)
www.gourmetcruelty.com
Hugs for Puppies
www.hugsforpuppies.org
Humane Society of the United States
www.hsus.org
In Defense of Animals
www.idausa.org
Mercy For Animals
www.mercyforanimals.org
People for the Ethical Treatment of
Animals
www.peta.org
Sea Shepherd Conservation Society
www.seashepherd.org
SHARK
www.sharkonline.org
Sonoma People for Animal Rights
www.sonomapeopleforanimalrights.org
United Poultry Concerns
www.upc-online.org
Vegan Outreach
www.veganoutreach.org
Woodstock Farm Animal Sanctuary

www.woodstockfas.org

BOOKS

For Activism

Ethics Into Action: Henry Spira and the Animal Rights Movement
Peter Singer

Get Political for Animals and Win the Laws They Need: Why and How to Launch a Voting Bloc for Animals in Your Town, City, County or State
Julie E. Lewin

How to Win Friends & Influence People
Dale Carnegie

In Defense of Animals: The Second Wave
Edited by Peter Singer

Made to Stick: Why Some Ideas Survive and Others Die
Chip Heath & Dan Heath

Making Kind Choices: Everyday Ways to Enhance Your Life Through Earth- and Animal-Friendly Living
Ingrid Newkirk

Making the News: A Guide for Activists and Nonprofits
Jason Salzman

Meat Market: Animals, Ethics, and Money
Erik Marcus

Move the Message: Your Guide to Making A Difference and Changing the World

Josephine Bellaccomo

For Cooking & Baking

The Artful Vegan: Fresh Flavors from the Millennium Restaurant
Eric Tucker, Renee Comet & Amy Pearce

Eat Your Veggies!
Beverly Lynn Bennett

How It All Vegan!: Irresistible Recipes for an Animal-Free Diet
Sarah Kramer

The Joy of Vegan Baking: The Compassionate Cooks' Traditional Treats & Sinful Sweets
Colleen Patrick-Goudreau

Vegan: Over 90 Mouthwatering Recipes for All Occasions
Tony Bishop-Weston

Vegan Planet: 400 Irresistible Recipes with Fantastic Flavors from Home and Around the World
Robin Robertson

Vegan Vittles
Jo Stepaniak

Vegan World Fusion Cuisine
Mark Reinfeld and Bo Rinaldi

For Support

Aftershock: Confronting Trauma in a Violent World: A Guide for Activists and Their Allies
pattrice jones

Animal Grace: Entering a Spiritual

*Relationship with Our Fellow
Creatures*
Mary Lou Randour
*Healing Through the Dark Emotions:
The Wisdom of Grief, Fear, and
Despair*
*The Inner Art of Vegetarianism:
Spiritual Practices for Body and Soul*
Carol J. Adams
Miriam Greenspan
*Vegan Freak: Being Vegan in a Non-
Vegan World*
Bob & Jenna Torres

CRUELTY-FREE PRODUCTS

Alternative Outfitters (US)
www.alternativeoutfitters.com
AnimalRightstuff (US)
www.animalrightstuff.com
Blissful Health & Vegetarian Products
(New Zealand)
www.blissfulvege.com
Comondi (Canada)
www.comondi.com
Cruelty Free Shop (Australia)
http://crueltyfreeshop.com.au
The Cruelty-Free Shop (UK)
www.crueltyfreeshop.com
A Different Daisy (US)
www.differentdaisy.com
Downbound (Canada)
www.downbound.ca
Downbound (US)
www.downbound.com

Ethical Wares (UK)
www.ethicalwares.com
Herbivore Clothing (US)
www.herbivoreclothing.com
Moo Shoes (US)
www.mooshoes.com
Pangea (US)
www.pangeaveg.com
PETA Mall (US)
www.petamall.com
Planet Species (New Zealand)
www.planetspecies.org.nz
Vegan Essentials (US)
www.veganessentials.com
The Vegan Food Mob (Australia)
www.veganfood.com.au
The Vegan Food Mob (New Zealand)
www.veganfood.co.nz
Vegan Line (UK)
www.veganline.com
Vegan Wares (Australia)
www.veganwares.com
Vegan Works (Canada)
www.vegan-works.com
VegBay Auctions (UK & US)
www.vegbay.com
The Vegetarian Site (US)
www.thevegetariansite.com

MAGAZINES

Animal People
www.animalpeoplenews.org
The Animals Voice
www.animalsvoice.com

Black Velvet
www.blackvelvetmagazine.com
Herbivore
www.herbivoremagazine.com
T.O.F.U.
www.twentertainment.ca/tofu/index.php
Vegan Voice
http://veganic.net
VegNews
www.vegnews.com

MULTIMEDIA
An Animal-Friendly Life
www.ananimalfriendlylife.com
Animal Voices – Toronto
http://animalvoices.ca
Animal Voices – Vancouver
www.animalvoices.org
Compassionate Cooks
www.compassionatecooks.com
Generation Vegan
www.generationv.org
Go Vegan
www.goveganradio.com
Go Vegan Texas
www.govegantexas.org/index.php

Toronto Vegetarian Association
www.veg.ca
Veg Cast
www.vegcast.com
Vegan Freak
www.veganfreak.com
Vegan Radio
http://veganradio.com
Vegan.com
Veganica
http://veganica.com

**ADDITIONAL ONLINE
RESOURCES**
www.animalconcerns.org
A clearinghouse for information on
the Internet related to animal rights
and welfare.
http://animalrights.meetup.com
Meet other local animal-rights
activists in your part of the world.
www.GoVeg.com
A comprehensive vegetarian Web site.
www.veganism.com
Answers to frequently asked questions
about animal rights.

BOOKS

O books
O is a symbol of the world, of oneness and unity. In different cultures it also means the "eye", symbolizing knowledge and insight, and in Old English it means "place of love or home". O books explores the many paths of understanding which different traditions have developed down the ages, particularly those today that express respect for the planet and all of life.

For more information on the full list of over 300 titles please visit our website
www.O-books.net

myspiritradio is an exciting web, internet, podcast and mobile phone global broadcast network for all those interested in teaching and learning in the fields of body, mind, spirit and self development. Listeners can hear the show online via computer or mobile phone, and even download their favourite shows to listen to on MP3 players whilst driving, working, or relaxing.

Feed your mind, change your life with O Books, The O Books radio programme carries interviews with most authors, sharing their wisdom on life, the universe and everything...e mail questions and co-create the show with O Books and myspiritradio.

MySpiritRadio

Just visit **www.myspiritradio.com** for more information.

SOME RECENT O BOOKS

Back to the Truth
5,000 years of Advaita
Dennis Waite

A wonderful book. Encyclopedic in nature, and destined to become a classic. **James Braha**
Absolutely brilliant...an ease of writing with a water-tight argument outlining the great universal truths. This book will become a modern classic. A milestone in the history of Advaita. **Paula Marvelly**
1905047614 500pp **£19.95 $29.95**

Beyond Photography
Encounters with orbs, angels and mysterious light forms
Katie Hall and **John Pickering**

The authors invite you to join them on a fascinating quest; a voyage of discovery into the nature of a phenomenon, manifestations of which are shown as being historical and global as well as contemporary and intently personal.
At journey's end you may find yourself a believer, a doubter or simply an intrigued wonderer ... Whatever the outcome, the process of journeying is likely prove provocative and stimulating and - as with the mysterious images fleetingly captured by the authors' cameras - inspiring and potentially enlightening. **Brian Sibley**, author and broadcaster.
1905047908 272pp 50 b/w photos +8pp colour insert **£12.99 $24.95**

Don't Get MAD Get Wise
Why no one ever makes you angry, ever!
Mike George

There is a journey we all need to make, from anger, to peace, to forgiveness. Anger always destroys, peace always restores, and forgiveness always heals. This explains the journey, the steps you can take to make it happen for you.
1905047827 160pp £7.99 $14.95

IF You Fall...
It's a new beginning
Karen Darke

Karen Darke's story is about the indomitability of spirit, from one of life's cruel vagaries of fortune to what is insight and inspiration. She has overcome the limitations of paralysis and discovered a life of challenge and adventure that many of us only dream about. It is all about the mind, the spirit and the desire that some of us find, but which all of us possess. **Joe Simpson**, mountaineer and author of *Touching the Void*
1905047886 240pp £9.99 $19.95

Love, Healing and Happiness
Spiritual wisdom for a post-secular era
Larry Culliford

This will become a classic book on spirituality. It is immensely practical and grounded. It mirrors the author's compassion and lays the foundation for a higher understanding of human suffering and hope. **Reinhard Kowalski** Consultant Clinical Psychologist
1905047916 304pp £10.99 $19.95

A Map to God
Awakening Spiritual Integrity
Susie Anthony

This describes an ancient hermetic pathway, representing a golden thread running through many traditions, which offers all we need to understand and do to actually become our best selves.
1846940443 260pp £10.99 $21.95

Punk Science
Inside the mind of God
Manjir Samanta-Laughton

Wow! Punk Science is an extraordinary journey from the microcosm of the atom to the macrocosm of the Universe and all stops in between. Manjir Samanta-Laughton's synthesis of cosmology and consciousness is sheer genius. It is elegant, simple and, as an added bonus, makes great reading. **Dr Bruce H. Lipton**, author of *The Biology of Belief*
1905047932 320pp £12.95 $22.95

Rosslyn Revealed
A secret library in stone
Alan Butler

Rosslyn Revealed gets to the bottom of the mystery of the chapel featured in the Da Vinci Code. The results of a lifetime of careful research and study demonstrate that truth really is stranger than fiction; a library of philosophical ideas and mystery rites, that were heresy in their time, have been disguised in the extraordinarily elaborate stone carvings.
1905047924 260pp b/w + colour illustrations £19.95 $29.95 cl

The Way of Thomas
Nine Insights for Enlightened Living from the Secret Sayings of Jesus
John R. Mabry

What is the real story of early Christianity? Can we find a Jesus that is relevant as a spiritual guide for people today?

These and many other questions are addressed in this popular presentation of the teachings of this mystical Christian text. Includes a reader-friendly version of the gospel.
1846940303 196pp £10.99 $19.95
.

The Way Things Are
A Living Approach to Buddhism
Lama Ole Nydahl

An up-to-date and revised edition of a seminal work in the Diamond Way Buddhist tradition (three times the original length), that makes the timeless wisdom of Buddhism accessible to western audiences. Lama Ole has established more than 450 centres in 43 countries.
1846940427 240pp **£9.99 $19.95**

The 7 Ahas! of Highly Enlightened Souls
How to free yourself from ALL forms of stress
Mike George

7th printing
A very profound, self empowering book. Each page bursting with wisdom and insight. One you will need to read and reread over and over again! Paradigm Shift. I totally love this book, a wonderful nugget of inspiration. **PlanetStarz**
1903816319 128pp 190/135mm **£5.99 $11.95**

God Calling
A Devotional Diary
A. J. Russell

46th printing
"When supply seems to have failed, you must know that it has not done so. But you must look around to see what you can give away. Give away something." One of the best-selling devotional books of all time, with over 6 million copies sold.
1905047428 280pp 135/95mm **£7.99** cl.
US rights sold

The Goddess, the Grail and the Lodge
The Da Vinci code and the real origins of religion
Alan Butler

5th printing
This book rings through with the integrity of sharing time-honoured revelations. As a historical detective, following a golden thread from the great Megalithic cultures, Alan Butler vividly presents a compelling picture of the fight for life of a great secret and one that we simply can't afford to ignore. **Lynn Picknett & Clive Prince**
1903816696 360pp 230/152mm **£12.99 $19.95**

The Heart of Tantric Sex
A unique guide to love and sexual fulfilment
Diana Richardson

3rd printing
The art of keeping love fresh and new long after the honeymoon is over. Tantra for modern Western lovers adapted in a practical, refreshing and sympathetic way.

One of the most revolutionary books on sexuality ever written. **Ruth Ostrow**, News Ltd.

1903816378 256pp **£9.99 $14.95**

I Am With You
The best-selling modern inspirational classic
John Woolley

14th printing hardback
Will bring peace and consolation to all who read it. **Cardinal Cormac Murphy-O'Connor**
0853053413 280pp 150x100mm **£9.99** cl
4th printing paperback
1903816998 280pp 150/100mm **£6.99 $12.95**

In the Light of Meditation
The art and practice of meditation in 10 lessons
Mike George

2nd printing
A classy book. A gentle yet satisfying pace and is beautifully illustrated. Complete with a CD or guided meditation commentaries, this is a true gem among meditation guides. **Brainwave**
  In-depth approach, accessible and clearly written, a convincing map of the overall territory and a practical path for the journey. **The Light**
1903816610 224pp 235/165mm full colour throughout +CD **£11.99 $19.95**

The Instant Astrologer
A revolutionary new book and software package for the astrological seeker
Lyn Birkbeck

2nd printing

The brilliant Lyn Birkbeck's new book and CD package, The Instant Astrologer, combines modern technology and the wisdom of the ancients, creating an invitation to enlightenment for the masses, just when we need it most! Astrologer **Jenny Lynch**, Host of NYC's StarPower Astrology Television Show

1903816491 628pp full colour throughout with CD ROM 240/180 **£39 $69** cl

Is There An Afterlife?
A comprehensive overview of the evidence, from east and west
David Fontana

2nd printing

An extensive, authoritative and detailed survey of the best of the evidence supporting survival after death. It will surely become a classic not only of parapsychology literature in general but also of survival literature in particular. **Universalist**

1903816904 496pp 230/153mm **£14.99 $24.95**

The Reiki Sourcebook
Bronwen and Frans Stiene

5th printing

It captures everything a Reiki practitioner will ever need to know about the ancient art. This book is hailed by most Reiki professionals as the best guide to Reiki. For an average reader, it's also highly enjoyable and a

good way to learn to understand Buddhism, therapy and healing.
Michelle Bakar, Beauty magazine
1903816556 384pp **£12.99 $19.95**

Soul Power
The transformation that happens when you know
Nikki de Carteret

4th printing
One of the finest books in its genre today. Using scenes from her own life and growth, Nikki de Carteret weaves wisdom about soul growth and the power of love and transcendent wisdom gleaned from the writings of the mystics. This is a book that I will read gain and again as a reference for my own soul growth. **Barnes and Noble review**
190381636X 240pp **£9.99 $15.95**

The Thinker's Guide to Evil
Peter Vardy and **Julie Arliss**

2nd printing
As a philosopher of religion Peter Vardy is unsurpassed. Dialogue Peter Vardy is the best populariser of Philosophy of Religion in Britain today.
Theology
    A challenging and wide-ranging discussion, clearly and engagingly written and thoroughly illustrated, it is an excellent book for anyone concerned to think seriously about these important issues. **Dr Jeremy Hall**, University of Glasgow
1903816335 196pp full colour throughout **£9.99 $15.95**

The Thinker's Guide to God
Peter Vardy and **Julie Arliss**

2nd printing
What a magnum opus! From Pluto's feet to Dawkin's Selfish Gene, this

provides a magisterial survey of Western thought about God. **Rev Henry Kirk**, Principal Examiner

An excellent modern introduction to the various theories. **Bishop William Kenney**

Vardy and Arliss have their finger on the pulse of today's world. **Dr Beverly Zimmerman**, Catholic Schools Office

190381622X 264pp full colour throughout **£9.99 $15.95**

The Thoughtful Guide to the Bible
Roy Robinson

A liberating experience. There is a great deal of factual information. The difficult questions are not avoided. Roy Robinson does not pretend that the Bible is always historically accurate or morally admirable. He has no time for a simplistic fundamentalism that trivialises the concept of inspiration. But from a critical position he offers a strong defence of the Bible as the church's main source of authority. **Reform**

1903816750 360pp **£14.99 $19.95**

The Thoughtful Guide to Christianity
Graham Hellier

A rough guide to the Christian faith for anyone within or without the Church, and a resource for teachers, preachers and discussion groups. Designed to give material for reflection, the guide is drawn from over 700 sources, including some of which are deeply critical of Christianity and the Christian Church. **Reform**

1903816343 360pp **£11.99 $17.95**

The Thoughtful Guide to Faith
Trevor Windross

2nd printing

This is a splendid book! Its author is ambitious for Christianity and his aim is the development of a voice coming from the Church that is truly radical and can be heard alongside those of traditionalists and fundamentalists, without trying to un-Church people from those backgrounds. Hasten to your bookshop. SoF
1903816688 224pp £9.99 $14.95

The Thoughtful Guide to God
Making sense of the world's biggest idea
Howard Jones

The wide scope of this fusion of theology, philosophy and science makes this an important contribution to a study of the divine that is easily readable by the non-specialist. **Dr Verena Tschudin**, author of *Seeing the Invisible*
1905047703 400pp £19.99 $39.95

The Thoughtful Guide to Religion
Why it began, how it works, and where it's going
Ivor Morrish

This is a comprehensive and sympathetic approach to all religions of the world, including the lesser-known ones, sects, cults and ideologies. Broader than "comparative religion", it uses philosophy, psychology, anthropology and other disciplines to answer the key questions, and provides a holistic approach for anyone interested in religious or philosophical ideas.
190504769X 384pp £24.99 $24.95

The 9 Dimensions of the Soul
Essence and the Enneagram
David Hey

The first book to relate the two, understanding the personality types of the Enneagram in relation to the Essence, shedding a new light on our personality, its origins and how it operates. Written in a beautifully simple, insightful and heartful way and transmits complex material in a way that is easy to read and understand. **Thomas O. Trobe**, Founder and Director of Learning Love Seminars, Inc.
1846940028 176pp **£10.99 $19.95**

Aim for the Stars...Reach the Moon
How to coach your life to spiritual and material success
Conor Patterson

A fascinating, intelligent, and beneficial tool and method of programming your mind for success. The techniques are fast to achieve, motivating, and inspiring. I highly recommend this book. **Uri Geller**
1905047274 208pp **£11.99 $19.95**

Amulets
Kim Farnell

This is a wonderful book for those interested in learning about amulets and how to create them. Farnell's expertise makes her the ideal guide. Her knowledge is sound and her instructions are always clear and easy to follow. The strength of this book lies in it being one of easy access and also very well presented in its structure and internal logic. It makes an ideal reference book for anyone of a serious interest, being equally suited to beginners and experts alike. **Deborah Houlding**, author of *The Houses: Temples of the Sky*
1846940060 160pp **£9.99 $14.95**

Developing Spiritual Intelligence
The power of you
Altazar Rossiter

This beautifully clear and fascinating book is an incredibly simple guide to that which so many of us search for. **Dr Dina Glouberman**
1905047649 240pp **£12.99 $19.95**

Happiness in 10 Minutes
Brian Mountford

Brian Mountford-in exploring "happiness"-celebrates the paradox of losing and finding at its heart. At once both profound and simple, the book teaches us that to be fully alive is to be in communion and that gratitude leads us into the mystery of giving ourselves away-the path of true joy. **Alan Jones**, Dean of Grace Cathedral, San Francisco, author of *Reimagining Christianity.*
1905047770 112pp b/w illustrations **£6.99 $9.95**

Head Versus Heart-and our Gut Reactions
The 21st century enneagram
Michael Hampson

A seminal work, whose impact will continue to reverberate throughout the 21st century. Brings illumination and allows insights to tumble out. **Fr Alexander**, Worth Abbey
19038169000 320pp **£11.99 $16.95**